BUFFALO COUNTRY

BUFFALO COUNTRY

Other titles by the author

A Piece of Paradise:
A Story of Custer State Park

Island in the Plains:
A Black Hills Natural History

BUFFALO COUNTRY

A NORTHERN PLAINS NARRATIVE

Edward Raventon

JOHNSON BOOKS

AN IMPRINT OF BOWER HOUSE

DENVER

BowerHouseBooks.com

Cover Design by Margaret McCullough
Printed in Canada

Library of Congress Control Number: 2003011143

Paperback ISBN: 978-1-155566-325-4

10 9 8 7 6 5 4 3 2

This book is dedicated to Beverly Marie,
who asked me to write a story about "her country"
and gave me the time and support to tell it.

Contents

Contents

Introduction

THIS BOOK IS A SERIES of journeys across and into the northern Great Plains, or more specifically, the northwestern unglaciated section of the northern plains, an area that was never deformed and buried by the glaciers. Its arterial system consists of a host of meandering streams that include the Musselshell, Yellowstone, Little Missouri, Knife, Heart, Cannonball, Grand, Moreau, Cheyenne, Bad, White, and Missouri, all of which were born fraternally with the rise of the Rocky Mountain wall and each in its own way a gatherer of waters, gravel, bones, and stories.

I follow old trails up into the forested buttes, across grass ridges and sagebrush prairies, and down into sculpted badlands and cobbled riverbeds. I think of it as the old buffalo country, a place where mystery and legend still haunt the landscape, a land of unique natural history that once evolved great herds of animals along with the native cultures that effloresced and disintegrated with them.

The following stories are about evolution, hunting, odysseys, dispossession, despair, adventure, transmogrification, and renewal of peoples, animals, and relationships that are still evolving within an awareness that connects and disperses. And through it all run the braided streams of the northern plains, swirling with mud, gravel, and sand in which I search for round stones to polish and smooth cedar sticks to burn.

Edward Raventon
Faith, South Dakota

Northern Plains Chronology

A.D. 900–1000 Ancestral Mandans introduce horticulture on the upper Missouri eventually establishing their main villages around the mouth of the Heart River in North Dakota.

1100 The Awatixa (Hidatsa) arrive on the upper Missouri and establish their main village at the mouth of the Knife River in North Dakota.

1350 The Astarahe (Ree) arrive on the upper Missouri in central South Dakota. Later migrations of Arikara follow.

1540 The Vore Buffalo Jump is used to slaughter bison.

1719 Charles Du Tisne and Jean-Baptiste Benard de La Harpe visit the upper Missouri and report Arikara living in forty-five villages.

1738 Pierre Gaultier de Varennes, Sieur de la Verendrye, reaches the Mandan villages.

1743 Sons of Pierre Gaultier de Varennes bury a lead plate near the mouth of the Bad River.

1750 The first waves of Sioux migrate from Minnesota to the Missouri River.

1781 The Ree/Arikara Indians are decimated by disease and the Teton Lakota claim the eastern part of the northern plains as their new domain.

1796 French traders, including Toussaint Charbonneau, take up residence with the Mandan, Hidatsa, and Arikara.

1804 Lewis and Clark visit the Mandans and Hidatsas and enlist the help of Charbonneau and his Shoshoni wife, Sakakawea, as interpreters on their trip to the Pacific.

1832 Fort Pierre Chouteau is built on the upper Missouri by the American Fur Company. George Catlin visits the Awatixa village.

1838 Fred Dupuis, a French Canadian, arrives at Fort Pierre from Canada via St. Louis.

1840 The Rev. Stephen R. Riggs, a congregational missionary, preaches the first recorded sermon at Fort Pierre.

1843 Toussaint Charbonneau, Indian trader and interpreter who accompanied the Lewis and Clark expedition, dies on the northern plains.

1872 The Rev. Thomas L. Riggs, son of Stephen R. Riggs, arrives on
the Missouri and builds the Oahe Mission on Peoria Bottoms
above the site of old Fort Pierre.

1880–1881 The winter of the "Big Snow" and the last winter buffalo
hunt of the Dakotas. The cattlemen begin moving their longhorn herds from the south onto the northern plains.

1883 The last free-range bison hunt takes place northeast of the Black
Hills in South Dakota and in southwestern North Dakota.

1889 The Cheyenne River Sioux Reservation is created and becomes
the home of the Mnikoju, Sans Arc, Two Kettles, and Blackfeet
bands of the Lakota.

1890 The Ghost Dance period ends in a fight at Wounded Knee
Creek killing Big Foot, a prominent Mnikoju leader from the
Cheyenne River Reservation and marking the end of the Indian
Wars and the open frontier.

1898 Fred Dupuis dies at his home on the Cheyenne River.

1904 The Matador Land and Cattle Company leases the eastern end
of the Cheyenne River Reservation while a host of smaller operations spread out west and lease the rest of the reservation
grassland.

1907 Burton "Cap" Mossman forms the famous Diamond A ranch
with headquarters at Eagle Butte, South Dakota.

1911 The Chicago, Milwaukee, St. Paul and Pacific (C, M, SP & P)
Railroad finishes laying track down the crest of the Fox Ridge,
founding a host of small towns, with its terminus at Faith,
South Dakota. A multitude of immigrant farmers and settlers
flood the country.

1913 The Verendrye lead plate is discovered.

1959 The Diamond A ranch is liquidated.

1962 Oahe Dam on the Missouri is closed and most of the great
river from Fort Peck, Montana, to Yankton, South Dakota, is
submerged.

Geologic Timeline

Era	Period	Epoch	Million Years Before Present (BP)	Principal geological events on the Northern Plains
Cenozoic Age of Mammals	Quaternary	Holocene	0.01	Widespread erosion and global warming
		Pleistocene	2	Extensive glaciation north and east of the Missouri Coteau with erosion west of the Coteau
	Tertiary	Pliocene	5	More erosion than deposition of materials
		Miocene	24	Another dramatic period of uplifting with continued deposition of light-colored clays and sands
		Oligocene	38	Deposition of a thick apron of light-colored clays and sands most notably eroded today in the White River badlands
		Eocene	55	Erosion of the western mountains with deposition of mud, clay, silt, ash, and gravel
		Paleocene	65	Uplifting of Rocky Mountains Deposition of shales, sandstones, mudstones with seams of lignite that comprise the Fort Union formation
Mesozoic Age of Reptiles	Cretaceous		138	Thick deposits of black and gray (Pierre) shales and Hell Creek shales are deposited across the entire Northern Great Plains; these shales contain the remains of dinosaurs
	Jurassic		205	
	Triassic		240	

James River Basin

Sinkholes

James River

Ree Hills

Wessington Hills

Bijou Hills

CROW CREEK SITE c. 1740

STANDING ROCK INDIAN RESERVATION 1889

CHEYENNE RIVER INDIAN RESERVATION 1889

KNIFE RIVER VILLAGES c. 1740 (AWATIXA)

MANDAN VILLAGES c. 1740

BISMARCK 1873

Missouri River

PIERRE 1880

Missouri Big Bend

MAIN ARIKARA VILLAGES c. 1740

Knife River

Heart River

The Oracle Stone

Cedar

Oahe Dam

OLD FORT PIERRE 1832

Bad River

White River

White River Badlands

White River

Pine Ridge

Wounded Knee

North Dakota
South Dakota

White Butte

Slim Buttes

FAITH 1910

FOX RIDGE

FOX RIDGE (Trail)

Cheyenne River

Killdeer Mtn

Badlands

Little Missouri River

Pretty Butte

Belle Fourche River

RAPID CITY 1882

DEADWOOD 1876

FORT MEADE 1878

BLACK HILLS

GLENDIVE 1881

Little Powder River

Bloody Red Kettle

Devils Tower

Belle Fourche River

Thunder Basin

The Six Horse Country

Big Sheep Mt

MILES CITY 1877

Yellowstone River

Powder River

Little Powder River

Tongue River

Little Missouri River

Montana
Wyoming

Big Horn Mountains

■ Historic Plains Indian Villages   ■ Historic Towns and Cities   ● Historic Towns and Cities

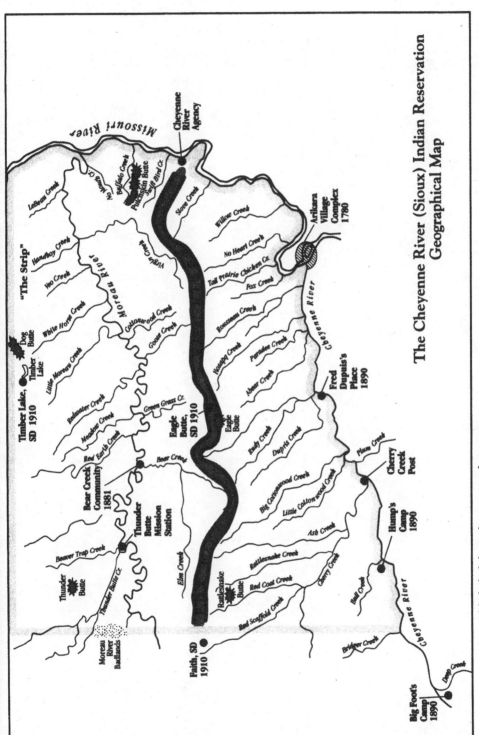

The Cheyenne River (Sioux) Indian Reservation
Geographical Map

Inset of dark shaded area from map on facing page.

Time is not a line but a dimension—you don't look back along time but down through it like water. Sometimes this comes to the surface, sometimes that, sometimes nothing. Nothing goes away.

—Margaret Atwood, *Cat's Eye*

Nothing out here stood still. Walking this prairie at night I could believe something rippled just beneath the sage, something immense and quiet. I could imagine the land crouching, pushing up a new hill each night, snaking a network of roots and rhizomes through the soil, then sitting back innocently as the sun rose. Who would notice?

—Judy Blunt, *Breaking Clean*

ONE

A Bloody Red Kettle

Certain Blackfoot decoys worked without camouflage, wearing only a loin-cloth. Advancing slowly on the herd, they would wheel in circles, alternately coming into view and hiding. As the buffalo, their curiosity whetted, moved closer to investigate, the decoys withdrew toward the wings of the pound, and the inquisitive herd trailed conveniently behind them.

—Tom McHugh

IT'S NEARLY DAWN. In the red valley north of the Black Hills, buffalo cows and calves form dark silhouettes against a pale sky streaked with orange clouds. The season is late, the air still and sharp without birdsong. Only the occasional low grunts of contented grazing bison punctuate the calm.

For weeks groups of hunters have spread out around this herd using stealth and man scent to slowly and inexorably push them together from all directions to the vicinity of a collapsed cavern.

The sunken cavern is rimmed by flecks of gypsum hardened to white alabaster. It is 200 feet in diameter, tapering to about 100 feet at the bottom. A pseudo-karst feature created over millennia as a result of the ground collapsing in the underlying limestone, the cavern eventually filled with red clay, forming a near-perfect circular sinkhole 70 feet deep with a shallow pond at the bottom. This deep red hole, appearing as if seamlessly cut into the surrounding red earth, blends in so well that from all directions at any distance it is invisible.

A dozen miles to the east in the shadow of a tall mountain peak, small nursery herds of bison began moving into the northeastern end of the red valley during the Moon of the Ripening Cherries to take advantage of a plethora of natural artesian springs, lakes, and streams that gush and flow with an abundance of pure, fresh water. In this vicinity, close to water and fresh grass, the Indians began to subtly maneuver small herds of cows and calves together. In the ensuing weeks they gently coaxed the unsuspecting animals west, closer and closer to the jump hole.

Now with the sun up, more than 400 head of bison cows and calves are bunched up 500 to 600 yards southeast of the sinkhole. They are becoming agitated and skittish. A band of eight heifers stands perfectly still looking east into a bright rising sun. They sense but cannot see or smell a presence and a movement not their own.

With the animals now expertly maneuvered into the proper position, a man sings a low chant to the bison. It is a hunt song asking for their permission to kill them. When he is finished, he stands tall and waves a great white buffalo robe at the herd. Next to him another man jumps up, waves a robe, and gives a great whoop. Down the line behind the herd, many robes are waving and men are yelling and shouting at the bison. "Run. Run fast, Run hard. Run."

Startled, the lead cows begin a fast trot west away from the noise only to be turned at a hard right angle by more men behind a makeshift drive line of boulders and brush south of the jump hole. Startled now into a panic, they stampede at a full headlong gallop the last 400 yards to the hole.

Despite their somewhat cumbersome appearance, bison are incredibly agile animals that can run hard, turn, and stop more quickly than horses. This is exactly what the first twenty or thirty lead animals do when they are abruptly confronted by the steep, gaping drop-off directly in front of them. But it's too late. Amidst shouts and boiling red clouds of dust, wild-eyed panic has set into the whole herd, and the rear animals push ahead like a loaded, out-of-control freight train moving down a mountain. In the end, pushed and harassed by yelling Indians, they are swallowed by the alabaster-flecked sinkhole.

When the dust clears, the death squeals and bellowing of bruised and maimed bison emanating from the sinkhole are both deafening and terrifying. The noise cuts to the bone and serves as a reminder for the next extremely hazardous part of the operation: the slaughter.

The sinkhole now is a kettle of writhing, frightened, angry beasts trying to breathe and move and climb. Most of the first runners are killed by the fall, their necks broken or suffocated by the later arrivals on top, while others sustain broken limbs and the last are relatively unscathed and desperate to get out.

The hunters begin a slow descent along the edges of the steep, unstable sides of the hole armed with spears, arrows, and grooved stone mauls. They stab and club the maimed and bloody survivors to death. For the hunters who lose their footing and slip into the hole there will be injuries, some serious. And always in the background are the cries of agony as flint-tipped spears pierce lungs and stone hammers repeatedly smash and thud into tough, wooly skulls.

Dispatching all the bison takes most of the morning. By midafternoon, butchering is well under way. As many as 100 people are now scattered out on the surrounding prairie, involved in the arduous labor of hacking apart and processing tons of meat. It is imperative that they work fast to jerk the fresh meat before vast swarms of blowflies move in and ruin it.

Processing the meat means zipping and stripping big muscle masses off the carcasses and hauling the flesh up by means of dogs and travois along a path that winds up and around the south and west side of the hole.

Most of the work falls to the women, who slice the muscle off the limbs into thin strips with razor-sharp stone knives. The thinness of the strips allows it to dry rapidly on wooden drying racks in the hot sun. The sundried meat forms a hardened surface glaze the flies cannot penetrate to lay their eggs. Drying also reduces the staggering weight of the meat by 70 to 80 percent without any nutrient loss.

During the butchering the Indians pause to crack open limb bones and feast on the yellow bone marrow, which is rich in fat. The men smash in nearly all the skulls to get to the fat in the brains, and they relish the raw entrails, liver, and kidneys. Occasionally the women throw large scraps of lean meat to fatten the wolf dogs, which in their turn will become food. The excess grease and marrow will be mixed with meat and stored in bison intestines where it will keep for two years as a supply of fat for the winter.

As the meat cures, ripening chokecherries growing in the nearby draws are stripped from the bushes and pounded together with dry meat to form a powdery, nutritious mix called pemmican, a portable, universal staple for the long term that can be eaten straight or used as soup stock.

As evening approaches and the sun slides down behind the Bear Lodge range, cooking fires appear and the soft twilight is filled with the rich savory scent of roasting buffalo tongues, humps, and ribs. After the feast the men tell their stories, recounting their bravery behind the drive lines and in the sinkhole. With their bellies full, many remember and recount how bravely the buffalo performed their deed of dying in the bloody red kettle.

For nearly three centuries, about A.D. 1540 to 1800, the jump was used at least twenty times. Some of the kills included as many as 800 bison. These big kills were separated by up to thirty years of inactivity while episodes of smaller kills may have taken place at an average of every eight to ten years, the minimum period required for the stench of rotting flesh to subside and for the bisons' memory of the kill site to fade. It would also take that much time for the local bison herds to increase and replenish themselves.

Following a kill, the Indians would return periodically to capture a host of scavenging carnivore furbearers as well as eagles attracted to the carrion. Evidence of wolf dogs has been found with the canine teeth broken off.

When the bones are picked clean and scavenging activity finally ceases, windblown sediments and silt runoff cover and eventually bury the bones in the red clay, setting the stage for the next kill. From the entire period of use twenty-two separate bone layers mixed with large heavy bison arrows have been identified, representing a total of possibly 20,000 slaughtered bison at what is now known as the Vore Buffalo Jump Site.[1]

The Indians who used the site have been variously identified by their projectile points and tools as bands of nomadic Kiowa, Kiowa-Apache, Crow, Shoshone, and Arapaho, along with Mandan, Hidatsa, Ree (Arikara), and possibly Cheyenne.[2] Groups of these tribes related by language, traditions, and kinship may even have hunted together. The lithic materials found have been identified as emanating from all the major prehistoric stone quarries of the northern Great Plains, including the vast Spanish Diggings of southeastern Wyoming, the Flint Hills quarry in the southern Black Hills, the Knife River Flint quarry of central North Dakota, and stone quarried from the Bighorn Mountains.

In prehistoric times before the advent of the horse and rifle, the "Bloody Red Kettle" may have been one of the most significant sites for the slaughtering of bison. In periods of drought and hunger, the site would have served as a crucial gathering place like nearby Bear Butte, where allied tribes came together on the northern Great Plains to celebrate the life and death of bison.

TWO

"The Big Gumbo"

The natural object is always the adequate symbol.
—Ezra Pound

I'VE BEEN WINDING SOUTH around bald hills and over ridges at a leisurely pace on a remote ribbon of gravel that roughly parallels the course of the Little Missouri River. It's a no-man's-land of rough clay hills and scattered pump jacks. Spindly groves of cedar cling to the steepest ridges with an odd ponderosa or two hiding in a deep draw, but mostly it's hardpan with cactus, sage, and shortgrass. Empty and unspoiled if you like coarse, gritty country.

A few miles south of a wide, desolate flat of dark clay known as the "Big Gumbo," I pause to admire a stand of tall waving switchgrass near a cluster of rugged badlands buttes. Shutting off the engine immediately immerses me in an immensity of solitary quietude that is at once awesome and disconcerting.

It's a fine morning in early September. The first cold front of the season has blown the dry, stifling heat of late summer south. The crisp fall atmosphere is blooming up a billowy battalion of cumulus clouds adrift in uneven ranks of gray, gun-metal blue, and creamy white. The landscape feels orderly, scrubbed, and invigorated.

Only the occasional rattling of an empty cattle hauler grinding gears as he downshifts to negotiate the tight curve and the narrow, single-lane bridge over Boxelder Creek reminds me of the confinement we call reality in the infinite vastness of time and space.

Fortunately the barbed-wire fence in front of me is loose enough to straddle through, and in a moment I'm walking across a landscape of bare humps, hardpan flats, and grassy hills. A half mile east beyond the road and out of sight in a low depression runs the Little Missouri. It carries a big name for a brown, skinny little stream in this obscure corner of North Dakota. Later and farther south I'll drive through it at a pleasant place shaded by cottonwoods called Salmen Ford. Right now, the object of my curiosity is a high, isolated mud butte standing like a sentinel between the river and the gravel road. After a short zigzagging route around the tall switchgrass and through a mine field of fat-eared clumps of prickly pear, I'm standing on its dull, gray base.

The butte is 40 to 50 feet high, the great bulk of it consisting of thick layers of undifferentiated Cretaceous shales—sediments of gritty mud laid down by the vast Cretaceous or Western Interior Seaway that was here 60 to 70 million years ago. This seaway stretched from the Arctic to the Gulf of Mexico, inundating the interior of North America for extensive periods of time. These shales make up the substrate for a great deal of the northwestern unglaciated plains that cover the western Dakotas, eastern Wyoming, and eastern Montana.

The dark shale that looks as if it were melting off the butte is either the Pierre shale, Fox Hills, or the Hell Creek formation. It's all late Cretaceous and looks pretty much the same. At this height and this far west along the Little Missouri it's probably Hell Creek. Farther east, if there is no unconformity, the formations all neatly pile up, the Pierre shale on the bottom followed by the Fox Hills and the Hell Creek on top.

The Pierre shale formation tends to be a dull, light gray to medium gray, with ironstone concretions, a couple of which lie here. Pierre shales were deposited over many millennia as the muddy, oxygen-poor, fetid bottom of the inland Cretaceous sea and consist of very fine-textured silt and sediments heavily permeated with former sea salts. Layers of shale that are lighter in color contain a significant amount of volcanic ash that blew in and settled out, forming the bentonite clays.

Pierre shale extends over a vast area stretching from the Missouri River in central South Dakota out to the Black Hills and beyond. The Hell Creek usually picks up where the Pierre shale leaves off, covering a good deal of northwestern South Dakota, the southwestern end of North Dakota, and much of northeastern Wyoming and eastern Montana. The Hell Creek shales tend to be in the warmer spectrum of colors, from gray to shades of umber, tan, and rusty yellow ochres. Both formations provide an excellent medium for badlands carving.

The great abundance of salts in these formations, particularly the Pierre shale, causes the very fine sediment particles to slake (disintegrate) when wet, preventing the percolation or infiltration of water into a soil substrate already devoid of moisture. When saturated with moisture, the shale/mud swells and becomes a sticky, slippery, adhesive substance locally called gumbo. Slaking makes shale beds, particularly the bentonite ones, treacherously gooey and nearly impassable when deeply saturated.

In the days when freight was shipped by wagon across the northern plains, drivers had to remove brake blocks when they hit wet gumbo, as it would build up and adhere so tightly between the brake and the wheel that it would completely halt progress. In his book *Dakota: An Autobiography of a Cowman*, W. H. Hamilton, who spent many years ranching southeast of here in the nearby Cave Hills, wrote, "I have gotten stalled going downhill with an empty wagon, and that is a bad predicament to be in, for you can neither unload nor back up."[1] Hamilton didn't add that all you can do is wait until the ground hardens up enough before you move again.

Walking through the gluey muck is also difficult, as it quickly accumulates around the foot of man or beast so that each step becomes progressively heavier and more difficult than the last. Fortunately this situation is short-lived for once the moisture has subsided, the abundance of salt in the shale gives it an unusually high evaporation rate. A hot sun quickly dries the upper-layer surface, which soon cracks and hardens like wrinkled piecrust.[2]

One spring day while traveling a remote trail west of the Black Hills in eastern Wyoming, I got stuck up to the axles in a deep gumbo hole. Miles back I had made the decision to keep going through a succession of mud holes that grew progressively longer and deeper. I had managed to maintain enough momentum to plow through the first four mud holes and still maintain control of the vehicle. But my luck ran out when I made the decision to run a hole 20 yards long with 3 or 4 inches of standing water. I gunned it and made the first two thirds, slinging a rooster tail of mud and packing it up into the fenders before thick, greasy paws finally stopped me. I spun the back wheels until they started to whine and smoke. No go. There were no trees, no fences, nothing for miles but perfect desolation and a 5- or 6-mile walk back to the nearest ranch. But it was a warm, early June afternoon, the sun was shining, and I could wait for the earth to firm up. Gumbo, as the sage might say, teaches patience and forbearance. Fifteen minutes later I started the engine and after a bit of rocking managed to drive out of the deep ruts I had just dug. The rear tires were clean but had a light metallic blue sheen that never quite wore off.

This phenomenally slippery, adhesive quality when wet, followed by a firming up and then a hardening, makes the Pierre and Hell Creek formations the perfect medium to form a badlands topography, as they have on the east side below this nameless butte. Sculpting a badlands works as follows.

First, of course, it takes the right materials: consolidated, nearly homogenous, fine-grained sediments in thin, hard, horizontal layers lying above the main drainage channels. The second requirement is a scarcity of deep-rooted plants. Normally, plant cover on the grasslands is continuous enough to cast a thin umbrella of leaves over the soil. When this is the case, raindrops strike the leaves first, then gently slide down into the soil. Plant roots and the burrows of a host of invertebrates (insects) and small mammals keep the soil porous and absorbent to surface water. This biodiverse community of plants, animals, and insects conserves water while retarding erosion. If, however, the plant cover and burrowing creatures are eliminated or absent, as they often are on a hardpan or a steep, nonporous clay slope, raindrops splatter directly onto the soil surface, pounding it tight and forming a hard, impermeable crust that brings into play the third element, climate.

The northern plains country is semiarid, with an average annual precipitation of 14 to 16 inches. That's a statistic, of course, but it's pretty close to the bar. Some years it may be as little as 11 inches, while a wet year can register as much as 26 inches. At any rate, if and when moisture arrives, it usually falls in April, May, and June in heavy, concentrated showers. Rain splash and heavy surface runoff become the active forces that carve, sculpt, and fissure a high, smooth clay surface into all manner of pinnacles, crests, crowns, vertexes, and 45-degree washboards. The salts in the clay, along with the high erosion/runoff factor of bare shale slopes, enhance the formidable ability of water to rapidly create badlands masterpieces.

On the other side of the equation, the northern plains country can be so dry over long periods of time that major erosional storms take place only infrequently during any given spring season or seasons. However, when a heavy rain falls in a burst, the storm and its results can be dramatic and intense.

Along the Missouri River, particularly near the mouth of the Cheyenne and Bad Rivers, Pierre shale beds reach depths in excess of 2,000 feet, creating a wide, desolate landscape characterized by low, conical hills and precipitous, sculpted out cutbanks. In vast areas above and surrounding the mouths of the Cheyenne, Grand, Moreau, and Bad Rivers, the highland has eroded into a stark, smooth, gray, treeless landscape that can be blazing hot in the summer and bitterly cold in the winter.

Lying directly over the massive Pierre shale beds, crowning the ridges, is the Fox Hills formation, characterized by loose sand beds along with scattered, broken slabs of sandstone and shell concretions. The Fox Hills is composed of coastal marine sediments that once formed the long, ragged, sandy reefs and lagoons of the Western Interior Seaway. This great coastal reef stretched in a long arc from present-day Wall, South Dakota, northeast almost up to Bismarck, North Dakota. Today it's a wide shelf of sand with accumulated depths of 200 to 400 feet. Much later, when the climate dried out during the late Eocene and Oligocene epochs, the sand was blown and cemented into dunes,[3] now petrified into eroded ridges and buttes of crossbedded sandstone. In a few isolated areas, eroded buttes of the Fox Hills formation are capped by large shell concretions that were once oyster beds.[4]

The last of the Cretaceous formations is the rugged Hell Creek. Composed of gray to light-colored sand and silt, it marks the areas where deltas, swamps, and sluggish rivers once ran along the edge of the seaway.

Across from the butte I'm standing on is a low ridge of shale with long, round, thick chunks of sandstone protruding horizontally from it. The sandstone appears oddly out of place, emerging from the hard mud like a long finger, but its presence is a sure marker of an ossified, long dead and buried stream course that once ran through this delta. It's a pretty good indicator that I'm standing on the Hell Creek above the benthic Pierre shale.

The Pierre shale beds harbor a repository of shells, armor left by giant squids and opalescent chambered nautilus, along with the fossilized bones of huge aquatic reptiles that flourished for eons above its murky benthic depths. The tropical shallow rivers and deltas that formed the Hell Creek formation became the resting place for the 8-foot-long stingrays, crocodiles, and turtles that had lived there. Also present in the Hell Creek are the remnants of massive Apatosaurus that grazed the fetid backwaters of the creek, along with herds of duckbills (hadrosaurs), troops of Triceratops, and their pursuers, the opportunistic scavengers *Tyrannosaurus rex* and *Edmontosaurus*, which preyed on the sick and wounded.

In the western Dakotas and eastern Montana, the Hell Creek and the related Lance Creek formation in eastern Wyoming reached depths of 450 feet. We can only imagine the dramas played out on the stage of the Hell Creek formation, now the vault for the monstrous creatures of earth's Middle Life era.

The Pierre shale, Fox Hills, and Hell Creek formations bear witness to the final events of the Cretaceous and close the era of reptilian dominance. How their dynasty collapsed after so many eons is still a mystery. What is clear is that reptiles were already dying out 10 million years before the end of the Cretaceous. Reptilian species had declined by nearly 60 percent[5] before a series of natural events, some cataclysmic and meteoric, others a combination of factors as mundane as starvation due to their small brains, massive size, and overpopulation. Whatever the reason, the great monsters were finally propelled into oblivion, forever changing the nature and direction of life on what would become the northern plains.

THREE

Northern Plains Genesis

The whole universe ... is nothing but change, activity, and process—
a totality of flux that is the ground of all things.

—Sogyal Rinpoche

IT'S MID-MAY and a brief early evening thunderstorm has just swept across the White River Badlands south of a sculpted ridge called "the castle." To the northwest, inky clouds flicker with lightning as they drag ragged tendrils of rain over white chalky buttes. In a matter of ten minutes the warm earth is dry again and the peach-colored clay I am walking on is a remarkably clean, polished surface with an odd, hollow thud to it.

The purity and freshness of the air and the earth are palpable. The washed clay and fine talc sand has a grit that I believe would cleanse my skin in a coarse, invigorating way. Beyond, on a small, elevated, flat, sodded hummock of earth, shy, tiny, pink phlox blossoms peer out from thick mats of short buffalo grass. Spread out around the hummock are shallow, damp depressions filled with slender green spears of sedge and tall stalks of flowering death camas. And below the long elegant death camas stems are the stubby spreading arms of purple locoweed, a lovely group of forbs, but potentially deadly.

On the other side of the sodded hummock, the soft peach-colored floor of the wash holds scatterings of small, rectangular, corrugated agates that look like neatly sliced slabs of backfat bacon. The slabs dribble and spill off ledges, arranging themselves into curious slides, rings, and mounds of odd shapes and designs. Washed, sorted, and cast out over the years by relentless erosion and the rush of rain-water, a neat pile is arranged in the form of a nearly perfect 20-foot tipi circle. Beyond this one, I find a nearly perfect conical pile 4 feet high that appears as if it were deposited by a dump truck with a funnel. This tall, tightly packed pile of agates has captured enough eolian sand and clay to create a thin layer of soil in its interstices to support a tiny garden of wildflowers.

An insistent grumble of thunder followed by a slight breeze distracts me. I stop to listen and watch the firmament. A meadowlark trills.

I continue to follow the odd scatterings of agate wheels, heaps, and pyramids, some with enough trapped soil to host more small plant communities. Each of the agate mosaics presents an artful, graphic demonstration of how rain, wind, and erosion inexorably drive change—natural dynamism on a microcosmic scale subtly raising the diversity of life by means of local destruction followed by regeneration. Each mosaic conveys a singularly unique and beautiful statement, nature unceremoniously ripping apart old systems, then recombining the fragments to build new ones. Always experimenting, revitalizing, renewing. Always searching for something slightly new and in the process formulating the unexpected and the unusual.

The sides of the wash are mostly white substrates from the Oligocene. They are a mixture of clay, sand, and volcanic ash that were washed down from the Rocky Mountains for 10 million years. Some of it has hardened to near rock while other parts of the same strata are nothing more than soft mud, layer after layer of gritty clay in hues of red, pink, and white standing 70 feet high above the wash. The sides of the wash are primer pages, rough and splendid, that hold and record the amazing evolutionary history of the mammalian megafauna that once inhabited the northern plains. Herein lie the remains of yet another life evolution experiment atop the tomb of the previous reptilian one.

Deep, low thunder again, but farther away. The frogs seem revitalized and chirp with patient insistence. The evening rain sky deepens into a froth of dark meringue. More low, sourceless rumbling followed by the serene quietude of darkness. Peering at the last dim shafts of twilight, I think about how storms are the wedges that often drive change into the vast, resilient force of life. Nightfall and the earth seem suffused with creativity. This must have been the feeling, the sense of charged anticipation and expectancy that ushered in the Cenozoic Era.

The story of the Cenozoic, the great Age of Birds and Mammals on the northern plains, began about 65 million years ago with the Paleocene epoch. By the end of the Cretaceous, the great Western Interior Seaway was beginning to recede for the last time from the interior of North America. This recession was coincidental as major features of the Rocky Mountains were forming. The internal geologic forces that were pushing, folding, and crumbling the thin crust on the west side of the continent gradually began lifting the western cordillera of North America along a narrow, north-south-trending belt extending from Mexico to Alaska. Barely discernible at first, this early mountain-building period was nearly cancelled out by erosion. The base of the mountains rose only 1,000 feet above sea level while the crests rose to 2,000 feet.

During the Paleocene and through the Eocene, the landscape of western North America was marked by great basins situated between the nascent Rocky Mountain chains. These basins luxuriated in dense, subtropical forests dominated by two types of palm trees, *Phoenicites* (feathered-leaf palms) and *Palmacites* (palm-leafed palms), while yellow water lilies and horsetail (*equisetum*) grew in and around the water's edge. But climatic change was under way and by the middle of the Paleocene, following a slight cooling of the climate, new deciduous plants like dogwoods and sassafras appeared and grew in abundance.

As the basins filled with sediments, the overflow spilled out across the adjacent plains in wide, shallow rivers heavy with fine silt, sand, and clay. These slow, sluggish rivers flowed out of their banks, depositing their tremendous loads of sediment over a broad featureless plain, only recently the bottom of the sea. As their velocities slowed, the rivers formed deltas and swamps, providing suitable habitat for what was left of the reptiles, including large boa constrictors and pythons newly evolved to prey on warm-blooded mammals along with a variety of soft-shelled turtles and crocodilians.

Ancient primitive mammals with rodentlike features and an ancestry stemming from a small, highly active, carnivorous, springing type of dinosaur[1] developed large cheek teeth for husking and cracking the fruits and nuts of newly dominant angiosperms (flowering plants). Insectivores, mostly small nocturnal animals such as shrews and moles and small, archaic ungulates, also appeared during the Paleocene.

On the northern plains, sedimentary Paleocene deposits changed from clay to sand that over time hardened into a soft, umber sandstone 2,000 to 3,000 feet in thickness, capping the Hell Creek formation in the western Dakotas and eastern Montana. All the members, or zones, of this vast sandstone formation contain seams of coal indicating periods of lush, tropical flora alternating with periods of inundation. In the North Cave Hills of northwestern South Dakota, the lowest member or oldest Paleocene deposit, the Ludlow, formed a rim of sandstone 350 feet thick.[2] Farther north and east in North Dakota, these Paleocene sandstone layers belong to the Cannonball member, a soft, coastal deposit filled with the fossil shells of small seawater clams and snails.

Above the Ludlow lies the Tongue River member, consisting of very thick sequences of sandstone and lignite coal deposits that make up the long rims of the Bull Mountains 30 miles south of Roundup, Montana. In eastern Montana and northern Wyoming the Tongue River member's vast lignite reserves would be mined extensively during the Holocene.[3]

The Ludlow, Cannonball, and Tongue River members,[4] deposited by deltas, lakes, and rivers, constitute the Fort Union group, accounting for all the sedimentary deposition that occurred during the 8 million years of the relatively quiet Paleocene.

During the Eocene the climate of the northern plains remains wet and warm and palm trees coexisted with early broadleaf trees. *Metasequoia*, the famous "dawn redwood" rediscovered in a small grove in China in 1941, appeared and soon dominated all Northern Hemisphere forests from the tropics to the North Pole through the remainder of the Cenozoic.

The Eocene, like the Paleocene, was also a period of relative stability, lasting 17 million years. There was fairly little mountain uplifting during this epoch, while intermontane basins continued to fill and host great freshwater lakes with more species of tropical and sub-tropical plants. The northern plains continued to be characterized by sluggish streams, deltas, swamps, and backwaters while deep weathering and erosion occured in higher areas, allowing for a widespread, strongly developed soil to form.

The predominantly forested landscape of the Eocene hosted an explosion of mammalian life that featured the appearance of the first true rodents. They were mostly small and inconspicuous, squirrel-like creatures that soon colonized all the available habitats, quickly becoming varied and numerous.

Placental mammals were clearly the main players of life. Their offspring possessed immensely important survival advantages over other life-forms. Born live, fully formed and well developed, they were nourished by their mothers' rich milk and nurtured and protected by her affectionate regard.

Their brains, larger than those of their reptilian antecedents, also gave them a distinct advantage in self-perpetuation which, coupled with increased speed and agility, helped them escape from the ever-growing array of faster and larger canine and feline predators.

Mammalian life quickly adapted to increasing changes in climate and vegetation, while evolution rapidly progressed from the simple to the complex, the simple appearing first and the more complex later. The rapid burst of evolution in the Eocene also produced many fully formed mammalian species. Some, like the titanotheres, persisted almost unchanged for millions of years before they disappeared, while others, such as the horse, the pig, the rhinoceros, and the camel, continually evolved upward in body and brain size, defensive techniques, feeding, social organization, and behavioral complexity.

As eons passed, a massive blanket of sediments known as the White River group extended the entire length of the Great Plains from Saskatchewan to Texas. Over some 15 million years of deposition beginning in the Eocene and continuing through the Oligocene, the old, flat silt rivers flowing from the mountains and basins managed to leave 650-foot-deep deposits of mud, clay, silt, ash, and gravel.

During this long period of deposition, new forests of deciduous trees evolved and flourished, continually adding new species of trees. Through the Oligocene and into the Miocene and Pliocene these forests grew to include poplar, willow, birch, ash, elm, sycamore, maple, sumac, hackberry, and walnut trees, which swarmed with birds and herds of small horses, rhinoceroses, and camels. And yet, just below the new splash of color and sound, these rapidly evolving animal species struggled ceaselessly for dominance and supremacy.

At the onset of the Oligocene, 38 million years before the present, mountain uplifting resumed along with stirrings of volcanism, which produced voluminous quantities of alluvia that inundated the northern plains via both wind and water. These deposits weathered into the pale, pinkish, cemented clays of the White River group of the Big (White River) Badlands in southwestern South Dakota and the long table of the Slim Buttes where deposits measure 500 to 600 feet in thickness.

Other hard, thick, chalky clay formations of the late Eocene and Oligocene on the northern plains eroded into the Long Pine Hills, the Ekalaka Hills, and the Chalk Buttes of southeastern Montana; the Slim Buttes and East and West Short Pine Hills of northwestern South Dakota; and the White and Chalky Buttes, East and West Rainy Buttes, and Killdeer Mountains in southwestern North Dakota.[5]

During the Oligocene, the continental backbone of North America, the Rocky Mountain cordillera, rose ever higher. As these immense walls of granite became elevated enough to effectively begin blocking most of the flow of warm, moist air from the Pacific, the western interior of the continent began to dry out and cool. By the end of the Oligocene a warm, temperate forest with ever-expanding savannas dominated the landscape.

The savannas of the northern plains continued to evolve their own unique flora, which included an ever-increasing array of cereals, grains, and grasses. Across these windswept landscapes of intense sun and waving grass, a complement of hooved grazing mammals, the ungulates, whose small antecedents had their beginnings in the subtropical forests of the Eocene, were now evolving specific physical adaptations to colonize them. Primitive at first, this host of ruminating herbivores quickly developed high-crowned cheek teeth that continued to grow from the roots to handle the abrasive grasses they were now forced to chew. Enamel, the most resistant tooth material, became folded so that when the tooth wore down, a system of enamel ridges continued to provide a hard, grinding surface.

The open plains environment also forced this growing host of herbivores to quickly evolve physical modifications for agile and speedy flight from the growing number of evolving mammalian predatory carnivores. Limb and foot bones lengthened and strengthened to permit rapid rotational fore and aft movement. Grazing animals also evolved the ability to run on their toes. In order to gain this advantage, the ungulates lost their side toes while their middle phalanges (toes) widened; they developed a hoof for greater protection when running over the hard prairie sod.

These ungulates (creatures that feed on grass and walk on hooves) evolved a four-chambered stomach system that improved the efficiency of their digestive mechanism for breaking down or ruminating the tough grassy materials they now fed on exclusively.

As mammalian life spread out to colonize the plains during the Oligocene and into the Miocene, all species continued to develop more efficient nervous and reproductive systems, greater speed and agility, reliable systems of body temperature control, larger brains with greater capacity for smell and hearing, and an innate instinctual animal intelligence that far exceeded anything reptilian that had preceded them.

In this amazing revitalization of life sweeping out across the northern plains, rodents, including mice, ground squirrels, prairie dogs, marmots, muskrats, and large burrowing beavers, proved the most successful, followed by the lagomorphs (rabbits, hares, and pikas). The development of carnivorous flesh-eaters, including weasels, raccoons, primitive cats, dogs, and bears, accelerated to take advantage of this great movable feast.

With the beginning of the Miocene, 24 million years before the present, the entire western region of the continent began yet another dramatic uplift. For the greatest part of the Cenozoic, some 50 million years of unrecorded time, streams for the most part had been depositing sediment *over* the plains, building up thick layers of sedimentary rock. Now, with a vigorous period of renewed uplifting, *all* the streams flowing east from the mountains across the northern plains were forced to cut down deeply *into* the plains.

This deep cutting began to build an arterial web of tributary streams leading away from the mountains. As stream excavation continued over broader areas, high grass ridges were left as divides between parallel river systems while other areas remained as broad, flat plateaus with eroded and disconnected buttes and mesas composed of various materials from their ancient past.

The climate also began to fluctuate by ever greater degrees between warm and cool, wet and dry, ushering in a distinctive rhythm of seasons that forced plants and animals to develop and adapt new strategies of survival. With the impulse of the seasons acting as a major force driving evolution, flowering plants inaugurated a cycle of bloom in the spring and fruition in the summer, followed by a cold period of dormancy. Mammals now gorged in the summer to store fat. They also developed thick coats of fur to insulate themselves through the coldest months in order to maintain their increasingly sensitive metabolic cycles.

As the Miocene progressed the two general types of ungulates, the odd-toed perissodactyls and the even-toed artiodactyls, continued their evolutionary journeys from a common plantigrade, five-toed ancestor.

The perissodactyls, made up of three families of creatures—the rhinoceroses, tapirs, and horses—represented the survivors of an original seven that once flourished on the northern plains. Of the three subspecies of rhinoceros that lived in large herds in the vicinity of the Black Hills during the Oligocene, only one remained to migrate into Asia and Africa and survive into the present.

The family of tapirs has remained virtually unchanged since its earliest days as a forest-dwelling creature, while the horse (*equus*) family became the classic model of evolution, developing from a 1-foot-high Eocene forest animal with four distinct toes that once ate twigs and leaves to a graceful, finely built creature with an intricate method of supporting its weight on the third or middle toe of its "foot" and raising its ankle to achieve more speed on the run.

The horse is an example of a successful generalized mammal that was able to occupy more than one habitat—to shift and evolve from forest to grassland, enabling it to survive for a longer period of time.

Another odd-toed creature distantly related to rhinos, tapirs, and horses that evolved on the northern plains during the Miocene was the chalicothere, *Moropus elatus. Moropus* appears to have evolved a rather ungainly and even grotesque body form and appearance. Although its head and neck resembled those of a horse, its heavy body maintained the general appearance of a rhino. Its muscular furry fore limbs were larger and longer than the hind limbs so that its back sloped rearward. Rather than hooves, its feet terminated in long, sharp, bifid, clawlike bones, combining in a peculiar aspect characteristics of both ungulates and carnivores. Its long, curved front claws probably forced *Moropus* to walk on its knuckles. These front claws may have been used to pull down tree branches in order to feed on leaves, which seem to have made up its diet exclusively.

The chalicothere is an example of a Cenozoic mammal specialized to a particular habitat where it was eventually trapped by its own evolution and declined to extinction as its preferred habitat, in this case the temperate forests of the northern plains, diminished and disappeared.

Another odd-toed, rhinolike ungulate found in South Dakota's White River Badlands also achieved elephantine status: the massive titanotheres, which to date are the largest creatures found in the badlands beds. There were five phyla, of which *Brontops* grew to be the largest. Developing slowly at first in the Eocene, near the middle of the Oligocene, titanotheres reached a massive size, comparable to that of a small elephant. One skeleton discovered in the badlands in 1895 indicated a beast 14 feet long and 8 feet high.

Titanotheres developed a thick skin covering and a head that resembled that of a rhinoceros, with a large, curved, saddle-shaped, hornlike protuberance that grew over its snout and three toes that splayed out on each foot. Like most of the early mammalian types that grew relatively quickly to a large size, its brain-to-body size was too small, dooming it to extinction.

Titanotheres evolved quickly during the Oligocene, and except for developing both in size and some minor special characteristics, they remained relatively unchanged. Their rapid, specialized, evolutionary burst in contrast to that of the equids was followed by a quick extinction near the end of the Oligocene, leaving no descendants.

Although the enormous titanotheres appeared ungainly and bizarre by today's downsized mammalian standards, they nonetheless possessed the survival skills that allowed them to endure for nearly 10 million years only to die out and be exterminated by the highly successful and aggressive members of the evolving cat and dog families.

It would be the artiodactyls, the even-toed creatures including ancestral pigs, goats, deer, sheep, cattle, and camels, that would achieve the greater evolutionary success both in species survival and in sheer numbers.

In the case of bovids (cattle, sheep, and goats) along with deer, elk, and bison, all of which evolved in Eurasia, the two middle toes evolved to be identical in size and shape, and, like the perissodactyls, they developed hooves for toe protection. When matched together, these two hooves made the foot appear to be split or cloven when in fact they were the two separate, middle phalanges of what was once a five-digit extension.

The White River Badlands have also yielded the fossilized remains of *Archaeotherium*, an ancestral giant pig resembling a hippopotamus. The most abundant fossil remains in the badlands, however, are the oreodonts, which one researcher describes simply as small "ruminating hogs." Oreodonts were squat beasts with a massive head, a small robust neck, and short legs with four toes on each foot. There were many species and varieties, measuring from 3 to 5.5 feet in length, and the vast quantity of their remains found in the bone beds suggests they were once great in number. They must have been a favorite, tasty prey of the prehistoric cat and dog families.

Protoceras was an ancient horned ruminant from the Oligocene with four functional hooves on the front feet and two hooves on the hind. *Protoceras* had a narrow face and developed a set of prominent curved horns on top of its head and at the end of its snout. Its descendants continued to evolve into various horned ungulates through the Miocene and into the Pliocene.

The third most abundant creature of the Oligocene after the oreodonts and horses were the camelids, including llamas and the long-necked, gazelle-like *Alticamelus* and *Procamelus*, ancestors of the modern camel. During the Miocene these ancestral camelids had hard hooves. This illustrious family of creatures passed their whole development on the North American plains, evolving in size and number, only to be one of the last to disappear from the continent near the end of the Pliocene.

The Pliocene, lasting 3 million years, is the last and shortest chapter of the Cenozoic. It is notable for the evolution of the antilocaprid family, whose descendants gave rise to the pronghorn (antelope), the only native northern plains ungulate that managed to squeeze through the bottleneck of the bitter Pleistocene Ice Age and survive into the present, a remarkable evolutionary achievement.

Perhaps the most important aspect contributing to the success of the artiodactyls was their ability to chew, digest, and ruminate the tough grasses of the Pliocene plains. Rumination, a process whereby ungulates are able to break down coarse grasses by passing their cud through a multichambered stomach, might be considered a kind of biological alchemy, the equivalent of plant photosynthesis whereby the sun's energy stored in grass is converted and transformed into blood, muscle, and bone.

This attribute allowed them to endure the cooler, drier conditions now prevalent during the Pliocene on the northern plains. The Pliocene clearly foreshadowed the Pleistocene Ice Age and was characterized by well-established seasons and a landscape that was primarily grassland, with only scattered forests of mixed deciduous and conifer trees (spruce and pine).

With the changing climate, rumination, reduction in body size, and a thick coat of fur became more important as conditions grew harsher and food and water increasingly scarce.

The most abundant and successful ruminants that had once dominated the northern plains during the middle to late Cenozoic would soon change to herds of cervids (deer and elk) along with massive mammoths, mastodons, wolves, grizzly bears, and bison, all of which crossed over the Bering land bridge from Asia during the Pleistocene, replacing the great herds of ancestral camels, llamas, swine, rhinoceros, and horses who escaped extinction only by migrating the other way.

FOUR

Bison and the Ice Age

Ice crystals are all six sided stars, flat hexagons, each with its own unique design. When they hit the earth, they interlock forming a vast sheet of crystalline whiteness. —*The Book of Urantia*

ON AN EARLY WINTER AFTERNOON in the eastern foothills of the Black Hills, I linger to observe a small cow-calf herd of bison ruminating on a terrace above a narrow, oak-clotted draw. Getting a closer look means slowly crunching my way up the draw through knee-high snowdrifts. When I am opposite the herd, I belly up the edge of the gully and stand behind a large, bison horn–scarred pine. The herd is small, maybe sixty animals, most of which are standing quietly 50 yards away.

My movements, subtle as I believe them to be, have nonetheless attracted the immediate scrutiny of four heifer yearlings standing in the front of the herd. They study me with a curious, rapt attention. Most of the animals behind them are actively engaged in brushing away snow with their snouts and grabbing meager mouthfuls of dry grass. A half dozen are lying down ruminating.

The heifers and I stand motionless and silent facing each other across the snow. Then, subtly as if on cue, the animals begin to slowly move and shift positions. Somewhere, unnoticed by me, the old lead cow, reacting perhaps to my presence, has given the signal to move. The animals lying down are getting up; those standing or grazing begin to perambulate at an easy gait up and out of the draw away from me.

I back down a few feet into the shelter of the draw, using the bur oaks to break up the shape of my form. The heifers all turn away.

Responding to the herd instinct, they too now begin to amble slowly up the hillside. The wind picks up. Hard, grainy crystals of swirling snow fly into my face, and I drop all the way back down to the bottom of the draw to escape the bite and sting of snow and wind.

Above me the cold wind saws through the oaks with an occasional hard gust that rattles dry, bronze, brittle leaves. On the north edge of the draw, wands of tall, blond grass bend at the wind's insistence to the southeast. Somewhere in the distance a crow caws twice. Then twice again. A pair of horned larks chirp sweetly nearby for a moment before flying off together. Feeling refreshed, I crawl to the top of the draw and peer south again. No buffalo. Only snow, wind, and the low, dim orb of the late December sun.

I walk to where they were standing. Interspersed amidst a crisscross of meandering trails are piles of fresh, steaming dung. There are brushed areas where they shoved away the snow to get at the grass. There are also large oval holes in the snowpack half-filled with frozen slush where a warm bison body recently lay.

I start to follow their meandering course south out of the draw, noting track sizes, use and depth of various trails in the snow, dung freshness, and their general direction of travel, along with the direction and velocity of the wind. It's instinctual and exciting. Then I realize I'm getting a primal adrenalin rush. I am subconsciously hunting and have become a predator. My senses are flushed and heightened to a single purpose and a single focus: to find and move up to the bison herd. How many generations of hunters have followed the trail of wild bison in the snow intent on the chase and the kill? The plot and drama of the hunt must be timeless.

Above the rise of the draw a quarter mile away to the south, the bison are grazing at the edge of a dark copse of pine, heads down in snow-covered grass, cinnamon-brown backs and rumps all turned into the wind. Slowly, methodically, I move up to their downwind flanks, the preferred position of the hunter when not wishing or able to employ an ambuscade from the trees. None take notice of me.

A high, broad line of cirrus, serving as an opaque lens, slides in front of the sun, darkening the already dim shadows cast on the snow. The herd of bison, their hides now a deeper hue of brown, blend so harmoniously in tonal quality with that of the pine curtain behind them that they are nearly invisible. Only their slow and easy movements betray them.

They keep moving and I follow at their pace, slowly edging up and closing the distance to 50 yards. I gain their downwind east flank. A few stop to notice and peer at me, their wide, dark, curly-haired faces flecked with snow. My heart is pounding. Now is the time to hurl the spear dart or loose the arrow.

The wind kicks up a swirling snow devil that passes between me and the herd. The sun slips from behind the cirrus and glares off the snow. I turn away, breaking off the hunt, crunching my way back through finger drifts, thinking about how it must have been this way from time immemorial. The drama of the hunt by the end of the Ice Age would prove to be the measure of both men and bison.

How the Ice Age or Pleistocene came into being remains a matter of mystery and conjecture. A recent theory suggests that the primary cause of this great cataclysmic climatic change was the movement and subsequent collision of continents that began some 60 million years ago coinciding with the Rocky Mountain uplift. Deep tectonic movements in the earth punched up hardened pieces of brittle crust at its thinnest, weakest junctures, forming the present great mountain chains of western North America, Europe, and Asia. The rise of these great mountain walls created a chain of events that slowly began to profoundly alter the earth's climatic cycles.[1]

Prior to the start of the Pleistocene, some 2 million years before the present, the entire planet enjoyed a relatively mild climate. Maritime influences for the most part dominated global weather patterns. Gradually, however, the ever-increasing height of massive mountain ranges began to deflect warm, moisture-laden seasonal wind currents of oceanic air upward, greatly cooling it. As the heavily saturated atmosphere was forced over high granite mountain walls of the newly formed northern highlands, they produced almost constant moisture that fell in the form of snow.

Snow began to accumulate first on the elevated, cooler regions of the Northern Hemisphere and continued to fall until it had attained depths of 1 to even 2 miles. The areas of greatest snow depth and elevation eventually determined the loci of subsequent glacial pressure. As this enormous mantle of snow grew, it compressed and metamorphosed into solid, creeping ice.

At speeds that varied according to icepack depth and plasticity, glaciers advanced over North America from the northeast to the south and west, moving and retreating as much as a half mile per year and leaving a devastated landscape in their wake. With each season's advance, rivers and valleys were blocked and subsequently flooded. Glaciers advancing from the northeast from a locus around Hudson's Bay eventually altered the flow of all the major river courses of the northern plains by effectively damming their preglacial courses to Hudson's Bay, forcing them all finally to become tributaries of the Missouri, which prior to the Pleistocene did not exist.[2]

As snow continued to blanket the earth around the boreal highlands for six to eight months every year, a new season, winter, came into full being with temperatures that routinely dropped to −60° F accompanied by windchills at −120° F. The Age of Ice had arrived.

Spring in the glacial zones consisted of warmer winds blowing over miles of pocked snowfields so deep, and so ubiquitous, that the ambient air temperature hovered almost constantly at 40° F during a sunlit day.

Summer consisted of a few short weeks of intense radiation, long enough for great, shallow lakes and marshes of ice-cold meltwater to form in front of the glaciers and spread out across the half-frozen land. When summer temporarily halted the advancing glaciers, lowlands east of the Missouri River turned into a vast network of marsh, wet meadows, and outwash lakes that provided nesting areas to great flocks of breeding waterbirds and still ponds and puddles for the hoards of insects they fed on.

Prior to this extensive, large-scale advance of ice, the plains of North America were overrun with an amazing array of horses, camels, llamas, pigs, pronghorns, and giant burrowing beavers, along with an interesting variety of creatures representing the feline and canine families. As the extreme severity of the climate increased, however, both numbers and species of animals declined. So precipitous was the reduction in mammalian species that by the end of the Ice Age, some 10,000 to 15,000 years before the present, the majority of ungulates that had once been so prominent and numerous across the northern plains were either greatly diminished or had became extinct on the continent of their grand evolution.

Beginning 10,000 years ago, the Holocene, or modern warming era, finally superseded the Pleistocene. And although temperatures moderated greatly and rapidly after the Ice Age, the northern Great Plains still maintained the signature aspects of this severe period with a dry, continental climate marked by long, bitter, cold winters and short, hot summers.

East of the Missouri, a high belt of hummocky, "dead-ice" morainal material created by the repeated advance, stagnation, and retreat of countless ice sheets, formed a series of low hills known as the Missouri Coteau.

The Missouri Coteau (hills) takes shape in northeastern Montana where it shadows the north and east side of the Missouri River through eastern Montana, North Dakota, and down through south-central South Dakota varying from 20 to 75 miles in width. In north-western North Dakota around old Fort Union, it attains its maximum elevation of 2,400 feet. The Swiss painter Karl Bodmer painted great scenes of and from it on his trip up the Missouri in 1833.

The Coteau's east- and northeast-facing escarpment forms the easternmost boundary of the Great Plains province proper, separating it from the Central Lowland province to the east. In North Dakota the Missouri Coteau is commonly 200 to 300 feet higher than the surrounding landscape with some conspicuous features, while in South Dakota it is generally less prominent.

Near the end of the Ice Age this escarpment acted as a buttress to later, lesser advancing ice sheets and played an important role in determining the direction of ice progression along with the positions of end moraines and other glacial features.

West of the Missouri the earliest ice advances left evidence of their visit in the form of large, erratic boulders scattered as far as 25 miles west and south of the great river in Montana and the Dakotas. The Northwestern Plains province proper (the unglaciated plains) escaped the grind of glaciation and was not buried under the 300 to 500 feet of glacial till that now forms the rich farmland of the Lowland province.

The attractive, contoured landform of the northwestern plains, which for the most part was created over the last 2 million years of the Ice Age, is the result of wind, winter runoff, and spring floods, not glaciation. These elemental forces of nature created the meandering stream courses of all the present northern plains rivers, carving out the divides and highlands fissured with creeks, coulees, and draws.

The divides of the western Dakotas have developed into a topographical ladder of rivers each separated from the next by a highland and a corresponding lowland river valley running in a west-to-east direction beginning in the south with the Niobrara, White, Bad, Cheyenne, Moreau, Grand, Cannonball, Heart, and Knife.

With the Little Missouri the ladder begins to shift to a more southwest-northeast direction, draining the Bighorn highlands through the Yellowstone and its tributaries and the Montana Rocky Mountain Front through the Musselshell, Judith, and Smith. All these highlands to varying degrees have been further incised and fissured by a vast arterial network of tributaries, most of which are gently winding draws and coulees. When fire and overgrazing are absent, the bottoms of the draws and coulees fill out with chokecherry, buffaloberry, wolfberry, and plum thickets. Along the lower ends of these draws, ash, hackberry, American elm, boxelder, willow, and cottonwood skirt the riparian fringe.

This is the landscape that greeted the first clans of nomadic big-game hunters at the end of the Pleistocene when they wandered up first from the southwest and later from the northwest onto the great northern buffalo plains. It was still a cold, windswept region when the first human migrants followed the tracks of mammoths and the well-worn herd trails of the great Ice Age bison. Armed with atlatls (long-handled spear throwers) and flint-tipped spear-darts, they were canny and expert in the pursuit of their quarry.

Their greatest hunt prize was certainly the Columbian mammoths that, during the Ice Age, had become well adapted to a cold steppe environment characterized by active glaciers, huge glacial lakes, and long, winding moraines through which they roamed and foraged for the tons of rough grasses they had to eat and ferment to sustain their great bulk.

The mastodon, a smaller elephant relative of the mammoth with straighter tusks and a different tooth structure, roamed through the birch, aspen, and alder thickets, preferring to strip trees of their leaves, twigs, and bark. Both proboscideans, after a long species life-time as a dominant mammal on the northern plains, disappeared at the end of the Ice Age, victims of a rapidly warming environment and overhunting.

While the great elephants left no descendants on this continent, one species of bison managed to survive the onslaught of early hunters and the drastic warming of the climate. In fact the later de-scendants of this great Ice Age beast thrived and multiplied on the nutritious grasses of the northern plains.

The progenitor of all species of North American bison, like most of the successful artiodactyls, evolved in subtropical Eurasia and Africa millions of years before the Ice Age. The earliest bison were small, short-horned beasts that gradually migrated north to colonize the evolving open grasslands of Europe. Migrating from the temperate regions, they eventually concentrated on the cold steppes of Eurasia and northern Europe. These creatures quickly evolved as fast runners for wolves were always nearby ready to cull the slow, the confused, the sick, and the unlucky.

With the onset of the Ice Age, the Eurasian steppe wisent (or bison) migrated farther north to exploit the nutrient-rich, fertile ecosystems that were forming and evolving under the influence of continental glaciation. One species, *Bison priscus*, possessing an attractive set of curving horns and a head and body reminiscent of a longhorn cow, crossed the Bering land bridge into North America 300,000 years before the present.

Bison priscus is the same elegant animal whose painted images still adorn walls of the Ice Age caves of Lascaux, France. And though no proof exists, it is an easy leap to imagine a herd of *Bison priscus* being shadowed across the Bering land bridge by packs of wolves and clans of red men as they entered a new, unoccupied continent.

Responding to severe predation pressure as well as the abundance of grass in prehistoric North America, *Bison priscus* quickly grew into the gigantic *Bison latifrons*, which evolved a larger, woolier head, a wide sweep of thick horns, and a larger hump, all without sacrificing any of its speed or agility.

Bison latifrons, an immense and regal beast, must have dispersed across North America, quickly occupying all available habitats. As forage and space became filled to capacity, however, populations of bison as well as other ungulates had to compete for the best forage. This competition triggered another evolutionary direction that selected for the most efficient grazer and forage converter. Bison had to do more with less so natural selection sacrificed body mass for reproduction efficiency, producing a scaled-down species version called *Bison antiquus*, which appeared on the plains near the end of the Ice Age. This animal was hunted extensively and successfully by the first bands of archaic hunters on the northern plains.

One final cold phase at the end of the Pleistocene, lasting a millennium from 11,000 to 10,000 years before the present, allowed the moose, the elk, and the grizzly bear, along with one final species of bison called *Bison occidentalis*, to cross from eastern Siberia into western Alaska.

Bison occidentalis, already probably reduced in body size when they made the Bering crossing,[3] joined what was left of the few surviving species of the dwindling North American Ice Age fauna, including whitetail and mule deer, pronghorn, black bear, wolf, and coyote.

Bison occidentalis's reduced size was probably the direct result of Siberian hunters who had over generations selected out and killed the largest, boldest specimens of bison, those who had chosen to stand their ground and fight rather than flee. Having been culled by hunters, *Bison occidentalis* spread quickly over the range formerly occupied by the now-diminishing remnants of *Bison antiquus*. The two species may have hybridized before *Bison antiquus* disappeared from the living animal species record.[4]

Midway through the Holocene epoch, *Bison occidentalis* was replaced by a relatively small-headed, short-horned "dwarf" of a bison called *Bison bison* that was 30 percent smaller in mass than its predecessor. Culled by wolves and native hunters for millennia, *Bison bison* had developed speed, agility, and endurance. For a time the match between a man on foot with an atlatl and a wary, fleet-footed bison was an even one, with the bison having the edge in speed and strength, but this underestimates the intangible guile, spirit, courage, and determination of the hunter.

FIVE

"Calling the Buffalo"

Sometimes at evening I sit looking out on the big Missouri. The sun sets, and dusk steals over the water. In the shadows I seem again to see our Indian village, with smoke curling upward from the earthlodges; and in the river's roar I hear the yells of the warriors, the laughter of little children as of old. —Buffalo Bird Woman

THE AWATIXA (ah-wah-TEE-khah) Hidatsa village, located near the mouth of the Knife River, was immortalized by George Catlin, who painted it in the summer of 1832. His portrait depicts a rich, sensuous scene of life and activity on a warm, lazy afternoon 170 years ago. Wading deeply into his idyllic scene, one can smell the warm, brown water of the Knife River as two young boys race through the shallows below the village where people are absorbed in daily activities or lounging together on the rooftops of the earthlodges. It's a dreamy rendition of a time hardly imaginable today as I look at the site on a late October afternoon in the early twenty-first century.

The Knife River is only 30 yards wide and shallow with a thin skim of ice. It's late in the year after a dry summer and the river is but a trickle of water compared with Catlin's rendering of that summer stream now so long past. Of the village nothing structural remains. All the earthlodges were destroyed when a Sioux raiding party torched it two years after Catlin painted it. The Hidatsa never returned. Today only thirty-one of fifty-three lodge depressions remain. Cutbank erosion and channel shifting have completely washed away six depressions and partially destroyed another half dozen while modern farming obliterated ten more sites on the east side.

Catlin stayed at Awatixa for several weeks during the summer of 1832 and painted a variety of the wonderfully animated scenes he witnessed around him. Thirty years earlier, Toussaint Charbonneau[1] lived in this village with his now-legendary teenage wife, Sakakawea. It was at Awatixa they met Lewis and Clark in the fall of 1804 and left with them the following spring for the Pacific.

Awatixa was one of three separate villages or groups speaking a distinct dialect of Hidatsa. The Awatixa Hidatsa probably first arrived at the Missouri River in the twelfth century. The Awaxawi, who built a neighboring village, came later from the Devil's Lake area, followed by the Hidatsa proper, who moved there from the same northern region. Buffalo Bird Woman, an Awaxawi Hidatsa, told Gilbert Wilson that Itsikamahadiś, a powerful spirit from the distant past, told the Awaxawi to follow him "to a better place on the Missouri River." They did, and he led them to a bluff on the east side of the river opposite the mouth of the Knife. "There," he said, pointing to the west side of the Missouri, "shall be your village. You shall grow up like red willows, so numerous shall you become." They crossed over to the west side of the river and built a village on the south side of the Knife, and increased rapidly as Itsikamahadiś promised. They called themselves the People of the Red Willows for, as Buffalo Bird Woman explained, "Red willows grow quickly. When the water of the Missouri goes down and leaves a sand bank, this is soon covered with shoots of this kind of red willow."

The newly arriving Hidatsas allied themselves with the numerous Mandans whose main villages clustered around the mouth of the Heart River to the south. Both people spoke Siouan languages and became close friends to the extent that they freely mingled and cohabited in each other's villages. Even their ceremonies and creation myths were similar, presenting an interesting perspective on how they perceived the creation of the northern plains.

For the Mandans and Hidatsa, Itsikamahadiś, or First Worker, was the first creator. "He made the world and all the people," Virginia Peters writes in her excellent book on the Mandans and Hidatsas, *Women of the Earth Lodges*. Itsikamahadiś's first name was "Amamikśaś, or Female Earth, because he made the south (west) side of the Missouri

River country. When First Worker created the world he wanted the earth to be solid, immovable, and everlasting. But this was no good; nothing ever died and nothing moved. So he covered all the earth, except for one hill, with water. A man ran down the hill; he was called Lone Man because he was the first man and alone."[2]

Lone Man, however, was also a Creator Spirit and he, along with First Worker, created the earth in one day and made the grass grow the second day. On the third day they made the different kinds of trees that grow on both sides of the Missouri, and early on the fourth day they started making the animals. First Worker created the buffalo and elk that lived primarily on the west side of the river while Lone Man created the moose, elk, and cattle that lived on the east side. On the fifth day they made the birds and on the sixth day they made the creeks and other running waters. The Mandans, noting the obvious differences in the landscape between the unglaciated northwestern plains west of the river and the glaciated lowland lake country east of the river, explained that First Worker made big and little springs that emerge from the earth on the west side of the river while on the east side Lone Man made the clear, beautiful, glacial pothole lakes.[3]

After all this work the two creators met to see what each had made. First Worker thought the land that Lone Man had made was good, except that it was too flat and open to be best suited for people (Mandans). He also believed the buffalo he had made were better than the cattle.[4]

Next, they both visited the west side of the Missouri. Lone Man liked the people (human beings) First Worker had made and the elk and buffalo, especially the white ones that all future generations would esteem.

Before the two creators made the grass and the trees, they traveled all over the world and found the ground to be only sand devoid of living plants, but they found tracks and were able to talk to some animals. Eventually Lone Man found a buffalo bull who taught him how to plant and dry tobacco and who sent him to meet Ear-afire, who taught him how to make fire and light his pipe to smoke it. Lone Man then said, "I will make people resembling me and I will give them ceremonies." And because the buffalo had helped him, Lone Man decreed that the people must have a buffalo skull in every ceremony, and so they did.[5]

Buffalo hunting and the cultivation of corn became the central focus of Mandan and Hidatsa life. As their primary source of sustenance and survival, these totems were sacred, iconic symbols in their rich, developing ceremonial culture.

While the Mandans and Hidatsas traveled far to the west in their pursuit of bison, their center of activity and culture revolved around their respective villages, the majority of which were built on terraces on the west side of the Missouri to give them close proximity to water and firewood.

The women tended gardens 3 to 5 acres in size, which were located nearby on the rich alluvial soil of the floodplains. In these family gardens owned by the women, they planted corn, beans, squash, and sunflowers. Each planting season was preceded by a dream about who would preside over the spring seed and planting ceremonies, as well as the arrival of the waterbirds (cormorants) from the south who brought with them the warmth of spring and the answered prayers and blessings of Old Woman Who Never Dies, goddess of all vegetation and patroness of the propagation of cultivated crops.[6] Every aspect of the planting cycle, beginning with the seeds, had its ceremony and function to ensure a bountiful harvest of food. In these important life-renewal ceremonies and work the women were leaders.

The plains village people maintained a seamless holistic view of their life and universe. In their view, plants, animals, people, and spirits all possessed an anima. They also shared and inhabited the same world. Shamans who acted as intermediaries were responsible for maintaining the balance and welfare of this entire world community. Their ceremonies were entreaties and supplications for help, power, and protection from the supernatural beings that lived around them. Gratitude and thanks to these spirits were always important.

In the specific case of bison, their skulls might be lined up in rows with their eye sockets stuffed with sage. This would appease their departed spirits and prevent them from apprising the living bison of the danger they encountered in approaching the village.[7]

All tribal members believed that each and every serious endeavor whether planting or hunting bison, required supernatural power to accomplish their goals or to overcome the many dangers, obstacles, and vicissitudes they might encounter. The acquisition and use of supernatural power were a lifelong quest and an obligation for both men and women. Supernatural power was acquired through fasting; participation in the numerous ritualized, sacred ceremonies; and acquisition and use of sacred bundles.

The Mandans employed the *Okipa* ceremony and the Hidatsa the *Naxpike* as public vehicles for the acquisition of power. These ceremonies required the male participants to fast and to suffer before the spirits and were believed to serve the practical function of assuring an adequate supply of meat, hides, and other buffalo by-products.

The centerpiece of the *Okipa* and *Naxpike* required that men be suspended from long poles using thongs inserted under the skin of the chest and back. The men hung from these poles until they fainted and were cut down by the older men.

During the summer months, the Hidatsa left their villages to enjoy an outing, often going west as far as the plains of central and eastern Montana to hunt buffalo or other game. The pleasure of the young men was muted by the knowledge that before the hunt ended, they would be required to drag heavy buffalo skulls by thongs inserted in their legs until they collapsed or fainted under the severe pain and exertion. This ritualized ceremonial torture proved their courage and endurance both to the people and to the spirit guides. They also hoped that this ordeal would induce a vision or bring them power.[8]

In addition to the *Okipa* and *Naxpike* ceremonies the Mandans and Hidatsas had a Bull Society, which was open only to males who owned sacred bundles that contained buffalo skulls. These bundles also gave the owner the right to instruct men in the ceremonial painting of buffalo skulls. Ownership of these bundles and their rights was hereditary rather than based on vision experience.

The Bulls met and danced in public four times a year, representing the buffalo in each particular season and direction. Women also formed a group, known as the White Buffalo Cow Society, whose specific function was also to represent the buffalo in dance. In the Bull Society's dance several young girls were given the duty to bring water for the Buffaloes when the society met to dance. While the Bull Society was painting for the dance, an announcer went through the village proclaiming, "The buffalo herds are coming to the Missouri. Everyone come out and see them drink."[9]

All of these ritual dances were mindful dramatizations of the importance of the buffalo and its return to the village. This ancient reenactment of "calling the buffalo" to the people was a ubiquitous and widespread ceremony conducted in a variety of ways in villages and encampments throughout the Great Plains.

In the calling-the-buffalo ceremony, no group's effort or "power" was more respected or esteemed than that of the White Buffalo Cow Society. The principal function of this society, which originated with the Mandans, was to call the buffalo for the critical winter hunt. All rites for the ceremony took place after the harvest had been gathered. The calling rituals of this society were believed to be so potent that even mentioning the ceremony or humming one of its songs might lead to an early frost and cold weather. Only older, postmenopausal women could be members of the White Buffalo Cow Society, and because their efforts ensured ample food for their families and the village, they enjoyed the enormous respect and admiration of all.

A remarkable example of the buffalo-calling ceremony was described by Henry A. Boller in his book *Among the Indians: Four Years on the Upper Missouri, 1858–1862*. The Mandans and Hidatsas during this period all lived together in Like-a-Fishhook village on the north side of the Missouri. The people were very hungry, and the White Buffalo Cow Society assembled when every means to attract the buffalo to the river had failed. It was winter and, although the bison were numerous, they were too far away for the men to pursue and return the same day, as there was fear of a Sioux attack.

Several young men had already tried to call the buffalo and failed. Two other men, Four Bears and Red Cherry, had both fasted and "made their medicine" on a distant hill, but this too produced no effect. Four Bears was waiting for his prayers to be answered and to receive the right dream to let him know when it was time for him to perform another ceremony. In the meantime, the Black Mouths Society, who served as the tribal police force in keeping order on the hunt and in the village, had enforced complete quiet so as not to frighten away any nearby buffalo. No hunting was allowed anywhere, and the women were forced to occupy themselves quietly inside their earthlodges. Unless a strong wind was blowing downwind from the herd's direction, no fires were permitted lest the buffalo smell them and flee. Hence the lodges were cold and dark. Travel had also been banned. With starvation lurking in the village all were forced to wait quietly for the buffalo.

The White Buffalo Cow Society, some forty or fifty strong, soon gathered in a large lodge wearing their deerskin dresses. Each woman had a spot of vermillion on her cheek and wore her long black hair carefully combed and dressed with marrow grease over her shoulders. Her hair was held back around the forehead with a headband of white buffalo skin. One of the women wore a white buffalo robe, which was common property of the band, very scarce and highly esteemed. Boller reported that three male drummers sat at one end of the lodge, singing a monotonous chanting strain. After the dance commenced, the people took heart that relief was on the way. The women continued dancing at various intervals for over a week while scouts kept watch to the west from the high tops of the surrounding hills.

Boller noted that across the river stood a solitary butte and on its summit lay two buffalo skulls with pieces of scarlet cloth fastened to each horn. Nearby stood two poles with pieces of calico flying from them—all gifts to the supernatural powers to induce them to send the buffalo. The butte was a famous lookout with a view that extended for many miles. It was here that Boller was sitting with two other Indians when he heard an "unearthly din" below him. Across the river a huge buffalo was charging wildly about less than 20 yards from the lodge where the White Buffalo Cow Society was dancing. The buffalo dashed headlong between the lodges and, according to Boller, was quickly shot on a sandbar in the river and died. "While his limbs were yet quivering ... a multitude of knives were busily at work and in a few moments only a pool of blood which the dogs were eagerly lapping up remained."[10]

The appearance of the lone buffalo was a good omen, and the White Buffalo Cow dancers left the lodge and began to dance around the village. Shortly thereafter, a young man rode in on a lathered-up horse to report a fine herd of buffalo cows nearby. The following day, the men returned from a successful hunt, their horses heavily packed with meat. Everyone agreed that famine had been averted by the dancing of the White Buffalo Cow Society.

Back at Awatixa, the Canada geese flying overhead remind me of the other important plains village women's society: the Goose Society. Second in importance only to the White Buffaloes, the Goose Society was open to women in their thirties and forties, who performed their dances and rituals in connection with the blessing of the fields and the planting of corn. These ceremonies commenced when the geese returned in the spring to the big river. The Goose Society also formally welcomed the waterbirds (cormorants) back in the spring and danced for rain in the summer during times of drought. The departure of the waterbirds and geese in the fall signified the end of the growing season and the beginning of winter.

The closing of another year's cycle is easy to imagine as I lie in one of the old earthlodge saucer depressions that was once a home owned and carefully tended by the women of the lodge. Gazing up into a cold, cobalt-blue October sky flecked with cirrus, I watch Canada geese rise and lift a mere 20 feet above me on steady, pumping wings. As they honk and form into skeins, I can imagine the women of the Goose Society watching them from the edge of their frosty fields and bidding them farewell as they disappear south beyond the round umber hills.

SIX

The Astarahe

The people looked all around and knew this was their place, the place upon which they would live forever, they and the buffalo together.

—Pawnee legend of Buffalo Woman

THE FRENCH TRADERS CALLED IT *Le Grand Détour*, the Americans simply the Big Bend. It was a geographical river curiosity for all the nineteenth-century river travelers en route on the upper Missouri. The Big Bend was a 26-mile loop the river carved around a narrow neck of hard Pierre shale 1.75 miles wide. It took a steamboat the better part of a day to run it, while a man could stroll across it picking his way through the cactus and tall grass, dally for lunch, and still make it in an hour. The Missouri was nothing if not capricious.

I have spent a good many hours poking the ridge of that narrow neck, and though a good deal of the bottom is submerged under the waters of Lake Sharpe, it still holds archaeological mysteries. On the heights, small groves of cedars may be centuries old, while a half dozen glacial erratics are tantalizingly aligned in a fashion to suggest they were dedicated in the distant past as plant and animal effigies.

On the tops of small, conical hills, pungent skunk brush might be draped with tobacco ties made as offerings to spirit guides. But mostly there is tranquillity and silence during the long, hot summer days when the river water below the highest ridge spangles with sunlight.

Seven centuries ago the Big Bend was the destination of migrants who called themselves the *As-ta-ra-he* (Ree). Like the Hidatsa, the first Ree who arrived at the Big Bend were probably led by a visionary, for that was the way of the world then. From these first settlers began a

dynasty followed by migrations of more people of their kind looking for the timeless resources that sustain life on the Great Plains: fertile earth, fresh water, wood, and bison. From their ancestral lodges
on the central plains they carried with them the seeds of corn, beans,
squash, and sunflowers that flourished in the fertile Missouri valley.
They also brought the concept of round earthlodges with doors
aligned to the southeast and the winter sun and away from the sharp
prevailing northwest winter winds.

Their largest villages consisted of an average of thirty-five dome-
shaped earthlodges built on the highest river terraces above the floodplain and clustered near the mouths of both small and large streams.
It was usual for two related extended families to share one lodge.

On the lower river terraces, women cultivated gardens of corn (*Zea
mays*), beans, and squash. They also raised pumpkins, small melons,
sunflowers, and tobacco. Surplus grains and vegetables from the harvest were stored in deep, undercut, straight-sided cache pits dug between the lodges. Subsistence agriculture was the mainstay of their
survival through the lean times of winter. Their garden produce was
augmented by their extended spring and late fall bison hunts on the
vast buffalo plains to the east and west.

The Ree were followed later by larger groups of Arikara who spoke
a dialect of the same Caddoan mother tongue (Pawnee). *Arikara*
means "antler," and it has been hypothesized that these people broke
from the original Pawnee group sometime after the earlier Ree migration north, settling first on the Elkhorn (Antler) River in northeastern
Nebraska from which they received their name. They moved again
after their sojourn on the Elkhorn and arrived in the mid-sixteenth
century in the upper Missouri River valley after the Ree had already
become well established.[1]

The two groups probably maintained distinct dialects, which varied
from each village until the historic era when they eventually became
culturally indistinguishable from each other. By the late sixteenth
century the combined groups of Ree/Arikara had established a number of villages along the Missouri stretching from Scalp Creek near

the present Nebraska state line up the Missouri to the present North Dakota line. Their domination of the river gave them an early proprietary control of the vast buffalo country of western South Dakota from the Missouri west to the Badlands, Black Hills, Slim Buttes, and Cave Hills.

At Crow Creek (north of present Chamberlain) they constructed a strongly fortified village on a high, flat terrace that served as their main southern guard outpost. This village, along with another extensive fortress village (Arzberger) south of Pierre, commanded a position that took advantage of natural features including steep cutbanks and draws on the west. On the exposed sides to the east, these villages were fortified by deep ditches and ringed by palisades 5 feet high reinforced with packed earth. The palisades were made of stout willow, cottonwood, or cedar poles set upright into the ground and banked with 2 feet of earth. These log-and-earth structures also incorporated bastions. The entire village/fort complex exhibited a sophisticated understanding of the art of fortification and the principles of good design and building. They also clearly indicated a concern for raiders and invaders.

The largest of the earthlodge villages were constructed in the vicinity south of Pierre, South Dakota, and around the mouth of the Cheyenne River to the north and at Crow Creek to the south. Many of the villages covered areas of 130 to 150 acres, indicating a cooperative, well-organized society and a population of 10,000 people, including 4,000 warriors at its zenith about 1760.[2]

The Arikara, who had become numerically dominant over the Ree, were also traders who supplied agricultural products to the later-arriving plains nomads, such as the Cheyenne, Arapaho, Kiowa, Crow, and Teton Lakota (Sioux).

For their semiannual bison hunts, the various villages were organized into village hunting groups who usually moved together in concert out onto the western bison ranges. Tabeau, a French trader who spent a few years in their villages on the Grand River in the late eighteenth century, writes of the Arikara that in

autumn and spring seasons [during] the annual passage [migration] of
the cow [bison], no one is allowed to meet her and, even if there is the
greatest distress [i.e., hunger], she is allowed to approach and even the
first herds are allowed to pass as they serve as guides to [the] other[s],
since all follow the same route. When the soldiers judge that the cow
is sufficiently invited [called by dancing, etc.] they make speeches and
order the surround. This hunt is made in partnership and this is how
it is undertaken: As great a number as is possible advance within a
certain distance from the animals and to a place designated by the
soldiers. The best archers, runners, and horsemen have their places
assigned. The old men begin their ceremony. They offer the pipe to
the sky, earth, and the four cardinal points; then they present all the
shanks of the pipe to the cow [bison]. While she is supposed to smoke,
the old men bellow very softly and make the same grimaces as at the
festival for attracting her. The partisan of the circle then speaks thus to
the herd, "Oh, you cows, you learn every day from the talk of our old
men that you are our only resource. Have pity then on us today. You
know that we are hungry; grant us some of your young ones. You see
that ours are weak, that our horses are poor and will not, perhaps, be
able to join you; flee not then with all your strength, and, you others,
lands, winds, and especially rocks, grandsires of the [people], aid us
today, give courage to the cow [bison]. Tell her not to be foolish and
not to harm our young men!" After this bit of eloquence, he gives the
signal to the others, who leave him and advance in a way to surround
the herd that is to be attacked.[3]

These hunting expeditions proceeded along well-established migration trails that wound along the ridges dividing the river valleys
of the Grand, Moreau, Cheyenne, Bad, and White Rivers as far as the
badlands and Black Hills on the south end and the Slim Buttes and
Cave Hills on the northwest end. With its mixed grasslands, woody
draws, shallow rivers, springs, and ephemeral lakes, this may have
been the best buffalo country on the northern plains. Farther west of
the Black Hills into the Thunder Basin and the Powder River country
of eastern Wyoming and Montana, the elevation is higher, the wind
incessant, the grass sparser, and the water less plentiful.[4]

In the spring, Arikara women planted their crops and remained at their villages long enough to give the corn one hoeing before all the people deserted their towns to go in pursuit of the bison. If the people were fortunate in the spring, they might find buffalo carcasses outside their door floating down the Missouri during the spring rise. These carcasses would have been the buffalo that had fallen through the ice during the winter and spring and drowned, and there were usually thousands of them. When a carcass floated by the village, young men would swim out to it, rope it with a braided leather rope, and drag it ashore. People then cut into the bloated body and ate the "innards raw." A bloated bison was relished by the Arikara. In fact the Arikara were known to bury a freshly killed bison in the earth for a few weeks to age and improve its flavor, waiting until the flesh attained a gelatinous consistency. They would then dig up the animal and scoop the rotting flesh out with a bison-horn spoon. It must have been an acquired taste that has since been lost.[5]

By late summer the Ree/Arikaras would return home from the buffalo hunt laden with dried meat in time to harvest their crops. In the fall, after the vegetable harvest had been dried and stored, they set out once again for the bison ranges and might remain on the hunt until spring, when they returned again to their villages to begin again their highly ritualized cycle of life.

About 1690, French traders began penetrating the Missouri River country from the east and south in search of beaver pelts. One of the first to visit may have been Pierre LeSueur, who traveled across country from the Mississippi via the Minnesota River, then southwest as far as the great Blood Run village complex near the mouth of the Big Sioux River where a large group of Omahas, Poncas, Iowas, and Otoes lived.

In 1714, Etienne Venyard, Sieur de Bourgmont, wrote a memoir describing the course of the Missouri as far upstream as the Arikara villages, three of which he placed on the west bank of the Missouri above the mouth of the Niobrara, and forty more still farther upstream on both banks. He described them as a very numerous people engaged in the fur trade.[6] He was followed by two more Frenchmen in 1719, Charles Du Tisne and Jean-Baptiste Benard de La Harpe, who reported the Arikara living in "45 villages of Pani [Pawnee]." In 1723 the villages were recorded as being 10 leagues (25 miles) from the Omaha (Blood Run?) with whom they were allied.

By 1734, French traders from St. Louis were living with the Pawnee and trading with the lower Arikara villages. The traders, by all accounts, described the Arikara as friendly, peaceable people on good terms with them. The Arikaras were, according to Tabeau writing some sixty years later, "long known for their customary mildness."[7]

While the Creole French of St. Louis were probing the northern buffalo country for furs, French-Canadian traders operating out of Quebec and Montreal were trying to contact the Arikaras as well as the Mandan and Hidatsa villages 200 miles farther up the Missouri. The travels of one French family, the Verendryes, to the buffalo country in the early eighteenth century are the first on record and present a fascinating story filled with confusion, misdirection, Indian warfare, and adventure.

Bison Shield motif petroglyph carved in sandstone (Fort Union formation) located near the ceiling of Ludlow Cave in the North Cave Hills, west of Ludlow, South Dakota. Sometime after this photograph was taken in the early 1980s, this handsome glyph was removed/stolen.

Bison herd roaming north into stiff breeze on a June morning, Thunder Canyon Bison Ranch, Butte County, South Dakota.

The rugged landscape of the Missouri Plateau country looking east from the high "Jumpoff" divide that separates the drainage of the Little Missouri River on the west side and the headwaters of the south Grand and north Moreau Rivers on the east. It was in this vicinity that a circle of bison skulls was unearthed from a cutbank west of Buffalo, South Dakota. This was also the area of one of the last wild buffalo hunts that took place in the summer of 1883.

The soft yellow light of sunset bathes the west side of the Slim Buttes near the vicinity of J.B. Pass, Harding County, South Dakota.

Bison herd grazing a high ridge on the Terry Bison Ranch south of Cheyenne, Wyoming. The mountains in the background are the north end of the Colorado Front Range.

Native stone-wall ruins of a homesteader's house on Beaver Dam Creek in Meade County, South Dakota.

This view from the historic site of the Yellow Clay Mandan village (Double Ditch State Historic Site) is looking north up the Missouri River. It is the likely site of the "river Mandans" visited by Louis-Joseph (Verendrye's son, the Chevalier) in early December, 1738. The site is located on a high bluff on the east side of the Missouri, about eight river miles due north of Mandan, North Dakota.

"Nameless" Butte is a classic high, rough shale outcrop about a mile west of the Little Missouri River located in the far southwest corner of North Dakota.

A view of the Dry Creek badlands country in the eastern Montana "flatiron," where taxonomists Hornaday and Elliott respectively searched for the last remnants of the wild Northern Plains bison in the mid-1880s.

The original hand pump for water sits in the front yard of the historic Jones House on Rabbit Creek, Perkins County, South Dakota. Gilbert Jones still tends the place and keeps the pump in running order.

Sandstone Boulders (Fox Hills formation) located near the Oracle Site (Medicine Hill) high above the Cannonball River, Grant County, South Dakota.

Thunder Butte, a landmark in western Ziebach County, South Dakota, significant to all the old plains Indian tribes from time immemorial.

A typical abandoned homestead house once common across the Northern Plains of western South Dakota.

Prehistoric teepee ring exposed after the 1999 grass fire on the Mason Ranch, Perkins County, South Dakota. The large round stones were used to anchor down the teepee flaps against the wind, and were left in place to be used again.

A typical Missouri Plateau badlands scene in northwestern South Dakota.

Capitol Rock, a chalk (Oligocene) outcrop near the south end of the Long Pines in the far southeastern corner of Montana, a few miles west of Camp Crook, South Dakota.

SEVEN

River of the West

Stories are lessons of a year or a decade or a life broken into chunks you can swallow.   —Judy Blunt

IT IS A DREARY, OVERCAST MORNING in late October, but it's not cold where I am standing on the south bank of the Souris River a few miles downstream from Velva, North Dakota. The roads and trails along the river bottom are muddy, sloppy affairs with skiffs of deep, wet snow. The Souris, or "Mouse," River is unfrozen. It is a deep, meandering ditch with steep, 20-foot-high cutbanks while the river itself is 15 to 20 yards wide and a few feet deep.

The Souris flows southeast out of Saskatchewan into North Dakota, where it makes a big loop, turning north at Velva to head back into Manitoba and its confluence with the Assiniboine. Here, at the bottom of the big loop, the floodplain forest is mostly a tangle of boxelder with a few big ashes and cottonwoods. The large trees bear old scars of girdling by beaver and most are dead. The boxelder saplings, dead falls, and old rotting logs create a riparian tangle that is nearly impassable, while the river itself is choked with logjams at strategic points.

When Pierre Gaultier de Varennes, Sieur de la Verendrye, entered the Souris valley in late October 1738, there would have been groves of old cottonwoods, their twisted stems protected from prairie fires by thick, gray, stringy bark. Underneath and around the groves there would have been stands of tall prairie grass—big bluestem, Indian, and switch—along with shrubs and forbs such as wild currants, prairie rose, and buckbrush.

Beyond the gallery groves of cottonwoods, old meanders abandoned by the river would have formed sloughs, some of which remain

47

today, fringed with cattails and cordgrass that create a haven for ducks, waterfowl, blackbirds, and small mammals.

I climb 70 feet or so out of the narrow Souris valley at Velva and take a southerly course, as Verendrye did, onto the Missouri Coteau (Coteau du Missouri), a rolling, treeless landscape punctuated with sloughs, wet prairies, and clear, cold kettle lakes. Two centuries ago it was criss-crossed by buffalo trails and Assiniboine travois ruts that wound a route around the wet holes south to the Mandan and Hidatsa villages along the Missouri.

After a few miles, a high, long glacial ridge looms up on the south-eastern horizon. This is Dogden Butte, an important cultural land-mark to the Mandans, who believed that all the wild animals were imprisoned there and had to be ritually freed every spring as part of their annual *Okipa* ceremony.[1] At nearly 2,300 feet, Dogden Butte is one of the highest points on the Missouri Coteau. As the crow flies it's only 30 miles, a two-day march from where the Missouri makes a big turn and heads south.

Scattered around the foot of Dogden, named for the wolf dens that once probed its slopes, are pothole lakes, some of which are begin-ning to ice over at this time of the year. Above the lakes, the steep, fis-sured flanks of Dogden are choked with wild currants, roses, buckbrush, chokecherry, and hawthorn, all stark and leafless in this season. At the foot of the butte in the shelter of the deep ravines on the northeast side is an unexpected surprise: a forest of tall bur oak, ash, and stands of aspen.

Dogden is a handsome landmark with its 2.5-mile-long ridge crest and its steep slopes littered with massive pink granite boulders splotched with orange and mint-green crustose lichens. Every trav-eler and trader coming from the Canadian prairies to the Mandan villages in the nineteenth century must have paused here for a drink of cool springwater or to pick berries while keeping a wary eye out for an ambush by Sioux or Assiniboines.

From the sopping-wet, muddy calm of the Souris valley it is only a score of miles to the north flank of Dogden, where the lakes are iced up and a fierce wind screams out of the north. This is the very direction Verendrye and his large Indian entourage had come that October more than two and a half centuries before to meet a Mandan chief who was awaiting him perhaps here, near the butte.

Verendrye, who had looked forward to this important meeting with the Mandans for years, was born in 1685 at Three Rivers, Quebec, on the shores of the St. Lawrence. Trained as a French military officer, he took a bullet and four saber cuts at the murderous battle of Malplaquet in Flanders before returning home to Canada, where he took part in French guerilla raids against the English in Massachusetts and Newfoundland. At the age of thirty he entered the fur trade and by 1729 was appointed commandant of the posts at Lake Nipigon and Kaministiquia (Thunder Bay, Ontario).

Two years later he formed his own business partnership. Still in the king's service, he was ordered to explore the "high country" of New France and establish a route of fur posts along the way to Lake Winnipeg. But his chief task was to find the Western Sea, believed to be a deep inlet of the Pacific and a sea connection to China. For this effort he was granted a monopoly on the fur trade of the western region and was to use the proceeds to pay for these explorations. It would prove a bad bargain from the outset.

The trade in beaver furs was already well established by the time Verendrye entered it in the early eighteenth century. Fur trading had started as an ancillary activity some 200 years earlier when French, English, and Portuguese fishermen began plying the Gulf of St. Lawrence to harvest shiploads of cod. Whalers soon followed, building seasonal camps on the North American coast to render the blubber into oil. Groups of Indians visited the camps on a regular basis to barter animal skins for beads, ceramic pipes, buttons, and especially manufactured metal products: kettles, knives, nails, and fire steels. Matchlock muskets were especially coveted.

Whaling and fishing captains considered the fur trade secondary to their more lucrative cargoes of cod and whale oil. Although Europeans found the beaver pelts attractive for their warmth and beauty, it wasn't until 1540 that French hatters discovered that the beaver underhair made a superior felt for hats.

In 1582 a handful of French investors from Brittany earned a handsome 1,500 percent return on a shipload of beaver pelts. The following year, trader/captain Etienne Bellenger returned from Nova Scotia with a load of furs that brought him a staggering profit of 3,250 percent.[2]

The astronomical profits in peltry created a demand in furs that the Indians, craving metal goods and firearms, were only too happy to satisfy. The result was the methodical depletion of beaver, from the East Coast of North America to the west. As one tribe cleaned out their territory of furbearers, they acted as middlemen for the Europeans to the next tribe west who were busy trapping beaver.

This worked well for a while, but as the value and volume of the fur trade expanded west like a pebble dropped in a still pond, intertribal tensions increased. Each tribe sought to monopolize the trade in pelts and set the price while controlling the distribution of manufactured goods. This was important not only from the standpoint of maintaining and increasing a tribe's wealth, but also for controlling the proliferation of firearms to hereditary enemies.

French-Canadian traders, however, always seeking ways to maximize their profits, began to bypass Indian middlemen in favor of dealing directly with their source suppliers. This in turn forced them to move their posts ever farther west, pushing French-Canadian expansion in the same direction while inadvertently fueling longstanding intertribal competition, rivalries, and warfare. By the early eighteenth century the frontier of the beaver trade had shifted far beyond the nexus of Quebec and Montreal on the St. Lawrence to the northern shores of Lake Superior.

In the spring of 1731, Verendrye was paddling a North Canoe[3] on what was by now a well-known route out of Montreal that headed west up the Ottawa River to the Mattawa River, to Lake Nipissing, down the French River to Georgian Bay, and then west along the shore of the North Channel to the great post of Michilimackinac on the St. Mary's River. The latter, which connected Lake Superior to Lake Huron, had to be portaged before the long North Canoes could embark across the vast inland sea of Lake Superior.

Verendrye paddled the icy water along the wind-buffeted north shore of Superior, stopping briefly at the Kaministiquia post on Thunder Bay before setting out for the Grand Portage at the mouth of the Pigeon River (Minnesota). The Pigeon River/Grand Portage route was a new trail for the French into the interior "high country," and many of Verendrye's superstitious voyageurs balked at going into the vast unknown forest where many believed demons of all types lived and moaned in the pitch-black night forests.

If demons were not bad enough, the Grand Portage itself was an arduous 9-mile uphill carry around Pigeon River Falls and rapids that stretched all the way to the big lake. The route had never been used by the French, and though it was shorter than the old Kaministiquia route, the first portage was difficult and took many days.

Grand Portage was one of three major canoe routes or trails into the interior forest that led west to the northern plains. All three were drawn on a map by a "savage" whom Verendrye called Ocha-gach, probably Cree, and a man Verendrye seems to have trusted implicitly. Ochagach drew a map for the explorer years earlier at Lake Nipigon showing how all three routes converged at Lac la Pluie (Rainy Lake).

The Kaministiquia route already in use had twenty-two portages around rapids and falls and was the most circuitous. It left Lake Superior at Thunder Bay, following the Kaministiquia River north to Dog Lake, then west to Mille Lacs, and finally by a series of smaller lakes and rivers to Rainy Lake.

The second route, called Nantouagan by the Indians, went up the Pigeon River along the international border between present-day Minnesota and Ontario. Because the mouth of the Pigeon River is blocked by numerous rapids, it required a 9- to 10-mile carry that later came to be known as Le Grand Portage (The Great Carry).

Verendrye eventually improved and used this route exclusively when he made his numerous voyages to Rainy Lake. And although it had forty-two portages, more than twice as many as the Kaminis-tiquia route, there were no rapids to hold back the canoes except for the Grand Portage. The big payoff was that the Nantouagan was one third shorter. The last route, never popular, was the Fond du Lac trail, which began at Fond du Lac (head of the lake [Superior]) below present-day Duluth, Minnesota, and wound its way north up the St. Louis River, ultimately reaching Rainy Lake.[4]

The Indians estimated that the Grand Portage trail took twenty-two days to reach Rainy Lake. From there it took four more days to paddle via Rainy River to the Lake of the Assiniboines (Lake of the Woods), and ten more days by canoe from Lake of the Woods via the Winnipeg River to Lake Winnipeg.

The last leg of the trip, the paddle down the Winnipeg River, which headed at the north end of Lake of the Woods, was a wild and scenic, 145-mile roller-coaster run with numerous "shocking" rapids and cascades that required thirty portages.

The Winnipeg River is a grand boreal affair, with its water-filled chutes, fast rapids, eddies, whirlpools, and cascades that posed great danger to the voyageurs. It drains a boreal paradise rich with creatures of the North: moose, caribou, black bear, and furbearers of all types. All the materials necessary for building and maintaining birch canoes were abundant: cedar for the slender ribs, birch for the covering, juniper rootlets to stitch up the bark, and plenty of pine and larch for the gum and resin that sealed the seams and crevices.

The Winnipeg drains a vast, soggy landscape laced with black spruce muskegs, swamps, string bogs, marshy peat lands, wildflower fens, and waterways and lakes mottled with rocky islands. The boreal forest that grows in the thin, rocky soil is a patchwork of birch, aspen, poplar, and evergreens, including spruce, cedar, and white pine. To the French in 1731 it was the frontier that lay just beyond the known. To the Cree and Monsoni who inhabited the country between Lake Superior and the Red River it provided a bounty in furs and meat. The Scot trader Alexander Mackenzie, who saw it many years later, believed there to be "no finer country in the world for the residence of uncivilized man."

Forced to stop and regroup that fall at the foot of the Grand Portage by his superstitious and recalcitrant men, Verendrye made plans to return to Kaministiquia for the winter while sending his trusted nephew, La Jeremaye, on to Rainy Lake with half his voyageurs to build a trading fort he named St. Pierre. That winter, Verendrye must have sat in front of the great log fires at Kaministiquia making plans for his excursion into the unknown Red River country of the North.

In the spring of 1732, with new contracts and the rest of his men now willing to take on the Grand Portage route, he quickly reached newly established Fort St. Pierre at the head of Rainy River near present-day International Falls, Minnesota. He followed the Rainy River west to Lake of the Woods with its vast maze of islands, coves, and inlets. Paddling across the great lake that borders the provinces of Ontario and Manitoba and the state of Minnesota, he established his main headquarters on what is now known as the Northwest Angle inlet in Minnesota and built a major trading post he named Fort St. Charles. He spent the next winter there trading and interviewing visiting Indians, searching for clues of the great river he believed flowed across the plains to the Western Sea. It was an old search with its origins extending back two centuries earlier in Quebec with the explorations of Jacques Cartier on the St. Lawrence. Its discovery (never mind its actual existence) had consumed generations of traders and explorers, and Verendrye now confidently believed it would be his destiny to unravel the mystery of its location via a great river he knew little about.

Verendrye was told by the Assiniboines who lived on the plains west of the Red River that the river he sought flowed south through the Mandan country to a salt sea. He was so confident of impending success that he wrote a dispatch to Quebec stating to his superiors, "You will see by the map the road that must be followed to get to the Sea of the West."[5]

Dark rumors of an impending war among the Indians, however, changed Verendrye's timeline. In mid-June 1733 the Cree and their close relatives, the Monsoni, planned to make war on the Saulteur (Ojibway), who lived around Chequamagon (northern Wisconsin) and the Sioux of the Plains (northern Minnesota). Cognizant of the fine muskets and munitions the French possessed, the Cree saw an opportunity to change the balance of power in their favor over their hereditary enemies. On a fine spring morning 300 Cree stood at the gates of Fort St. Charles and begged Verendrye for French arms and munitions.

Verendrye responded first by scolding the Cree for making war (it was bad for the fur business) and then made the grave political mistake of appeasing them with guns, lead balls, powder, flints, and other items.[6] Seeking to gain the French as allies, the Cree also requested that Verendrye's eldest son, Jean-Baptiste, join them as a gesture of his support. It was a complicated situation. Aware of being greatly outnumbered by the Cree who were in a high lust for blood, Verendrye gave in again, thinking that perhaps it was better they hit the Sioux than hit the French.

The Cree obtained their Sioux scalps while Verendrye spent a cold winter at Fort St. Charles. In the spring of 1734, no doubt tired of war and Indian intrigues, he returned home to Montreal where he spent the winter of 1734–35 with his wife and three younger children. He must have seemed a stranger to his family after being in the wilderness for three years. In his absence he arranged for his son and his nephew, La Jeremaye, to establish a fort he named Maurepas near the mouth of the Red River on the shores of Lake Winnipeg. Verendrye was inching his way ever closer to the northern plains.

At home the trader found himself in serious financial difficulties. Dishonest merchants had skimmed his furs, creditors had been negligent in sending supplies, and his explorations had been far more time-consuming and expensive than anyone could have predicted. The governor-general of New France, Pierre Beauharnois, and the French minister of marine in Versailles, Comte Maurepas, were adamant that his duties as a pseudo-explorer must come before his business as a fur trader; Verendrye was forced to rent out his trading forts, which had other disastrous outcomes.

In the spring of 1735, he set out again for the three-month canoe voyage into the "upper country." He reached Fort St. Charles in early September and found his men gaunt and destitute. His thoughts turned to Fort Maurepas on Lake Winnipeg and he sent two of his sons down the Winnipeg River to check on the condition of the men stationed there.

Arriving at Maurepas, they found the men also destitute and starving. And there was more bad news: La Jeremaye, Verendrye's sagacious and trusted nephew, was dead. The situation was grave as the men struggled through the bleak winter of 1735–36 at Fort St. Charles. The year 1736, however, would be worse.

The Achilles heel for the French traders had always been the long hazardous trips from Montreal to their far-flung wilderness outposts and the brevity of the boreal summer, both of which had worked against Verendrye in the fall of 1735. The Monsoni and the Cree were also aware of the depleted stocks of the French, but stayed their tomahawks against their onetime benefactor. Only the Sioux now gave Verendrye real worries. That spring they went on the warpath against the Cree, carrying a nasty grudge against the French who had armed their adversaries.

The prairie Sioux were regarded in every way as comparable to the fierce Iroquois of the eastern Great Lakes who had summarily destroyed the Huron and Erie Nations. Like the Iroquois, they would prove themselves implacable warriors. Proud, boastful, and arrogant, they were continually at war with their neighbors the Cree, Ojibway, and Assiniboine.

In desperate need of provisions, which had failed to arrive during the spring of 1736, Verendrye sent his eldest son, Jean-Baptiste, along with a Jesuit priest and a contingent of voyageurs east to the post at Michilimackinac. While camped on a small island a day out from the post, they were ambushed by more than 100 vengeful Sioux warriors.

On June 22, a sergeant, after making a search of the nearby area, delivered the grim report: Twenty-one men "seven leagues [18 miles] from the fort have been massacred on a little island. Most of the bodies were found, all decapitated, and lying in a circle against one another ... the heads being wrapped in beaver skins."[7] Decapitation was the Sioux signature on the deed. The heads wrapped neatly in beaver skins showed both disdain and irony.

It was the first significant massacre of white men in the west by the Sioux whose main camps were then located around Mille Lacs and Red Lake (Minnesota). The Sioux, always inclined toward hostility, now had something to brag about—they had struck a brutal blow against the French whose persons up until that point had been held sacrosanct. They now assumed an air of importance and contempt for the French and began to terrorize and commit depredations against the French traders at all the outposts from Lake of the Woods south to Lake Pepin (Minnesota) and Prairie du Chien (Wisconsin). Their disdain for the white man was becoming everywhere apparent.

The deaths of Jean-Baptiste and La Jeremaye stunned the commandant, and plans for a major expedition west were again halted. The French, who had never numbered more than sixty in the West, were now reduced by one third. The debacle at Massacre Island had been devastating both politically and emotionally, and Verendrye needed to take stock of the situation.

The Cree were more outraged by the massacre than the severely weakened French. War between them and the Sioux, which had seemed imminent following the massacre, was only narrowly avoided by Verendrye's insistent pleas to the Cree to desist.

After visiting Fort Maurepas in the winter of 1737–38, Verendrye returned to Fort St. Charles and left the following spring for Montreal. He was now fifty-two, and although he had experienced devastating personal and financial setbacks, he was still determined to find the route to the Mandans and the Western Sea.

In mid-June 1738 he started out again from Montreal, following the old canoe route west to Michilimackinac where he arrived a month later. In two weeks he was at Kaministiquia, where he paused only briefly before setting course for Fort St. Charles, reaching the latter at the end of August. There he implored the Cree and the Monsoni chiefs again not to go to war against the Sioux, even though "the lake was still red with the blood of the slaughtered Frenchmen."[8] He knew revenge must be discouraged. War was always bad for the fur trade Verendrye so desperately was trying to build. Three weeks later, he was at Fort Maurepas gazing out across the tannin-stained waters of Lake Winnipeg for the first time. He was finally out on the prairie. After all the delays, he desperately needed to get to the "River of the West," the great Missouri.

From Fort Maurepas, Verendrye paddled around the south end of Lake Winnipeg to the mouth of the Red River and then headed south upstream to the point where it forked with the Assiniboine. There he found ten cabins of Cree, including two war chiefs awaiting him with a large quantity of meat. He requested their permission to build a post on the site, which would later become the city of Winnipeg, Manitoba. He also stated his intent to canoe west up the Assiniboine. The Cree chief warned him that the Assiniboine was very low because it had not rained that summer and that he ran the risk of damaging his canoes. He also cautioned the French that they "would be going among people who did not know how to kill beaver and whose only clothing was buffalo skin."[9] Nevertheless, Verendrye told the Cree that he intended to ascend the Assiniboine as far as possible to increase the number of French subjects and to find the Mandans.

The water was low and the Assiniboine proved a typical prairie stream, broad and shallow with meandering loops, fallen trees, and numerous sand bars. It was a dramatic change from the cold, deep lakes and waterways that characterized the north woods. He noted that the river was bordered by fine trees along the bank, and beyond were prairies as far as the eye could see filled with buffalo and deer.

Verendrye, observing that it was shorter to walk over land across the prairie than to paddle a canoe, left his men to navigate the river shoals while he set out afoot. He marched steadily west for six days until October 2, when he met a band of Assiniboines who informed him that owing to the low level of the water it was not possible to ascend the river any higher by canoe. He decamped the river at this point, not wishing to damage his canoes as there was neither proper gum nor resin trees in the area to mend them, and built a trading fort he named Fort La Reine (the Queen's Fort). It was situated on a well-traveled trail between Lake Manitoba in the north and the Mandans to the south. A year later he relocated the fort 15 miles west to the present site of Portage la Prairie, Manitoba.

Fort La Reine was quickly constructed during the quiet autumn of 1738 and consisted of only a few log huts with a protective palisade. Verendrye held a council with the nearby Assiniboines, giving them gifts of powder, ball, tobacco, axes, knives, chisels, and awls, "all being things they valued greatly," as he put it, "owing to their lack of everything." The Indians "shed tears of joy." There was the usual ceremony of laying hands on the heads of the Indians, whereby the red men became the "children of the Great Father." Verendrye further exhorted them, saying, "We have given you presents which have come from a great distance. You ought to be sensible of their value."[10]

Verendrye was finally about to set off across the northern plains on an adventure that would exhaust him beyond any point he had ever known.

On October 16 he gave the drumbeat to arms, assembling the men and distributing gifts and supplies including powder, balls, shoes, an axe, a kettle, twists of tobacco, gunflints, gun screws, and steels— everything they would need for the long journey south. He ordered the Indians, men, women, and children to form a rough column while the French formed up apart.

The cavalcade was a great spectacle we can only imagine. The Assiniboines, or Stoneys,[11] as they were sometimes called, when in large numbers usually traveled in three columns with some scouts ahead and on the flanks and a good rear guard. The old and lame marched in the middle, forming the central column.

The column also had a contingent of barking wolf-dogs pulling travois loaded with bundles containing utensils, folded tipis, dried buffalo dung for fuel, and winter clothing that included moose-skin choppers, leggings, and capotes.

During the march Verendrye described the behavior of the Indians: "When as often happens the scouts catch sight of a heard of buffalo along the way, they raise a cry, which is at once carried to the rear guard. Then all the most active men of the column join the vanguard to surround the animals. Having killed a number of them, each takes as much of the meat as he wishes. This is done without stopping the march. The vanguard choose the campsites, beyond which no one goes."[12]

Verendrye described the Indian men as naked except for a buffalo robe hung loosely over their shoulders. The women dressed much the same except for a leather apron about a hand's width in front attached to a girdle. Both genders wore moccasins. The French voyageurs standing apart wore cloth or buckskin jackets, shirts, and woolen pants and packed capotes and a cap of coon fur and mittens for the winter. Matchlock muskets or flintlock muskets were standard equipment along with an axe and a trenching tool. Their haversacks, which they also carried, contained a sleeping bag, a cup, spoon, a knife, a fork, and an extra pair of moccasins.

Verendrye himself was conspicuously dressed as the marine lieutenant he was in a red quarter-length coat with broad cuffs, a tricorn hat, a sword attached to a waist belt with hilt protruding, buckled leather shoes, and a cane. He brought a writing case, which also contained medicine and personal effects, carried by an assistant who was aided by a slave. Verendrye's baggage also contained an astrolabe and a cross-staff to determine the latitude. All this, along with kegs of sundry supplies and staples, had to be either carried or hauled by dog travois. The horse at this date had yet to reappear on the northern plains.

And so the party proceeded south from the Assiniboine River at a brisk walking pace headed for the Pembina Hills, about 26 leagues (65 miles)[13] from the Assiniboine. On the third day out, forty Assiniboines overtook them and begged them to stay one day for a feast and a council, to which the commandant reluctantly acquiesced.

On October 21, five days out of Fort La Reine, they reached the north side of the Pembina Hills, a low escarpment stretching some 80 miles along the north side of the Pembina River. Verendrye vaguely referred to a point on the hills as "the first mountain."[14] From here they struck a westerly course, marching 24 leagues (60 miles) toward the "mountain that glows night and day."[15]

This tantalizing reference probably pertains to a point in the Turtle Mountains, a large glacial drift area composed of high rolling hills and studded with more than 200 lakes that straddles the Manitoba–North Dakota border.

The Turtle Mountains rise 800 feet above the surrounding prairie
and cover a wide area. The highest elevations are cloaked in hardwood forests of aspen, oak, birch, ash, elm, and Manitoba maple,
along with an assortment of pines and evergreens. The depressions,
including bogs and lakes, are filled with boreal elements while the
lower slopes are covered with prairie shrubs and grasses. The Turtles
are still a wild sanctuary for a host of native animals. Unfortunately,
the location of the glowing mountain has been lost to history.

It is doubtful that Verendrye entered the Turtle Mountains. He
probably skirted them, but from there it's difficult to ascertain exactly
which way the French and Indians went because the Assiniboine
guide on whom they depended took them all over the area to visit
other Assiniboine camps, some perhaps as far west as the great loop
of the Souris River, for councils and buffalo feasts. Verendrye was exceedingly vexed by these constant meandering delays and wrote:

> To go directly from the top of the second mountain [Turtle] to
> the Mantannes [Mandans] we should have gone southwest by west.
> But we were unable to follow a straight course; to make two or three
> leagues in a straight line we had to go three or four. From the fort the
> distance is 120 leagues west southwest but our guide lengthened this
> by some 50 to 60 leagues and a number of stops, to which we were
> obliged to consent in spite of ourselves, letting the finest fall weather
> slip by encamped. Thus we spent 46 days in accomplishing what we
> should have been able to do in sixteen or twenty days.[16]

Verendrye needed to be patient. Nothing he could say persuaded
his guide to make haste. To Verendrye's chagrin the guide took them
22 leagues out of their way to visit an encampment of 102 Assiniboine
families who insisted on meeting and feasting with the French.
Verendrye, however, never missed an opportunity to gather the Indians
into the arms of the French with gifts and promises never to abandon
them if they behaved "sensibly and brought them their furs."

The Indians, for their part, made a great display of gratitude with
profuse tears accompanied by the ceremony of placing hands on the
explorers' heads, taking Verendrye as their father and his company as

brothers, and the explorers likewise placed their hands on the Indians' heads and wept. It was traditional (and good policy) for Indians to adopt outsiders into their families particularly if the outsiders were wealthy or powerful and might prove advantageous to them.

On November 20 the ever-expanding party of French and Indians were headed south once more having criss-crossed the Souris plain and river valley following the southerly fall migrations of the buffalo herds. They now set a direct course for the Mandans. The Assiniboines marched steadily over the prairies, up hills and through valleys, always taking to the high areas when possible to avoid a surprise Sioux attack. The march "never ceased to be fatiguing, ascending, and descending many times a day," wrote Verendrye, who nonetheless was impressed by the sight of "magnificent plains" that stretched for many miles.

On the morning of November 28 the party reached the chosen place where they were to meet a small party of Mandans, "an elevation 17 leagues [43 miles] from their village." The Mandan chief surveyed the size of the traveling camp, which according to Verendrye "made a fine appearance." They all continued marching south and on the afternoon of December 3 the party reached a Mandan village somewhere east of the Missouri River.

The village has never been positively identified. The Menoken site, because of its location 15 miles east of Bismarck, has long been the favored location, but it's difficult to correlate its small size with the description in Verendrye's account. What Verendrye described was a village of some 130 earthlodges situated on an open plain and protected by a log palisade complete with four bastions.

Surrounding the palisade was a ditch 15 feet deep and 15 to 18 feet wide. Verendrye thought it was impregnable by other Indians. Inside he described a village of broad streets and open plazas in which "some of our Frenchmen often lost their way."

What he observed of their lifestyle and manners must have intrigued him. He described the Mandans as a "nation of mixed blood, white and black. The women are fairly good looking, especially the light-complexioned ones; many of them have blonde or fair hair."

Both genders were very industrious, he wrote, and "everyone sleeps naked" in separate compartments in their neat, large, and spacious huts. The men went "completely naked all the time except for a buffalo robe covering. A great part of the women are naked like the men with the difference that they wear a small, loose loincloth, about a hand-breadth wide and a span long, sewed to a girdle in front. All the women have this kind of covering even when they wear a skirt, so that they are never embarrassed or keep their legs closed when they sit down, as all other Indian women do. Some of them wear a kind of shirt of antelope hide, well softened."

He observed that the Mandans cultivated crops of squash, pumpkin, corn, tobacco, and beans. Grain, food, fat, dressed robes, and bearskins were stored in holes in the ground lined with straw. These supplies, he wrote, were the measure of a person's wealth. The Mandans ate corn and meat, the latter consumed practically raw. They were, he noted, "great eaters, always eager for a feast."

He described the men as large and tall, active, and the greater part as fairly good-looking. The women, he observed, did not have the typical dark Indian features, and both genders had a fondness for tattooing, but never more than over half of their body. The men also enjoyed various kinds of ball games.

On December 6, Verendrye sent a subordinate, Sieur Nolan(t), and his youngest son, Louis-Joseph the Chevalier, along with six Frenchmen to visit one of the main Mandan villages along the river. Sieur Nolan and Louis-Joseph returned the evening of the following day pleased with their journey, having been well received. They reported that the village was once again as large as this one and with fortifications in better condition. They found the waters of the Missouri running rapidly with many shallows, and the overall course heading in a southerly direction. And the water, they reported, was not potable, being somewhat brackish.

The river Mandans also told them that there were men like the French, very numerous on the lower part of the river, who carried on wars with "a great number of Indians." Gaining information from the Mandans was extraordinarily difficult because the Frenchmen required a long translation chain, from French to Cree to Assiniboine to Mandan and then back. When their Cree/Assiniboine interpreter deserted them just after their arrival at the Mandan village, the explorers were reduced to communicating only by means of hand signs and gestures. That they learned anything at all regarding the river, the Western Sea, and the country and people beyond it is amazing.

The winter season was now well advanced. Verendrye's trade goods were nearly exhausted and he had no presents to give to his hosts (Verendrye's box of belongings and gifts for the Mandans had been stolen by the Assiniboines). Therefore, the commandant chose to leave the next day for La Reine before snow closed the trails. It was a decision that would make for a desperate journey north.

On the eve of December 8, after all the preparations had been made, Verendrye became ill and was confined to his bed for three days. He recovered enough by December 13 to bid the Mandans farewell, leaving them with a few gifts and a lead tablet decorated with ribbons so that they might forever remember his "having taken possession of their lands in the name of the king."[17]

On Christmas Eve 1738, Verendrye reached the Assiniboine village of his guides, probably in the vicinity of the Turtle Mountains, but was still very ill. His box had been recovered with his belongings intact and only the presents for the Mandans missing. He was angry with the Assiniboines, whom he accused of deceit regarding their stories of the Mandans and of a country and a sea far to the south. An Assiniboine chief remonstrated Verendrye, saying he had spoken the truth and that he had in fact killed a conquistador by first killing his horse. Furthermore, he said, there was a great river "the other side of which cannot be seen; that the water is salt; that it is a country of mountains; and that there is a great extent between the mountains of fine land with many cattle, big and stout, white and of different colors. ... I have seen their wheat fields, where no women are to be seen; what I tell you is without deceit; you will learn further of it afterwards."[18]

After a rest of three days, Verendrye doggedly headed east, reaching the first mountain on January 9, 1739. He was very weak and had great difficulty walking in the bitter winter weather. With aid from the fort he was able to reach La Reine on February 10, taking thirty days to cover the last 105 leagues (88 miles) to the fort. "Never in my life," he wrote later, "have I endured so much misery, sickness, and fatigue as I did on this journey."[19]

He would never again travel south over the northern plains. All future explorations into the interior would be undertaken by his sons, and their journeys would present a fascinating glimpse of the life and times of nineteenth-century northern plains Indians.

EIGHT

The Way to the Western Sea

You must take this country for itself, for what it reveals, its enchantment and terror, its unutterable loveliness, the ghosts it forces upon you ...
—Ellen Meloy

THE ORACLE STONE of the Mandan and Hidatsas sits mute on a hilltop far above the meandering loops of the Cannonball River in southern North Dakota. The view from the rock, a brown slab of sandstone, is 360 degrees offering timeless, shadowy vistas of long distant ridges, low hills, and lonely buttes.

The stone crowns the top of a low, crossbedded sandstone butte that was once part of a late Cretaceous dune field extending 150 miles from here down to the Cheyenne River. The northwest side of the butte, which receives the brunt of the prevailing wind, is deeply cracked and broken into crevices and alcoves that bear scat evidence, indicating use by rabbits, raccoons, and coyotes. Boulders scattered at the foot of the outcrop lie in thickets of chokecherry, currant, rose, and buckbrush. All the exposed sandstone is daubed with orange, yellow, and mint-green crustose lichens.

The north slope of the butte is carpeted in a mosaic of big bluestem and Indian grass punctuated by smaller, crossbedded sandstone outcrops that are flat, even, and unbroken. The southeast slope features small clumps of buffalo berries laden with ripe, red fruit still perfectly tart and succulent at the end of October. The main approach up the south side is a gentle slope covered with little bluestem and curly grama that leads up to the crest of the butte and the foot of the oracle stone.

The stone serves as the highest point of the butte and is an outcrop 20 feet long and 9 feet wide. The state has built a 6-foot chain link fence around it through which someone has taken the liberty to cut a big hole. Areas of the still-standing fence are festooned with strips of colored cloth. The colors are symbolic of direction and significance in the beliefs of the Mandan and Hidatsa. Yellow decorates the southeast, green the south, blue and white the north and west, and black the west.

With respect, I step through the fence hole and touch the oracle stone.

The stone is one large layered slab of gritty, umber-hued sandstone 10 feet high that tilts down on the north side and up on the south. The north side is rough and stained with dark splotches of dead lichen. The smooth south side holds the mystery of etched effigies. Still clearly visible are two incised turtles, the larger one about the size of my palm. Also etched there are a pair of perfect life-size elk tracks complete with dewclaws, a small bison effigy, an incised bear track, and a human hand.

Lewis and Clark, who did not see the oracle, wrote in their journal on February 21, 1804, that

> the medicine stone is the great oracle of the Mandans, and whatever
> it announces is believed with implicit confidence. Every spring and
> on some occasions during the summer, a deputation visits the sacred
> spot where there is a thick porous stone ... with a smooth surface.
> Having reached the spot the ceremony of smoking is performed
> by the deputies, who alternately take a whiff themselves and then
> present the pipe to the stone; after this they retire to an adjoining
> wood for the night ... in the morning they read the destinies of the
> nation in the white marks on the stone.[1]

The Hidatsas called the stone *Me-ma-ho-pa* and traveled two to three days to reach it from their villages at the mouth of the Knife River. Upon arriving at the stone they performed a tobacco ceremony, and then a portion of the rock was washed and an offering was left. The supplicant would pray nearby and upon his return to the rock, his presents are no longer there, and he believes them to have been accepted and carried off by the Manhopa [Me-ma-ho-pa, i.e., the Great Spirit] himself. Upon the part of the rock, which he had washed, he finds certain hieroglyphics traced with white clay, of which he can generally interpret the meaning. ... These representations are supposed to relate to his future fortune, or to that of his family or nation; he copies them off with pious care and returns to his home, to read from them to the people, the destiny of himself or of them.[2]

The smooth area washed by the oracle seekers is still plain to see because the color of the sandstone is lighter and worn as if slightly bleached.

Just below this spot, wedged in a crevice, is a thin prayer stick, 18 inches tall, painted in red and black stripes and tied with tobacco ties (tiny pouches of tobacco). Leaning over and nearly touching the earth, I consider it proper to set it straight again.

While the mystery of the oracle still lingers, the character of the land and the people surrounding it has been altered. The great herds of "wild beasts" the Verendrye brothers saw when they passed north of here with their escort of two voyageurs and two Mandan guides are gone. And who knows how long it's been since the oracle presented a hieroglyphic message writ on stone.

I wonder if it predicted the arrival of the French as the last rays of orange evening light peek through a low, narrow slit of deep purple clouds over the western horizon. A cold wind picks up while I sit on the edge of the oracle waiting for the earth to turn one more time away from the sun and slide into the swirl of night.

In the winter of 1738, Verendrye left two Frenchmen in the Mandan villages on the Missouri that now lie under the small city of the same name. He instructed them to learn the Mandan language and customs and specifically to learn more of the great "River of the West." When the Frenchmen returned to Fort La Reine the following September of 1739, they related stories that clearly implied the presence of Spaniards to the southwest and other Frenchmen to the south.

They also noted that during the spring, a host of Indians mounted on horses arrived at the Mandan villages with trade goods consisting chiefly of skins trimmed with feathers and porcupine quills. The previous spring, they said, some 200 Gens du Chevaux (People of the Horse) had arrived and encamped on the farther bank (west side) of the Missouri. They were not all the same tribe, they said, but rather a group of tribes, possibly eight or nine, who claimed to have come from the land of the setting sun where there were white men living in forts of brick and stone.[3]

There were also enemies, the Frenchmen said, of the white people. These Indians were the Gens du Serpent (People of the Snake), a powerful, hostile nation, and it was necessary to make a long detour to avoid them.

The Mandans gave them more information about the white men's habits of sleeping on elevated beds and praying in specific houses that left little doubt that the "white people" were the Spanish living in New Mexico and along the Gulf Coast.

So where was the Western Sea, that illusive inlet of the Pacific that existed somewhere west of a height of land out beyond the plains no more than 100 leagues (250 miles)? And did the great River of the West lead to it? The Frenchmen still had no answers.

The following spring, 1740, Verendrye ordered his second son, Pierre, to make another trip to the Mandans and learn more about the River of the West and its connection with the Western Sea. In the meantime the commander returned to Montreal where he found himself besieged with debt and political difficulties. He was also now a widower. Undaunted, he made plans to return west the next spring.

He arrived at Fort La Reine the following October to find that Pierre had returned without making any important discovery, which the latter blamed on the lack of suitable guides. As usual, reliable guides and language translators were difficult to acquire and retain.

Pierre had tarried for two months at the Mandans awaiting the arrival of the "Horse Indians," but they never showed. He then took it upon himself to venture out on his own and traveled south, giving no specifics regarding his route. He related to his father that he had gone south to a place not far from certain Spanish forts, where a fear of enemies turned him back. The party in pursuit, he later learned, was the Sioux of the Prairie, which prompted him to hasten back to Fort La Reine.

Pierre showed his father a coverlet of embroidered cotton and porcelain beads that was said to have come from the strange white people. Another novelty, a more useful one, was two horses he acquired from the Mandans, who had traded for them with the Horse Indians.

Still, he could add no new geographical information to what was already known. The River of the West was surely the Missouri, but where was the Western Sea? Over the long northern winter at La Reine the question must have been debated over and over again.

Verendrye would next turn to his youngest son, Louis-Joseph, known as the Chevalier, to go once more in the spring to the Mandans to search for the elusive body of saltwater that he believed connected to the Pacific. The Chevalier must not fail.

In the spring of 1742, arrangements were made for another small party to make a dash to the Mandans. Louis-Joseph would lead and take his older brother, François, along with two experienced voyageurs, Edouard La Londette and Jean-Baptiste Amiotte.

On April 29 the party departed La Reine on foot, following the trail south. They reached the Mandans on May 19, a mere twenty days later, the same length of time their father had predicted it would take four years earlier. Like Pierre in the previous spring, the group patiently awaited the arrival of the Horse Indians, but again they never appeared. On July 23, with two Mandan guides, they set out from the river in a southwesterly direction hoping to find the "People of the Horse."

For twenty days the six men headed west-southwest. Assuming an average of 5 leagues (12 miles) per day over rough country, they could easily have covered more than 200 miles. During this time, the Chevalier reported, they encountered "no human beings, but many wild beasts."

They traveled across the handsome grasslands of southwestern North Dakota with its long ridges and buttes, entering the Little

Missouri River badlands country, which Louis-Joseph vividly described as having "soils of different colors, such as blue, a vermillion shade, meadow green, shining black, chalk white, and others
the color of ochre."

On August 11 they reached the "Mountain of the Horse Indians,"
where they set to work building signal fires on all sides of the mountain hoping to attract the attention of any Indians, "being resolved
to trust themselves to the first tribes that might appear." A brave act
indeed and one certainly born of long frustration and desperation.
Ten days later, one of their Mandan guides departed.

For a month Louis-Joseph went out or sent someone every day to
explore the hills. Patiently they waited for the Indians. Finally, on
September 14, their scouts sighted a column of smoke rising to the
south-southwest, and to everyone's joy, they found a group of Indians
they called the Beaux Hommes (Handsome Men).

The Beaux Hommes were likely Crow (Absaroka), and their
"mountain" may have been Pretty Butte, a tall, handsome mountain
with timber located northwest of Marmarth, North Dakota, near the
Little Missouri where Crow Indian territory began, and some 200
miles west of the Big Missouri.

They spent three weeks with these Indians before continuing their
search for the Horse Indians. Moving south-southwest, they met a
village of people they called the Petit Renards (Little Foxes), who
were also glad to meet them. Still they sought the Horse People (ap-
parently all the Indians they had met thus far were unmounted) who,
they hoped, would show them the route to the Western Sea. Continuing their sojourn, they met a larger group of the same people,[4] who
guided them to a village of Pioya (Kiowa), which they reached on
November 15.

The question they asked every tribe they met was "Can you show
us the way to the Western Sea?" Two days later, still heading in a
southerly direction, they encountered another large group of Pioya.
They were all now marching together before they finally met up with
the Horse Indians probably southwest of the Black Hills of South
Dakota.

The "Horse Indians" Louis-Joseph reported were in a state of "great desolation. There was nothing but weeping and howling, all their villages having been destroyed by the *Gens du Serpent* (People of the Snake)[5] and only a few members of their tribe having escaped." The Chevalier continued:

> These Snake Indians are considered very brave [fierce]. They are not satisfied in a campaign merely to destroy a village, according to the custom of all other Indians. They continue their warfare from spring to autumn, they are very numerous and woe to those whom they meet on their way!
>
> They are friendly to no tribe. We are told that in 1741 they had entirely destroyed seventeen villages, had killed all the old men and old women, and made slaves of the young women and had traded them at the seacoast for horses and merchandise.[6]

This may explain why the Horse Indians (Plains Apaches)[7] never appeared at the Mandan villages in 1741, 1742, and 1743. They were systematically being decimated and driven out of the area by the Snakes.

Proceeding farther south, the French encountered yet another large group of Indians, whom they describe as the Gens de l'Arc (People of the Bow) and "the only tribe who by dint of their bravery, do not fear the Snakes. They have even made themselves dreaded by the Snakes through the wisdom of good leadership of their chief."[8]

After marching steadily to the southwest, on November 18 they came upon a large village of the Gens de la Belle Rivière (People of the Beautiful River).[9] Again they found another large village of "Bow People" who had "a large number of horses, asses, and mules; these they use to carry their baggage, and to take them on their hunting parties as well as on their expeditions."

The French were treated very graciously and courteously by the Bow Chief, in "a manner," the Chevalier wrote, "not at all characteristic of the Indians. I became attached to this chief, who merited all our friendship." Thanks to the chief's patience and instruction, in a short time they were able to communicate in his language.

Again they persistently posed their question. The chief's reply was tantalizing, persuasive, and cryptic: "We know them [white men] by what the prisoners of the Snake Indians, whom we are to join shortly, have told us of them." Then he changed the subject to war. "Do not be surprised if you see many villages joined with us. Messages urging them to meet us have been sent out in all directions. Every day you hear the war song chanted; that is not without purpose: we are going to march to the great mountains which are near the sea, to seek the Snakes there. Do not be afraid to come with us, you have nothing to fear, you will be able to see there the ocean for which you are searching."[10]

With an ever-growing group of Indians, the French continued to march sometimes south-southwest, sometimes northwest, picking up groups of allied Indians along the way. "Our band was continually augmented by the addition of a number of villages of different tribes," Louis-Joseph wrote.

On New Year's Day, 1743, they came in sight of the mountains[11] riding with some 2,000 mounted warriors accompanied by their families and all their possessions. It must have been a grand spectacle with clouds of dust rising from the herds of horses and mules along with the lines of horse-drawn travois loaded with tipi skins, children, baskets, and stores of buffalo meat packed in brightly colored parfleches.

The entourage would have included packs of dogs and noisy boys practicing with their bows and arrows on any small animal they might scare up. The young women, arrayed in tunics of fringed buckskin embroidered with porcupine quills and mounted on fine ponies, would have ridden ahead of the old women who were walking and scolding the lagging horses or screeching at the packs of wolf-dogs.

Most of the young warriors would have been mounted and armed with round shields of bullhide, feathered lances, war clubs, bows, and quivers of arrows, while a few of the elders, wrapped in buffalo robes, might have been walking in groups with a stately air chatting and laughing.

This great entourage, the Chevalier wrote, marched "through a magnificent prairie where animals are plentiful. At night there is singing and shouting [war dances] and they weep continually, begging us to accompany them to war." The thoughts of his father echoed in the Chevalier's statement to the chiefs that "we were sent to pacify the land, and not to stir it up."

The chief of the Bows used the same ploy the Cree did to entice the Chevalier's support to fight against the enemy: He asked only that the Chevalier accompany them as spectators for "surely they know the Snakes have no friends."

Like his father earlier, greatly outnumbered by the natives in a strange land and virtually at their mercy, and also wishing desperately to see "the sea from the summit of the mountains," he acquiesced to the chief's request. The next day they endured long harangues from the members of each tribe concerning the safety of their families if the men were away to attack the Snakes. The Indians also begged the French not to abandon them, to which the Chevalier replied that "they seek peace for all nations but will accompany them if only to advise if required." The Indians thanked them effusively and then proceed "through long ceremonies with the calumet."

They continued to march with the village in tow through the first week of January 1743. On the ninth the men left camp to march (ride horseback) on to the foot of the mountains, which they reached on the twelfth. The Chevalier described the mountains as "thickly-wooded with all kinds of wood and appear very high."[12]

Upon approaching the main part of the Snake village, they found it abandoned; the Snakes had fled in great haste, leaving their tipis and a large part of their belongings. Instead of elation, the men felt terror, for the enemy, having discovered them, could now be on their way to massacre their own villages of women and children.

The chief of the Bows tried in vain to persuade them to the contrary, but panic gripped the great war party. "It is very annoying," the chief told the Chevalier, "to have brought you to this point and not be able to go farther."

What had been an orderly pursuit of the enemy became a disorderly rout, and the Chevalier was "exceedingly vexed not to be able to ascend the mountains." He could now only return with the rest of the group.

The warriors rode back to the main village as if pursued. The French eventually became separated from the Bow chief in the ensuing melee as well as from one another. In addition, the Chevalier and his brother had to stop and go back to find their two missing voyageurs. Retracing their route for miles, they spotted them grazing their horses at the "tip of an island."

After joining them, they noticed fifteen men approaching from the woods, "covering themselves with their arrow quivers. There was one far ahead of the others and we let him approach within half range of a rifle shot. Seeing that they were preparing to attack us, I thought it well to fire several shots at them, and this obliged them to retreat hastily, this weapon being much respected by all those tribes which do not have the use of it and whose arrow quivers cannot save them from the bullets."[13]

They remained in place until nightfall before starting out again in the hope of finding the Bow Indians. "It was difficult," the Chevalier wrote, "as the prairie was dry and barren, and the hoof prints of the horses cannot be detected." Nonetheless they continued riding into the night, "not knowing whether or not we were on the right track." Their instincts were good, however, and they managed to reach the Bow tribe on February 9, nearly four weeks after their separation and scare at the Snake camp.

The Bow chief, who arrived five days later after an exhaustive search for the Frenchmen, was overjoyed to see them. The Chevalier wrote that they were especially fortunate to arrive at the camp prior to a great winter storm that buried the camp under 2 feet of snow.

The French now moved with the Bow tribe in an easterly direction. En route east they came into contact with the Gens de la Petite Cerise (People of the Little [Choke] Cherry)[14] on March 15, 1743, who were returning from their winter villages and were two days' march from the Missouri. Four days later they all reached the Arikara summer "forts" on the river.

One of the Arikaras had been brought up among the Spaniards and spoke Spanish as well as his native tongue, which the Chevalier found "very easy to learn," suggesting that their language was similar to that of the Bow chief.[15] When Louis-Joseph asked him how far it was to the Spanish country (New Mexico), the Indian replied that "it was very far and there were many dangers to be met on account of the Snake tribe, and that it took at least twenty days to make the trip on horseback."

He further added that the Spaniards made articles of iron and carried on a large trade in buffalo skins and slaves, giving in exchange horses and merchandise, as the Indians desired, but no guns or ammunition. Verendrye also learned that three days' distant was a Frenchman who had settled there several years before to trade. To this news the Chevalier responded by sending a message to the Frenchman to visit them, but regrettably nothing came of the invitation.

The time had now come to return north, and even though the Verendrye brothers had penetrated deeper into the interior of the northern buffalo country than anyone before, they must have been disappointed. They found the Spanish far away and the French nearby, but there was no River of the West that led to a Western Sea.

By early April, with their horses rested and in good condition, they headed north to the Mandan villages, but before taking their leave the Chevalier placed on a hillock near the fort a lead plate bearing the arms and inscription of the king. Over it he formed a pyramid of stones, telling the Indians only that the stones were a memorial of their visit to their country.[16]

They departed on April 2, "much lamented by the whole tribe." A week later they came to a village of twenty-five lodges of the Gens de la Flèche Collée (People of the Glued Arrow), identified as Prairie Sioux, who were moving camp at the time. Although they were friendly, the French kept a guard all night.

In the morning they continued north, following the river, and met no one until they reached the Mandan village on May 18, six weeks later.[17] They left the Mandan villages in a hurry on May 26 to catch up with a large village of Assiniboines heading north, joining them for mutual protection against the Sioux. It was well they did, for on the last day of May their scouts perceived thirty Sioux waiting in ambush on their route (they may have been in the vicinity of Dogden

Butte). The Sioux, however, were greatly surprised to see so many men advancing on them and "retreated in good order," skirmishing along the way. The Chevalier wrote that it wasn't the overwhelming odds that deterred the Sioux—who considered the Assiniboines "cowards"—but the guns of the French. There were many wounded on both sides and one Sioux was killed.

They arrived on June 2 at the Assiniboine village near the Turtle Mountains and stayed until the twentieth, then left with a couple of Assiniboine guides who took them to La Reine, which they reached on July 2 after an incredible journey of fifteen months.

The Verendrye brothers learned that the Western Sea[18] was too far, if anyone still believed that inlet existed, and that all the direct routes to the southwest were blocked by hostile Indians. Although the brothers found a large group of allied tribes living in a state of relative peace and harmony on the northern plains, they also found a vicious war under way that was disrupting all travel and trade in hides and horses.

Ironically, a century later, the trade in peltry and buffalohides that the Verendryes had so earnestly sought would be centered a scant 3 miles from where they buried their now-famous lead plate.

NINE

Nomads

The buffalo was part of us, his flesh and blood being absorbed by us until it became our own flesh and blood. Our clothing, our tipis, everything we needed for life came from the buffalo's body. It was hard to say where the animal ended and the man began. —Lame Deer

IT WAS EARLY JUNE and I was riding horseback over an unbroken carpet of tender, new grass under a high, windswept arc of blue sky. The landscape was the high plains of southeastern Wyoming, open and empty without a trace of man's stamp on it. Late in the morning I crested a high hill and there, quietly spread out as far as the eye could see, were random but evenly spaced groups of grazing bison just as Catlin had portrayed them on the upper Missouri. I dismounted and stood in amazement at the tableau before me. I had ridden into an old earth dream that perfectly matched the description John Townsend wrote in *Early Western Travels*, when his party "on rising a hill were suddenly greeted by a sight which seemed to astonish even the oldest amongst us. The whole plain, as far as the eye could discern, was covered by one enormous mass of buffalo. ... It was truly a sight that would have excited even the dullest mind to enthusiasm."[1]

The peaceful harmony of the scene was inspiring beyond words. I could feel the wind on my face and hear the sweet, flutelike warbling of larks. J. R. Mead described the same sensation in *Hunting and Trading on the Great Plains*: "There were buffalo on all sides of us and mingled with them were groups of antelope grazing or playing over the hills. It was the most beautiful scene I ever beheld: an abundance of game on every side, quietly feeding or reposing in the sunshine, and at home as the Great Creator placed them."[2]

There was a glory in it that might be described as a mixture of joy and humility. The anima of the earth and the buffalo, the plains and springtime, is a potent elixir when encountered complete and natural. The experience far exceeded anything I could have imagined. It was pure and primal.

Seldom in the history of humankind has one animal shaped and determined the life, the culture, and the spirit of so many plains people in so many ways. For those who love the plains the bison is an icon. For the old nomadic hunters it was the physical essence of life itself.

Next to warfare, the buffalo hunt demanded all of a man physically, mentally, emotionally, and spiritually. This drama, which usually ended with the death of the antagonist, had been played out over and over again since before anyone could remember. From time beyond memory everyone knew that being men involved killing, and the killing involved subterfuge, mysticism, courage, bloodlust, and violence.

In the earliest days, maneuvering and killing bison on foot with primitive weapons made of hardwood and tipped with sharp stone projectile points required an astute knowledge of landscape and animal behavior, along with a tenacity that involved total abandonment of personal safety. Undertaking the challenge of hunting and killing bison, with its outcome a matter of tribe or clan survival, was never taken lightly. Nothing could be left to chance; buffalo dancing, magic charms, incantations, and divination all became essential factors in determining the success of the hunt. All the people of the buffalo country had a full appreciation and a direct understanding that other creatures must die so that they might live. They even went one step further, believing that buffalo could be induced to sacrifice themselves for the good of the human community.[3] And to make this sacrifice the most meaningful to the bison anima, the people, particularly the nomads who followed their movements and lived and died with the herds, adopted them as "relatives"—a gesture that at once elevated the animal's persona and humbled the hunter's. In effect they became equals.

Purity of spirit and intent was believed to be tantamount to gaining "power" in ensuring a successful hunt. In some instances those in charge of the hunt would fast and abstain from profane activities for weeks in order that they might be worthy of leading the hunters. Medicine men might be chosen to propitiate the bison, to beg their spirits to cooperate with the endeavor of the hunters, and finally, to let themselves be killed so that the people might live. Human intent in a focused mind is a potent force.

Many methods of hunting bison on the plains evolved to take advantage of every landscape pattern or circumstance in which bison might be encountered. One of the earliest methods before the horse was the foot surround, by which a long line of men gradually encircled a small herd of bison and moved in for the kill. Ideally, the surround was held on a still day, when the bison would be less likely to catch the scent of hunters on the wind. If there was wind, the hunters would be forced to approach the bison from the upwind side last. As the line of hunters formed around the herd, the men gradually drew closer to one another and to the buffalo, forming an increasingly tighter ring. When an animal finally became alarmed and tried to break the circle, the hunters would yell, throwing their robes in the air before loosing a barrage of arrows and spears into the herd until all the milling beasts were slain. And it was important that all the animals be killed; survivors, they believed, could warn the others.

Nicolas Perrot, a French fur trader, described the events of a successful pedestrian hunt he witnessed in the seventeenth century. According to Perrot, a village or several villages of people were gathered together during the bison's late-summer rutting season. A leader was selected for the expedition; until the hunt was completed, everyone without exception accorded him absolute obedience. Strict order prevailed to prevent anyone from going out alone and frightening the herd away. The leader organized all the participants to form a large circle around the herd and then, on cue, they slowly closed the circle, careful not to alarm the animals. As they did so, they fired (torched) the grass, further enclosing the herd, and then began shooting the trapped animals with arrows. With this method, Perrot wrote, "there are some villages which have secured as many as fifteen hundred buffaloes."[4]

Subterfuge was another technique for bringing the bison into closer range of the village, thus saving the hunters the effort of hauling hundreds of pounds of meat on their backs or by dog travois. Two methods were used. The most dramatic involved a hunter or hunters masquerading as bison by draping themselves in a hide complete with head and horns. These decoys would then advance toward the herd on foot or on all fours downwind from their quarry. Occasionally they would pantomime the gestures of bison and flawlessly mimic their grunts and bellows. Once the decoys attracted the attention of the lead cow, they would entice her to move the herd over to the ambush site, where other hunters waited behind rocks, brush, or convenient landforms. Sometimes they might lead the herd into a makeshift corral where they could all be killed or stampede them over a high cutbank.

In the spring or early summer, decoys might guide them into a bog where they could more easily be approached and slain. In the winter, scouts would try to herd them into deep snowdrifts at the bottom of draws where they would founder and could be speared.

Another daring subterfuge occurred when the hunters disguised themselves as wolves. Wrapped in a wolfskin tied at the neck and the waist, the hunter, hunched over on hands and knees, would move slowly downwind in the direction of a slow grazing herd. Because bison were fully habituated to the presence of wolves, who pursued them on an almost constant basis, the hunters' movement aroused little suspicion or alarm.

Upon penetration of the lead cow's comfort zone, the hunter might howl to assure her that he was nothing more than what he appeared to be: a wolf. Then, when she put her head down to graze, he would sit back on his haunches, wolf cape still in place, and let fly an arrow aimed at her lungs. A good lung shot would preclude her from running and drop her on the spot. At that point the hunters would continue to assault the herd one animal at a time until they had shot them all or spooked them away. The subtlety, danger, and skill involved in this stratagem cannot be overstated. Taking the life of a powerful, sentient creature at such close range and personal risk must have been exhilarating, for at any moment the hunter was subject to a kick or a charge from a wounded or angry animal.

With the introduction of the horse on the northern plains in the early eighteenth century, hunting odds began to shift in favor of the hunter. And everything virtually changed for the people who followed them.

An example of the effect of the horse can be found in the life of the Cheyenne, whose amazing odyssey from woodland hunter-gatherers to plains village farmers to nomads is a classic story of constant change and cultural revision.

According to their oral tradition, the Cheyenne reached the eastern banks of the Missouri River in 1676. Their stories suggest they arrived as harried refugees who had been driven out of their camps along the Sheyenne River in southeastern North Dakota by the better-armed Cree and Ojibway. Along the Missouri they found shelter with the Arikara and established small villages of their own on the banks of the Missouri north of the main Ree villages.[5]

In time, groups of Cheyenne drifted farther west onto the plains and stayed longer on their annual bison hunts, until at some point a vanguard of the tribe spent their entire time in conical, bisonhide tipis far out on the northern grasslands in continual pursuit of the herds.

Fewer people returned every year after the hunt to their earthlodge villages on the Missouri, and eventually all the members followed the pattern set by the more nomadic elements of the group. By the mid-eighteenth century the Cheyenne had adopted a completely nomadic lifestyle even as a dwindling minority of women still tarried long enough at a handful of remote terraces along the Cheyenne, Moreau, and Grand Rivers to plant a patch of corn and pumpkins before heading farther west to live the wandering life based on the migration of the herds.

By the end of the eighteenth century, the Cheyenne had completely transformed themselves into a nomadic culture. They had also managed to develop a strong, cohesive tribal society largely because of the advanced teachings of their legendary culture hero, Sweet Medicine. With his gift of the *mahuts*, or four sacred arrows, a high standard of ideals and principles was adopted by the tribal leaders. These unified the tribe culturally and spiritually.[6] As a reinvigorated culture, they located their main camps on the eastern slopes of the Black Hills in the vicinity of their sacred vision-quest mountain, Nowah'vose, known today as Bear Butte.

The migration of the Cheyenne west of the Missouri to the Black Hills appears to have been gradual and bloodless. They seem to have mingled peacefully with the other nomadic tribes in the vicinity at that time, including the Kiowas, Apaches, and Arapahos. They shared a language affinity with the Arapahos and were on generally good trading terms with the Rees, Mandans, and Hidatsas. For the most part the end of the seventeenth century in the northern plains buffalo country appears to have been relatively tranquil.

In fact the Black Hills in the late seventeenth and early eighteenth centuries became a meeting and gathering place for "friendly nations"[7] that included the Arikaras, Kiowas, Kiowa-Apaches, Arapahos, Cheyennes, and Pawnee where maize, tobacco, and, later, horses, guns, and articles of Spanish goods were traded.

But the horse was about to change everything in ways few of the Plains Indians could imagine. According to Cheyenne folklore, the Comanches brought horses to the Cheyennes while they were still living in their earthlodge villages. The Comanches invited them on a horse-raiding expedition against the Pueblos of New Mexico. It was such a significant proposal that Cheyenne medicine men fasted and prayed for four days over the decision. The oldest medicine man spoke for the group, claiming that Ma'heo, their Great Spirit, said that: "If you have horses everything will be changed for you forever. You will have to move around a lot to find pasture for your horses. You will have to give up gardening and live by hunting … like the Comanches. And you will have to come out of your earth lodges and live in tents. … You will have fights with other tribes, who will want your pasture land or the places where you hunt. You will have to have real soldiers, who can protect the people. Think before you decide."[8]

Whether true or apocryphal, these would prove prophetic words of wisdom for the Cheyenne. The acquisition of the horse also began the transformation of the Arapahos, Assiniboines, Atsinas (Gros Ventres), Blackfeet, Crows, Kiowas, and Teton Lakotas, who had all at various times in their pasts as pedestrian hunters dwelt on the fringes of the plains. The Cheyenne, in their turn, would now become mounted buffalo hunters and warriors.

But, as in all political matters, consensus shifted within tribes and they differed regarding the adaptations and philosophies required for a completely nomadic existence.

The Hidatsas eventually broke up into three distinct groups. Those who became nomads changed their identity, calling themselves Absaroka (Hawk) and entered the popular literature misnamed the "Crow." One group, the Mountain Crow, moved from the Missouri to claim the rich hunting grounds of the Yellowstone and its upper tributaries, a region thick with bison that also encompassed the Bighorn Mountains. The River Crow established their main camps at the mouth of the Powder River, also on the Yellowstone. To the north the Piegan led the Blackfoot migration onto the northern plains ahead of their relatives, the Kaihahs and Siksikas.

Killing buffalo, which had once required all the people, now, with the help of the horse, became almost exclusively the work of men. In the case of the classic "surround," what had once been done carefully on foot could now be accomplished on horseback, thereby encompassing larger herds with more speed and agility.

In the horseback surround, two columns of mounted hunters formed twin crescents or pincers that, like the two lines of walking hunters, approached and enclosed the herd in a giant circle that might be 2 or 3 miles in diameter. Like the foot surround, the final approach would be made with the utmost caution and regard for what the Rees called "the bison's exquisite degree of scent."[9] The bulk of the hunters would begin to move downwind employing cover and/or landforms (hills or ridges) when available to keep the animals as unaware as possible of their approach. If the animals were not prematurely spooked by human scent or noise, the hunters would gradually tighten the ring. When they started to spook and begin a stampede, the horsemen would quickly close in from all sides and commence the slaughter.

Surrounded, hemmed in, and bunched tightly together by hunters loosing a barrage of arrows and lances, the bison became a milling mass of wild-eyed, frenzied animals bellowing in rage and pain. Under this withering assault, they fell by the score, littering the prairie. Sometimes a horse would be ripped apart by slashing horns and a fallen rider mangled or trampled under sharp, pounding hooves. But the other hunters kept up the deadly assault. Sometimes a bold animal would turn and bolt from the circle of riders, at which point it would be run down. The hunt ended when all the bison were killed.[10]

Catlin graphically depicted a horseback surround of buffalo the Hidatsas undertook in 1832. He reported that during the hunt, many Hidatsa hunters were thrown from their horses or squeezed in between the herd. His painting shows men running over the backs of the buffalo. Following the hunt, he noted that an entire herd of several hundred animals had been killed in the span of fifteen minutes.

In preparation for a hunt, each rider would carry fifty to sixty arrows to be shot from a short, 3-foot bow usually made of a pliant wood (ash) and sinew. A good bowman could keep an arrow in the air the entire time he was hunting while controlling his horse with his legs. In later times, when the fastest horses were specially trained to run the bison, these arrows would be shot and timed to hit at the exact moment the ribs of the animal were fully exposed and extended in a dead run. The hunter would endeavor to place his sharp, stone-tipped missile just behind the front shoulder of the beast, taking advantage of its natural shoulder rotation to drive the arrow tip back and deep into the heart.

Most experienced mounted bison hunters later asserted that arrows did more damage and could be fired faster than the black-powder muzzleloaders of Civil War vintage, which had to be reloaded on the run after every shot. Also, whereas a black powder–driven mini ball might pass completely through an animal, allowing it to continue running, an arrow was more apt to cause a mortal wound even if it did not immediately penetrate the heart. In both instances, if the hunter found his mark, the bison would blow blood from its mouth and nostrils and, after a few more yards of running, stumble and fall into a huge mass of muscle, bone, hide, and horn.

With the invention of breechloading firearms and faster, better-trained buffalo-running horses, "the surround" as a tactical maneuver lost its importance and gave way to "the chase." In the end the latter was not much more than a free-for-all inasmuch as the hunters with the best buffalo horses usually killed the most bison on a run. If the hunter had a good horse, he would not pause after killing a buffalo, but immediately pursue another bison until he had slain it. If he had a great runner, a "five mile buffalo horse," he would run down and get a third one. At this point the horse was spent and the chase was over.

The chase had formerly been employed only as an expedient measure to pursue every escaping bison from the surround, but by the late nineteenth century it was the method of choice. Good horses and repeating firearms gave an overwhelming technological advantage to the hunters, who were now capable of killing large numbers of bison, creating more competition and tension for resources and territory. Regrettably, history has been a litany of advancing technology outpacing human discipline, restraint, and wisdom. This imbalance would eventually sow the seeds of waste and war in the buffalo country.

TEN

The Teton Lakota

The Sioux, as warriors and as buffalo hunters, have become the symbol of all that is Indian—colorful figures ... they were the heroes of the Great Plains ... and the villains, too. —Royal B. Hassrick

HALLOWEEN NIGHT 1999, west of Faith, South Dakota, starts out quiet and uneventful. The thermometer on the bank in town indicates 61° at dusk. The air is very dry and the wind dead calm. At 7:30 P.M. I walk up Main Street in a T-shirt and ball cap headed for the grocery store. I make my purchase and am walking home when a 55 mph wind blast blindsides the town like a low-flying B-52. Anything not nailed down goes southeast ahead of the northwest wind. The air is immediately filled with clouds of dust, sand, and grit. Before I make it a few blocks, my eyes are stinging and my mouth tastes like a campfire. Then I realize there is smoke in the air.

Eight miles west of town on Avance Road, that first wind gust snaps an old Rural Electric Association pole like a matchstick. When the crossbar hits the ground, the wires arc in the tall dry grass, igniting a wildfire that quickly takes off. In the first twenty minutes, driven by 30 to 40 mph sustained winds, it burns 300 acres. By 9:00 P.M. the fire line is 5 miles long, racing southeast down the ridge that separates Stoney Butte Creek from Red Scaffold Creek. An old primal monster has been loosed from its chains.

The fire burns to within 4 miles of Faith and is clearly visible from town. I drive a few miles south of town to another ridge closer to the fire to get a better look. Through binoculars I watch bright red, 5- to 6-foot flames lick the night sky with volatile fury. It is a magnificent spectacle of elemental power that leaves me in awe with a thrilling sense of excitement and foreboding. It's a capricious monster out of control. If the fire manages to cross state Highway 73 south of Faith and enters the rough breaks and tall grass on the Cheyenne River Reservation, it will turn into a conflagration of biblical proportion that might go all the way to Cherry Creek.

In the meantime, some 200 to 300 people fight the fire from the west upwind side with pump trucks, effectively choking it down. Ten miles south of Faith, the leading point of the blaze hits a long stretch of plowed stubble field and dies a mile and a half west of the highway. It is 11 P.M. In three hours the Avance grass fire has burned over 11,000 acres of grass in a line about 15 miles long stretching northwest to southeast. No one is hurt. Some livestock are lost, a few hay piles burned, and a lot of fenceposts are charred.

Six weeks earlier, within a couple of miles of the same locality west of Faith, wheel bearings in a horse trailer heated up, igniting a ditch fire in the late afternoon. This time a strong breeze blowing from the southeast fanned the flames into a hot blaze and sent it north toward Flint Rock Creek. It burned slower than the Avance fire, consuming nearly 2,000 acres before it was extinguished a few hours later. Again, no appreciable damage.

Probing through the burn area of the Flint Rock blaze a week later I come across five stone tipi rings scattered over a low ridge above Flint Rock Creek. Tom Mason, who has lived there all of his eighty-plus years and whose parents homesteaded the place at the turn of the twentieth century, never knew they were there.

The rings on the Flint Rock are old. Archaeologists who have dated similar rings in western South Dakota place the circles at about 500 years. They base their estimates on how deep the stones have settled down into the sod. The people who set them there to hold down their tipi skins may have been buffalo hunters from the Missouri River villages on their annual hunt, or early nomads from the northwestern plains who had established a small seasonal camp here and hunted the area on foot.

Fire, buffalo, and nomads: the northern plains triumvirate, all three intertwined and restlessly moving in elliptical paths, curves, and circles through and around each other. Here today, gone tomorrow. Ephemeral like the wind feeding a fire.

And like a fire in dry grass before the wind, building slowly into a fierce and unpredictable force, the Teton Lakota entered the northern plains. They came slowly at first as eastern Prairie Sioux, migrants from the tallgrass prairies of western Minnesota, and made their way west, stopping to rest in the shady river groves of the sluggish Cansunsun (James River),[1] arriving on the banks of the broad, shallow Missouri sometime in the first half of the eighteenth century. They were probably small groups of Brûlés and Oglalas accompanied by big wolf-dogs dragging travois while their women and girls were heavily laden with packs.

They were poor and afoot when they reached the Big Bend country of the Missouri where, according to statements made by both the Arikara and the Sioux, they begged at the Arikara towns for corn, dried pumpkins, and native tobacco as well as a few horses.

"But the Teton Sioux," wrote George Hyde in *Red Cloud's Folk*, "was always a hardy beggar with nothing humble about him; and if these people came to the Arikara one day to beg, they returned on another day to waylay the Arikaras and kill them, and from the very first they must have proved bad neighbors."[2]

A second wave of Minnesota Sioux, sometimes identified as the Sharp-tail Grouse People, soon followed. They proved inconsistent in temperament and character and unpredictable in behavior. This later group may have represented an aggressive vanguard element of well-armed Yankton Sioux who had recently slaughtered and then driven out large groups of Omahas, Poncas, and Iowas from their large complex of villages south of the big S bend of the Big Sioux River, known today as the Blood Run site.[3] They were boastful, aggressive, and bore a proud arrogance born of successful conquest.[4]

The Sioux as a nation was a large one, consisting of some 25,000 people who spoke three major dialects: Dakota, Nakota, and Lakota. Within each of these major groups were subgroups and within each of these subgroups were further divisions of *tiospayes*, or family/clan groups.

Although united in language and culture, the Sioux were in no way a cohesive nation. Individualism and daring were always encouraged, making factional disputes frequent, divisive, and often bitter. Edward Denig, a clerk at Fort Pierre and Fort Union, observing the character of the western Lakota who traded there in the 1840s, noted that when two bands of the Sioux came together, "their opinions and interests clash, quarrel follows, and separation follows with bad feelings."[5]

Two different Oglala pictographic calendars record the year 1768 as the time the Oglalas and Brûlés, the two southern divisions of the Teton Lakota, fought a civil war against the Saones, a name of some derision applied early on by the southern Teton to the five northern divisions of Teton that included the Hunkpapa, Itazipcola, Oohenumpa, Sihasapa, and Mnikoju or Minniconjou. These seven tribes made up the Titunwan Oyate (Teton Nation).[6]

The Hunkpapa band to which Sitting Bull belonged was called Icira-hingla wicotipi, or "Everyone Is Always Disputing One Another." Other unflattering names applied to bands of Oglalas were Shoves-asides, Disregards-owns, and Bad-faces, all of whom were sometimes bitter rivals.[7]

Pierre Tabeau, a French fur trader from St. Louis living on the Missouri in 1803, recorded these observations in his journal:

> All these thirty tribes, particularly those of the Titons, yield still other divisions which are under the leadership of subordinate chiefs. If this nation had more insight and policy, it could form a chain that would render it yet more formidable to all of its neighbors than it is. But their separation and mutual remoteness, necessitated by their form of hunting which does not permit of their living together in too great numbers, divides its interests and causes those of the St. Peters [Minnesota River Santee], those of River of the Mohens [Des Moines River Yankton], and those of the Missouri [Teton] to regard each other as strangers. Then too, the spirit of unsociability and of discord which exists among the particular tribes; the ambition and the jealousy of the too numerous chiefs; and most of all the national character, naturally brutal and fierce, cause particular enmities to arise, which not only destroy the general harmony but especially that of the

various units. Individual quarrels arise which perpetuate, in families, hatred and revenge. Thus by a just defiance, which experience sanctions, a Titon is always armed even in his lodge.[8]

Although the Nakota division (Yankton and Yanktonais) tended to stay on the east side of the Missouri and the Teton Lakota on the west, both groups must have viewed the Arikara as an impediment to their access to an important river ford, trade, and the big bison herds across the Missouri. The symbol of Arikara power and dominance was their southernmost fortified village, located on the high precipice overlooking the Missouri at the mouth of Crow Creek.

With the arrival of more Sioux immigrants possessing firearms obtained from traders in the Minnesota country, Sioux war parties began to perceive themselves with a distinct advantage, even though they were still mostly on foot and lacking Arikara horses. Nonetheless, their warriors, hardened veterans of successful campaigns against the Iowas, Omahas, and Poncas, were a fierce, determined, and relentless force who were now focused on the Arikaras. Indian traditions verify forty years of war between the two nations.[9] In Baptiste Good's winter count, forty-four of the annual pictographs from the eighteenth century depict an ear of corn, the sign of a raid or attack against the Pawnees and Arikaras.[10] Warfare was the Sioux forte and the Arikaras were the prime target.

Eventually scattered bands of Sioux must have gathered a large war party and set out to attack the heavily fortified and well-defended earthlodge village at Crow Creek. It would have been an ambitious undertaking. The Crow Creek site was a pivotal one located above one of the best places to ford the treacherous Missouri, which is hemmed in here by steep cliffs with unstable slopes, gumbo banks, and narrow ravines. Hence, the Crow Creek fortress controlling the river passage was of critical strategic importance and had to be neutralized if the Sioux were to claim the river and proceed west unhindered.[11]

In spite of their determination, their first attempt to storm the palisades and bastions of the Crow Creek village was probably repulsed, and after taking a few scalps and horses and plundering the corn crops, they withdrew. Their initial attack may have seemed more of an annoyance than a serious threat to the Arikara. The Sioux would have to devise a new strategy, a deception in the form of a ruse; perhaps a pretext of friendly trade would get them through the gates and once inside with the Arikara guard down, they could implement their treachery. How they were finally able to subdue the village at Crow Creek is still a mystery, but get inside they did, and during the course of a bloody afternoon an entire village of nearly 500 men, women, and children was slaughtered. Most of their skulls were scalped, while the long bones were found disarticulated and cut through at the joints. All the victims' hands and feet were severed from their bodies and their heads decapitated, the unmistakable signature of the Sioux.[12] Heads of dead Arikaras may have been thrown into the river to float downstream, a proclamation unmistakable and terrifying to all the lower river Indians. The Sioux were in control of the upper river country.

A more serious threat to Arikara domination of the Missouri and the vast Buffalo Country to the west was even more insidious than Sioux treachery and arrived swiftly and unseen from the opposite direction.

In the late 1770s a virulent smallpox epidemic revisited the Valley of Mexico, the worst since Cortez had invaded the Aztecs and inadvertently decimated them with the same disease.[13] In 1779, upwards of 22,000 Indians succumbed to smallpox in Mexico before it moved to the Pueblos of New Mexico where it killed 5,000 people, or about half of the Pueblo Indian population at the time. In the matter of a decade, smallpox shifted the demographics of the Rio Grande valley, making the mestizos the new majority.[14]

From the highlands around Santa Fe the disease quickly moved northeast along the old trade routes to the upper Missouri. Now mounted, a warrior could travel much farther and faster while the virus incubated in his lungs without any ill effect for well over a week before displaying any overt symptoms. It hit the Pawnees first, then the Arikaras, Mandans, and Hidatsas where it spread like wildfire with devastating consequences.

Smallpox, genus *Variola*, is an old disease with numerous species or variants. All are spread as a highly communicable airborne virus that enters the body through the respiratory tract. It can also be contracted by coming into contact with a fresh pox scab or pustule. Once contracted, the virus incubates for about ten to fourteen days in the carrier before manifesting a host of symptoms that include nausea, extreme fatigue, chills, pounding headaches, convulsions. and debilitating back pain. These symptoms are followed by a high fever (106° F.) during which the victim may become delirious or comatose.

After a few days the fever subsides and the victim develops flat, red blotches that appear first across the face and forearms, then the abdomen, chest, back, and legs. These develop into painful red lesions and pustules that swell into clear blisters, which slowly fill with pus before oozing and erupting into sores and wounds that eventually cover the entire body including the face, which swells into an ugly pulp of pimply flesh.

Concurrent with swelling and the eruption of sores, the victim's fever spikes again and many of the early symptoms reappear. Every heartbeat reverberates as a pulse of headache pain while the victim's mind slips in and out of delirium. As the body is eaten away by the canker, the victim exudes a sickening stench of rotting flesh.

Mortality depended on the strain of smallpox contracted. Ninety percent of the victims of discrete smallpox in which the pox sores did not touch each other survived. Half of those afflicted with confluent smallpox in which the sores were close enough to touch died. All who contracted hemorrhagic smallpox, undoubtedly the most horrible strain, in which the pox attacked the victim's mucous membranes and internal organs including the lungs and throat, died.[15]

If the victim managed to survive the onslaught of one of the lesser strains of pox, his or her skin pustules would eventually mature after a week, split open, and dry into scabs. Within a month, the scabs would heal, leaving deep-pitted, disfiguring scars that formed a curious centrifugal distribution pattern over the entire body.

By the close of 1781, an estimated 80 percent of the entire Ree/Arikara nation, nearly 8,000 people, were dead from smallpox, which the upper river Indians appropriately called "rotting face."[16]

The smallpox epidemic all but destroyed the Arikara as a viable culture and a dominant force on the Missouri and the buffalo plains. A nation who had grown and prospered for nearly five centuries on the Missouri River had now entered its twilight.

Demoralized by disease and continually terrorized by the Sioux, survivors of all the Arikara towns migrated upriver and combined to form five new villages on the west bank of the Missouri just below the mouth of the Cheyenne.

But here also they remained an obstacle to the movement of the Sioux,[17] who were "feared and dreaded ... on account of the firearms with which they are always well-provided. Their very name causes terror, they have so often ravaged and carried off the wives and children of the Arikaras."[18] These Tetons, perhaps along with the fierce Yanktons, ultimately forced them to withdraw again farther up the Missouri to the mouth of the Grand River.[19] In 1795, Jean-Baptiste Trudeau, a French trader who visited the Arikara villages following the epidemic, wrote after watching them stockade their new villages that "a few families only from each of the villages escaped; these united and formed two villages" near the mouth of the Grand River.

Where once there had been 10,000 Arikaras living in more than forty large villages stretched out for nearly 300 miles along the Missouri, there were now only two villages with about 1,500 survivors, these the remnants of at least three waves of smallpox.

The way across the Missouri at Crow Creek and the mouth of the Cheyenne was now open all the way to the Black Hills.

The Teton, however, still regarded Minnesota as their home during the first few decades of their wanderings across the Missouri. They tended to stray west across the big river only for the late-summer buffalo hunt and to obtain horses from tribes near the Black Hills. In the fall, they returned again to Minnesota. By the end of the eighteenth century, though, their migrations ceased and the Tetons' main winter camps were now established on the Missouri near the sites of old, abandoned Arikara villages.

The former country of the Arikara, now in Sioux possession, must have seemed a poor trade compared with the lushness of Minnesota's lakes, rivers, forests, and prairies. The seasons, each in their own way, were a test of endurance and fortitude. During the winter the cold could be extreme, with low temperatures settling in at –20° F and windchills at about –70° F. In the summer the heat could be intense, with searing temperatures reaching 110° F. And then there was the inexorable wind, sometimes blowing steadily for days at a time, gusting at speeds of 40 to 60 mph—bending, probing, scouring out every landform and creature.

On the west side of the river the grass, although nutritious, was sparse, short, and brittle and the ground thickly spread with cactus. The rivers were shallow, muddy affairs. In the spring they were susceptible to wild flash floods while at the close of summer they reverted to dry, salt-encrusted beds punctuated with pools of brackish water.

The worst of the rivers in terms of flash flooding and alkalinity the Tetons simply called Shicha Wakpa (Bad River). The next major stream above the Bad, they called Wasta Wakpa (Good River).[20] South of the Bad was the White, which the Tetons called Earth Smoke or White Earth.[21] And below that ran the Niobrara, which the French called L'eau Qui Court (Running Water).

The southern and eastern parts of the northern plains were now the domain of the Teton Lakota. As the prominent streams of the buffalo country, beginning with the Grand down through the Niobrara, were inked onto the maps, their combined French and Sioux names would ultimately be anglicized, foreshadowing the mix and the addition of one last dominant group to come. But first the Sioux and Cheyenne would struggle for what would amount to a brief dominance of the northern buffalo country.

ELEVEN

Creek of Ghosts

The individual Indian fought just in his own way and took orders from no one.
—George Bird Grinnell

THE SIOUX CALLED IT WAKAN WAKPA (Ghost Creek). The early
settlers demeaned it to Spook Creek. It's like a hundred other draws
that wind and twist their way south from the Fox Ridge headed for
Cherry Creek and the Cheyenne River. It's mostly lined with small
ash trees, willows, and an occasional great cottonwood. But there's
an odd story connected with Wakan Wakpa from a long time back
when the Cheyenne and Lakota went head to head in a fierce pitched
battle over this prime piece of the buffalo country.

The Cheyenne, having been harassed unmercifully in their earlier
struggles in the Minnesota country by the Prairie Sioux, on the Sheyenne
River in eastern North Dakota by the Cree, and later on the Missouri
by Sioux war parties, it was perhaps inevitable that this shift to a less
secure nomadic existence also needed to include a new philosophy
that encouraged a fighting spirit among every man of the tribe.[1]

A warrior code that would become the litmus test of manhood and
bravery against an enemy soon became the ideal of the mounted
plains nomads. To risk one's life in battle would eventually be carried to the extreme of overtly courting death at the hands of the
enemy to prove one's courage. Such actions were accorded the highest honor in the Cheyenne camps. Prowess as a warrior would come
to rank as the highest pursuit any young man could achieve.

As Teton war parties crossed the Missouri in the late eighteenth
century, they met the Cheyenne amidst a host of other nomads already living in the vicinity of the Black Hills. In the Black Hills the

Cheyenne lived in an alliance with their linguistic kinsmen, the Arapaho, who had preceded them earlier onto the plains. The Cheyenne also seem to have been on amicable trading terms with the Kiowas and Apaches and were usually welcome at the earthlodge villages of the Arikaras, Mandans, and Hidatsas.

When they first met the Tetons, the Cheyenne described them as being very poor, lacking horses, and traveling with all their possessions by dog travois. They took pity on them, as had the Arikara earlier, and helped them make the transition to mounted bison hunting. The Tetons undoubtedly proved adept learners in the art.

With the continued influx of Tetons from the east, their numbers grew on the western plains. Well mounted and in the midst of the great bison herds, they prospered. Able to procure more protein, their families grew larger numerically as well as in strength and vigor. Their numbers, aggressiveness, and continued need for conquest and territory quickly allowed them to begin leveraging more power in a bid for domination of the heart of the buffalo country.

Although independence, disagreement, and infighting within the great Sioux Nation had always been a part of their collective personality, nonetheless, as an extended society they possessed strong cultural affiliations including language and blood ties that bound them closely together against outsiders. They believed that a great symbolic circle of kinship inscribed them, and that while they as kin lived inside the circle, only enemies lived outside of it. This strong ethnocentric creed was further reinforced by their language, in which the terms "stranger" and "enemy" were synonymous.

By the end of the eighteenth century, Sioux warriors of the plains had become a power to reckon with. Their relentless wolf packs of young men out to gain war honors, scalps, and horses had driven the Kiowas and Apaches south and out of the Black Hills, while the Crow had been pushed back into the Bighorns, the Pryors, and the upper Yellowstone country. Only the Cheyenne stood in the way of total Sioux domination of the buffalo country. And they, as a warrior force, were nonpareil.

Stories of battles between the Cheyenne and the Sioux are few, but records clearly indicate that the two tribes fought a handful of fierce, pitched battles.[2] Well matched in armament, skill, and bravery against the Tetons, the Cheyenne were numerically inferior, but they exhibited remarkable courage in battle, exacting a great toll on their adversaries. Both sides must have suffered such heavy casualties in their internecine conflicts that neither was able to claim an outright victory.

An oral legend passed down by early Sioux informants recounts one such battle that took place on the west end of Fox Ridge in western South Dakota.[3] At that time, the land between the Moreau and Cheyenne Rivers was a prize hunting territory. Two groups of disparate people, hunting separately, could invariably spoil the hunting for the other, chasing the bison far away from their camps before the other could get a chance to hunt them. A situation like this would certainly cause friction and animosity, not to mention the ultimate question of territorial preeminence.

A soldier society of Cheyenne warriors known as the Kit Fox would have responded to this kind of intrusion with force in a manner that may have happened as follows.

The Kit Fox Society, one of a handful of powerful military societies that protected the Cheyenne people and their territory, derived their name from the slender Swift Fox of the Great Plains. Admiring the animal's sleek, alert, and cunning ways, they sought to emulate its power of sustained running endurance. In tests of speed and running, members of the Kit Fox Society could be counted on to outstrip their fellows across long distances.

As a symbol of their society, their head chief carried a staff with a fox skin tied to it. The fox skin was powerful medicine. Wrapped in a similar skin, the great prophet, Sweet Medicine, brought the sacred arrows to the tribe. The men of the society regarded this talisman as the source of their power. Smearing their medicine on the foxhide as well as on themselves before a journey or battle imparted to them a sense of lightness and speed, allowing them to endure the rigors of traveling great distances with little water, rest, or food.

The society also had a rattle keeper who carried a red-painted gourd with special medicine stones inside. The rattle keeper marked time by shaking the rattle during their special songs and dances. On marches he helped maintain the pace at an easy trot across the wide and open country. The society had four sacred songs, part of which related to the fox, as well as four war songs and hundreds of dance songs that inspired them to perform feats of strength, endurance, and agility.

Preceding this particular foray to the hunting grounds between the Moreau and Cheyenne Rivers, the warriors of the Fox Society first began their preparation for the fight by setting up a special skin lodge in the center of the camp village. Within the interior of the lodge, facing the east, would be a fox skin with its head directed at the entrance. When the chief and his assistants were situated in a council circle within the lodge, the skin was set down before them in the middle of the circle. Four maidens, who were members of this society, sat in front of the chiefs.

With preparations set, the warriors entered. All members of the society were dressed alike. Each warrior had two feathers stuck vertically in his scalplock. Although each normally carried a sharp, flint-tipped spear from which hung various types of feathers having a specific, significant relevance for the owner, on the warpath each man would exchange his spear for a bow and arrows.

Preparing for a long march, they painted their faces and torsos, including the upper parts of their arms and legs, yellow, while their lower arms and legs were painted black to resemble the leg markings of a fox. Suspended on a rawhide thong around the neck of each warrior was a black-painted, crescent-shaped piece of hide. When all were present the drumming, rattling, and singing began. The dances may have lasted for days during which time the men jumped up and down rapidly like a fox pouncing, keeping time to the ever-increasing beat of the drum and rattle. The four maidens, daughters of the chiefs, wore dresses decorated with elk teeth. Their faces were painted yellow like the men's and they wore two eagle feathers upright in their hair. At the end of their dance, the warriors, their spirits honed and heightened to a razor's edge, departed eastward, disappearing into the dimness of dawn.

After a two days' march, the war party encountered what they had been looking for: a large group of Sioux hunters near a high ridge. Initially caught off-guard, the hunters quickly surmised their predicament and a battle began. The Foxes, having taken the initiative, quickly gained the upper hand, forcing the hunters to retreat. A Sioux runner was dispatched to the nearby main camps for reinforcements and soon they had the numerical advantage.

Meanwhile, the Kit Foxes fought with a spirit and intensity the Sioux had rarely encountered.[4] These men were superb warriors like themselves and took the lives of some of their best braves and yet, in the face of relentless and overwhelming odds, their numbers dwindled. The tide of battle shifted and the Foxes regrouped to make their last stand. All knew they would die in battle together for none wished to return alone to the camp to mourn their lost and fallen comrades.

The remaining Foxes chanted their death songs to prepare their way down the sunset path and into the next world:

> *It is a good day to die the death of a warrior.*
> *It is a good day to die the death of a Fox.*
> *It is a good day to die a Cheyenne.*

In the end each man stood alone, slaying as many as he could in bloody hand-to-hand combat before falling himself beneath the onslaught of the enemy. No survivor returned to the Cheyenne camps.

Following the battle, the victors tied all the bodies of the dead Cheyenne to the ash and elm trees in a nearby draw to acknowledge their prowess as warriors and to honor their spirit and bravery in the face of overwhelming odds and death. The Kit Fox did not flinch.

Finding the fox skin talisman tied around the chief and understanding that all the men belonged to one warrior society, the Sioux named this high ground, the place where all the Foxes died, Fox Ridge.

In time, the elements reduced the bodies of the slain warriors to sinewy skeletons of bleached bones dangling and rattling in the trees.

The draw below the ridge where the skeletons danced in the wind became Wakan Wakpa, the Creek of Spirits or Ghosts.[5]

It may have been one of the last bloody skirmishes between these two people, exacting a horrible price on both sides. Neither group spoke of it, but place-names and dim stories remained.[6]

Sometime in the nineteenth century a truce was called between the Sioux and the Cheyenne, stopping the slaughter on both sides and ending the brutal and debilitating warfare that threatened to cripple and destroy both entities. For the only time in their history on the plains the Teton Lakota accepted "strangers" as allies.

TWELVE

Old Fort Pierre

All this is now of the past. The buffalo have departed. The wandering
Indian of the plains has also gone. —Thomas R. Riggs

IT'S EARLY MAY and for four consecutive days rain has swept across
the Fort Pierre plain in central South Dakota, turning the dark Pierre
shale into thick, gumbo muck. When the leaden skies finally lift, bright
sunshine pours across a carpet of dandelions and tender blue-green
spears of grass that cover the small 35-acre Fort Pierre historic site. The
morning is animated by small darting flocks of lark buntings while the
air is thick with humidity and the rank odor of blooming mustard.

The old fort itself no longer exists, nor has it existed in the memory of any living being for three generations. It disappeared from the
Fort Pierre plain and the west bank of the Missouri River 150 years
ago, its likeness preserved only by a few scant drawings, its departed
spirit commemorated in the old dusty annals of fur traders and a
host of adventurers and travelers.

The old Fort Pierre plain stretches about 5 miles along the west
bank of the Missouri from the mouth of the Bad River to present-day
Oahe Dam. In ancient times it was a central location and river crossing along a trade route that wound its way up from the deserts of
Mexico and the American Southwest to the great pine forests of the
upper Mississippi and Lake Superior country.

In 1817, Joseph La Framboise (the Raspberry), a mixed French/
Ottawa fur trader, built a small fur trading post out of scavenged driftwood he had gathered along the Missouri River at the south end of
the Fort Pierre plain near the mouth of the Bad River. It must have
appeared as a great white bonfire pile with a door. Five years later, in

1822, the Columbia Fur Company erected a more substantial stock-aded post they called Fort Tecumseh near the confluence of the Bad and the Missouri. For a short time it served as their headquarters until it was sold to the more aggressive American Fur Company.

The two rivers conspired with a flood and managed to undermine Fort Tecumseh's east wall, so another fort was built in 1832. Relocated about 3 miles north of the Bad River's mouth, it was on higher ground situated on the east side of the Fort Pierre plain and adjacent to a good, deep-water steamboat landing.

Named for the great St. Louis fur purveyor and entrepreneur, Pierre Chouteau, Jr., Fort Pierre was built to tighten the American Fur Company's grip on the rapidly expanding buffalo robe and fur trade industry that had developed in the early nineteenth century across the northern buffalo plains. By the middle of the century, the old post had become the largest fur trading venue along the upper Missouri, serving as the field headquarters for all who went about "the Company's" business.[1] From 1832 to 1855 it, along with its sister post Fort Union,[2] located near the confluence of the Missouri and the Yellowstone, was the main port on the upper river, providing an access point as well as a unique window into time and place for travelers to look upon the life of the northern plains.

Based on a handful of descriptions and drawings made by sketch artists and military draftsmen, historians know that Fort Pierre consisted of a fortified protective enclosure of 16- to 20-foot cottonwood logs picketed upright that enclosed a nearly 300-foot squared quadrangle, or about 2.5 acres. Two log blockhouses 24 feet square and two stories high crowned the northwest and southeast corners. Jutting a full 8 feet beyond the stockade, they served as lookouts and protective bastions.

All roads and trails came into and connected at Fort Pierre: from the west, Fort Laramie; from the south, Fort Kearney; from the southeast, all the forts and posts along the Missouri; and from the north, the Indian villages. It was a handsome hub of activity situated in the midst of a lovely prairie bottom, which George Catlin described in near-rapturous terms when he first saw it in 1833:

The country around this fort is almost entirely prairie, producing along the river and streams only, slight skirtings of timber. No site could have been selected more pleasing or advantageous than this; the fort is in the center of one of the Missouri's most beautiful plains, and hemmed in by a series of gracefully undulating, grass-covered hills on all sides, rising like a series of terraces to the summit level of the prairies, some three or four hundred feet in elevation, which then stretches off in an apparent bound-less ocean of gracefully swelling waves and fields of green.[3]

All the visitors, who included a host of European dignitaries, scientists, explorers, and artists as well as seasoned traders, trappers, buffalo hunters, and Indians, entered through the larger of two front gates that faced the river (east). Upon entering they immediately found themselves in the midst of a small settlement of nearly twenty buildings enclosed within the stockade. Two long, single-story structures separated by a passageway that led into the post yard contained shops where tinsmiths, blacksmiths, carpenters, and saddlers labored at their trades.

Farther out to the right and left ran even longer buildings set out about 25 feet that paralleled the fort's walls. One of these structures contained a store of Indian trade articles that included mirrors and bells from Leipzig; clay pipes from Cologne; beads from Italy; cloth from France; guns and blankets from England; and tools, clothing, firearms, and a great variety of bric-a-brac from American manufacturers. The other long building provided housing for the employees.

At the rear of the fort another large building, complete with dormer windows, was used principally as a dormitory. By 1850 it had a porch along the entire front, with windows in the roof, and a bell on top complete with a weathercock. Next to the dormitory stood a neat log house with a pleasant little portico that was the home of the post bourgeois (BOOSH-way) or boss. Nearby stood the kitchens, a sawmill, an adobe powder magazine, horse stables, and smaller buildings used for pelt storage. And over it all in the center of the post yard, the American colors whipped in the wind against a clean, blue sky from a tall, traditional flagstaff.

Fort Pierre was the high point for weary steamboat travelers up the lower Missouri, most of whom had endured weeks on deck dodging cinders from belching smokestacks, fighting hordes of insects, and subsisting on a miserable diet of salt pork and biscuits and occasionally wild meat. The arrival of a steamboat, particularly the first one in the spring, was cause for immense excitement for fort residents, who had endured months of unrelieved boredom and physical isolation.

A steamboat brought a bloom of fresh faces and news from the outside world. Just the sight of tall smoke plumes and the throaty shrill of a steam whistle ignited a frenzied rush to the riverfront. As the vessel slowly churned into view rounding the north point of La Framboise Island, cannon salutes boomed alternately from the boat and the fort until the craft touched the landing. By this time the entire population of the fort, some 100, along with a sizable gathering from the nearby Indian encampment, lined the bank to welcome the boat and ogle the passengers. It was a meeting of two realms, and if the boat passengers were objects of immense curiosity by the fort denizens, the visitors in their turn were equally fascinated by what they encountered, particularly the "wild" native Indians who were more or less considered to be "tame" or "in captivity" at the post.

E. de Girardin, a French soldier of fortune and artist who accompanied Dr. John Evans, a geologist en route to the White River Badlands to explore and hunt for fossils, made these interesting observations on the Indians he encountered there in the summer of 1849 when his boat, the *Amelia*, landed at Fort Pierre: "A few steps from us on the shore, a group of Indians in holiday costume, their faces painted red, yellow, and white, [stood] as motionless as statues leaning on their guns, examining us with a somber and restless air. ... We have scarcely landed when some fifty young warriors and women swarm upon our deck, enter the lounge, the kitchens, everywhere in fact examining, touching and tasting everything, and in spite of the remonstrances of our Negro cooks, a huge kettle filled with boiled corn is emptied in an instant."[4]

Nearly every voyage included a group of preeminent passengers who were often scientists, artists, and members of European nobility.

The distinguished men of arts, science, and royalty often traveled at the expense and pleasure of Pierre Chouteau, Jr., and the American Fur Company. Upon landing at Fort Pierre, they were, as a matter of course, invited to a sumptuous dinner that, according to Monsieur de Girardin, featured fresh buffalo, cornbread, and pemmican served at the bourgeois's "high table."

In the evening, upper Missouri crepes suzette were prepared over an open bonfire in the center of the compound. So that guests might be properly warmed up and lubricated for the evening's festivities, each traveler was afforded two bottles of whiskey, one for each hand, ostensibly to ward off the cholera. Entertainment commenced with a pair of fiddlers standing atop barrels playing for a crowd who drank, smoked, danced, and reveled into the wee hours.[5]

These unabashed revelries were the exception, however. The reality of life in Fort Pierre entailed endless hours of monotonous labor strictly regimented by a rigid, medieval-like class system. Lord of the manor was the bourgeois, followed by his chief clerks, each of whom might earn as much as $2,000 per year. This frontier nobility dined at the high table on the best cuts of meat.

Also dining with the bourgeois and his clerks were the most favored old half-breed French traders, often referred to as the "white Indians." These traders were descendants of French-Canadian coureurs de bois and *hiverants* (winterers), who carried their language and culture among all the tribes of the upper Missouri country. Since most of these traders were illiterate, they kept their Indian account books by employing a unique succession or series of hieroglyphics understood only by themselves. Many, in marking down peltries received from the Indians, drew the form of the animal representing the skin beside the name of the Indian debtor, whose name might also appear as a peculiar hieroglyph or animal. Despite the idiosyncrasies of their bookkeeping annotations, each had mastered the mystery of ciphering and all amounts were correctly made and drawn.

Also essential to their success was their ability to speak a handful of Sioux dialects fluently and to move with equal assurance among the Indians and the whites. Inside the post walls the white Indians were the "big men of the country" and always figured prominently on the guest list of every major feast. When outside the walls, they could be observed strolling through the Indian camps in moccasins with a bowl of warm, puppy stew in one hand.

Beneath this upper class of clerks and traders, eating the less desirable cuts of meat at the second table, were the post hunters, who earned $400 per year and the craftsmen, who earned up to $250 per year. At the bottom of the pecking order were the boatmen and the assistant workmen, who might earn as much as $180 per year. These men, the majority of whom were also French Canadians, ate directly from the stew pot, which frequently consisted of bison meat one observer described as "very odorous and cooked in a large kettle which was always half full of bouillon three or four days old."[6]

The combination of low wages and the high price of staples like brown sugar, coffee, flour, and soap, all of which sold for a dollar a pound in the Company store, kept the hunters, workmen, and boatmen in a continuous state of penury and debt. Utterly demoralized by his wretched situation with no stake in "the Company" and little chance of promotion or salary increase, the average worker tended to be inefficient and lazy, avoiding work at every opportunity. Because many of the clerks, traders, and government Indian agents posted at the fort often drank heavily and quarreled, they set poor examples for the lower-echelon employees. Lax discipline, frustration, and short tempers encouraged violence, which was often vented during holiday celebrations at Christmas and on the Fourth of July when liquor was abundant and freely dispensed. These festivals often degenerated from feasting and dancing into drunken, boorish, free-for-all brawls.

Imbibing in hard liquor was an accepted practice at the fort. It was the coping mechanism of choice practiced by even the most sanguine of traders to escape the chafe of fleas, lice, biting flies, and stinging mosquitoes as well as complaining Indian wives, squealing offspring, dirt, grime, stench, and cholera.

For their part, the Indians who lived in the tipi encampments near the fort came to trade, beg, and in many cases leave their sick, lame, old, and infirm relatives who were unable to travel. These, they hoped, would be cared for by the traders. If circumstances proved propitious while they wandered around the fort, they might help themselves to a head of livestock grazing in the adjoining fields or merchandise and furnishings left unattended.

Because of the lack of sanitation and crowded living conditions, disease periodically scoured the fort and the adjacent Indian camps. During the winter of 1850–51 a virulent smallpox epidemic visited the Sioux camps near the fort.[7] Other years, cholera and influenza inadvertently introduced into the Fort Pierre population by steamboat passengers would run their course, killing whites and large numbers of Indians who often fled to the refuge of the Black Hills in the face of severe epidemics. Even though thousands of frightened natives were inoculated by the traders, the Indians invariably blamed them for the epidemics. And, contrary to later accusations of genocidal conspiracies perpetrated against native peoples, it was always in the best interests of the western fur traders to continually promote health and peace among all their Indian neighbors if they were to prosper as fur dealers and suppliers of goods.[8] Every good trader knew that internecine fights, tribal wars, and disease interrupted business and profits.

While the death toll on human beings at times was considerable at Fort Pierre, it paled by comparison with the waves of slaughter and death that rolled over the surrounding wildlife. Edwin Denig, a trader who visited the fort in 1833, reported a notorious buffalo hunt that had taken place a few years prior to his arrival. Although Denig did not witness the 1830 hunt, other traders told him that Yanktonai Sioux killed 1,500 bison on the east side of the Missouri across from the fort, taking only the tongues to trade at the fort. Stated another way, 1,500 magnificent animals, each weighing close to a ton, were killed for the express purpose of taking 4 pounds of its total body weight.

George Catlin, who also heard the story when he arrived in 1833, added a note that the tongues were traded for "but a few gallons of whiskey."[9] Catlin may have been exaggerating with his addition, but whiskey was an important and pernicious part of the trade at both

Fort Pierre and Fort Union, even though its use as a lubricant for trade had been strictly outlawed by the U.S. government. Enforcing the ban on the remote frontier, however, was another difficult matter.

With or without whiskey, the immense slaughter and waste of bison during the period of Fort Pierre's operation went on unabated. Twenty years after its opening and in the final days of its existence, Alfred Vaughan, Indian agent on the upper Missouri based at the fort in 1853, ascertained that the number of bison "annually destroyed in this agency does not fall very short of 400,000."[10] Hundreds of thousands of bison were literally slaughtered for only their tongues or their hides. The lion's share of the demand for hides shipped to eastern tanneries were processed into heavy machine belts that literally ran the pre- and post–Civil War industrial revolution. Fueling the tanneries deforested large parts of the northeastern United States and polluted vast stretches of numerous streams and rivers.

This early mass eradication of the bison as a commercial enterprise was initially carried out by the Plains Indians. Later, following the Civil War, it was undertaken almost exclusively by white buffalo hunters, but during the reign of Fort Pierre, it was the Sioux hunters around the fort, tempted by whiskey, calico, and hardware, who were the primary agents of this immense slaughter.[11]

Such was the tenor of life during the glory days of old Fort Pierre. But it was short-lived. No society can maintain for long such an extravagance of waste and despoliation. By the mid-1850s, after two decades of intense hunting pressure and trading, the great herds of bison had been nearly eliminated from the western Dakotas, with the survivors having been pushed into the northwestern reaches of the northern plains. With their depletion and disappearance the old post too faded as a commercial hub and fell into a general state of decay and disrepair. Chouteau and his partners in the American Fur Company were indeed pondering its ultimate fate when the U.S. Army showed an interest in purchasing it for use as a military post. Military planners entertained hopes of using it as a base for conducting "chastisement" operations against the Sioux. For Chouteau it was a stroke of serendipity.

Thoroughly aware of the fort's deteriorated condition and military shortcomings, Chouteau quickly went to Washington to pressure the quartermaster general into purchasing it. On paper, Fort Pierre commanded an ideal location on the crossroads of the northern plains from which to launch a host of strategic military campaigns. It was easily supplied by steamboat and only 325 miles from Fort Laramie and 150 miles from the Black Hills. And finally, the fort was already built. So the sales spin must have gone.

In April 1855 the army purchased Fort Pierre sight unseen for the exorbitant sum of $45,000. It was a small fortune for a big mess. When Maj. William Montgomery arrived to take command of the American Fur Company's "white elephant" on the upper Missouri in August, he found a group of rat-infested, broken-down, old wooden buildings unfit for human habitation. There were holes in the walls that had been eaten out by insects and the floors were too thin and rotted to support a man's weight. There was no mess hall or adequate latrine facilities. The lack of this critical sanitation left the stench of human excrement hanging over the entire grounds. As for fuel and forage, all the wood and grass had been stripped away for an 8-mile radius, making forage for animals difficult to find. Montgomery estimated that to make the fort serviceable would cost $22,000. With that said, he then made the inexcusable mistake of doing absolutely nothing to alleviate these deplorable conditions and departed.

Meanwhile, Gen. William S. Harney had commenced his military campaign of chastisement up the Platte River in the summer of 1855. His mission was to clear the immigrant road of refractory Indians who had been harassing westbound wagon trains bound for Oregon. After warning then decimating Little Thunder's unfortunate band of Oglalas near Ash Hollow (Nebraska), he pushed on to Fort Laramie, where he convinced the Sioux with his unyielding "take no prisoners" sweep up the Platte River, that the immigrant road was to be left unmolested.

Departing Fort Laramie in late September, Harney marched his men across southwestern Dakota and arrived, after a long, tiresome journey, at Fort Pierre in mid-October 1855. What he found must have infuriated him: a dilapidated fort, much smaller than he had expected and in a much worse condition than represented. All the grass around the site was dead because of the recent presence of many Indian lodges, while all the cottonwood trees had been destroyed (debarked) for feeding to the starving Indian ponies. The steamboat landing proved inconvenient as high water had shifted the channel and built a half-mile-wide sandbar in front of the post, forcing boats to discharge their stores a mile below. If there were any positive features regarding old Fort Pierre, Harney never mentioned them.

With winter rapidly approaching, Harney had to move fast. He spread out most of his command of 1,200 men into smaller groups along the river where there was more wood and forage. They were the lucky ones. The rest of his command were forced to spend the coldest months in flimsy, portable, prefabricated barracks that proved uncomfortable and miserably inadequate against a bitter northern plains winter. While the general was not responsible for the miserable conditions, his men, agreeing that it was typical of military administration, relieved their frustration by singing a little ditty they composed for the occasion:

> Oh, we don't mind the marching,
>   nor the fight do we fear,
> But we'll never forgive old Harney
>   for bringing us to Pierre.
> They say old Shotto [Chouteau] built it,
>   but we know it is not so;
> For the man who built this bloody ranche,
>   is reigning down below. [12]

That winter, frostbite and scurvy were rampant among the soldiers; many grew pale and listless as their teeth loosened from bloody gums and their flesh became soft and pallid. They were about as miserable as a corps of soldiers could be. Three men, unable to bear the misery, decided to risk the brutal cold rather than endure any more enforced hardship at the fort and deserted. It was a bad gamble. The following spring, their skeletons were found less than 100 miles out; all three had frozen to death. The livestock fared even worse, as fully one third of the cavalry's mounts perished from starvation. When the weather moderated, many of the younger recruits went off to visit the nearby Indian camps where they were able to trade for buffalo robes, hats, and mittens and join in the recreation of their winter games.

On the first day of March 1856, Fort Pierre saw the first and last of its official duties—and even that amounted to nothing. On that date, Harney addressed some 3,000 Yankton, Yanktonais, and Tetons assembled on the Fort Pierre plain. He scolded, warned, and threatened them about their behavior against the whites. Following this reprimand, treaty talks continued for a week and on March 8, 1856, the Treaty of Fort Pierre was signed (but never ratified by Congress), which in effect ordered the chiefs to control their respective bands, discipline their raiders, and encourage their young men to walk the "white man's road." Military planners believed the treaty laid the "Sioux problem" to rest.[13]

In late June, Harney removed most of his command downstream to the new chosen site of Fort Randall some 30 miles above the mouth of the Niobrara River. A handful of troops garrisoned Fort Pierre through the following winter of 1856–57. In the spring, as soon as navigation opened up on the river, the garrison loaded movable stores and government property on the steamer *D. H. Morton* and chugged downriver to Fort Randall. Fort Pierre as a military post was unofficially abandoned.

Charles Galpin of the American Fur Company, under contract to the army, agreed to take down and transport all the remaining cottages and other large, movable stores to Fort Randall. While doing so, he managed to convert about half of it to his own personal use. When Galpin walked away, the Sioux plundered what was left, smashing in the doors, breaking the windows, and plugging up the fireplaces.[14]

No one in the military seemed to have any idea of what to do with the old fort. Following Harney's lead, the army simply ignored it. Nevertheless, while some were busy scavenging it, others farther removed from the scene were advocating its repair. In November 1857, Captain Paige of the quartermaster's department visited the site and found little more than a shell, which he endeavored to repair by cutting off the southeastern corner of the rectangular structure and repairing the picketing. The quartermaster general eventually instructed Paige to the effect that the War Department was so thoroughly dissatisfied with its purchase and condition that no further expenditure for its repair would be allowed. Paige withdrew. There was a flurry of correspondence about who was to blame for plundering the fort, and meanwhile the elements of nature, in their subtle and inexorable way, ate away at what remained of the hacked-out, broken-down, cannibalized structures.

In June 1859, Capt. W. F. Raynolds of the engineers stopped at the site and held a parley with the Dakota in the vicinity before proceeding on his exploration of western South Dakota and the Yellowstone country. Returning down the Missouri in September the same year, he noted in his diary that little was left of old Fort Pierre, "the remains consisting of the shell of one row of houses and the demolition of this was in progress, the material being used in the new fort [Randall]."[15]

Old Fort Pierre, once the premier gathering place on the plains and the headquarters of Chouteau's great Western Fur Department, was reduced to ruin in less than a quarter century. And yet even as a pile of rubble, it never failed to be remarked upon by all the steamboat passengers who passed it recounting its part in the glory days of the old buffalo country.

THIRTEEN

Fred Dupuis's Odyssey

Old Fred had a loud voice and he made a lot of noise.
Bruce Siberts

QUEBEC PROVINCE IS THE HEART and soul of French Canada. The old city of Quebec still stands high and dignified on a point above Orleans Island where the wide St. Lawrence transforms from a great river to a deep seaway. And yet there are still pockets along the river where towns like Les Becquets and St. Croix remain small, quiet affairs and the most prominent building is a red-brick Catholic church.

Fred Dupuis was born in Quebec about 1818, and like generations of young French-Canadian men before him, he left home as a teenager (fourteen was the usual age) to seek his fortune in the western fur country. There are no details regarding his departure, but he must have signed on like hundreds before him as an *engagé*[1] in the early 1830s with the intent of learning the vocation of a trader.

Engagés usually started out as boatmen paddling an eight-man, 35-foot-long North Canoe. These great canoes were 4.5 feet wide, had a frame and ribs of cedar, and a shell consisting of quarter-inch-thick sheets of birchbark. The sheets were sewn together with spruce roots (*wattap*) and the seams were sealed with pine gum and resin. Cargo, including trade goods and supplies, was packed into bales that weighed about 90 to 100 pounds apiece. Sixty bales were packed into each canoe along with eight men who were each allowed a 40-pound haversack of belongings. Fully loaded with men and cargo, each North Canoe weighed in at about 4 tons. The standard complement of North Canoes was a brigade that consisted of three or four fully loaded and manned canoes.

The youthful men who provided the muscle to move these barks across the water were referred to on their first outing out as *mangeurs du lard* (pork-eaters) because they cooked their dried corn and peas in lard. The name also signified their status as "greenhorns." Each year a handful of the best pork-eaters stayed in the fur country outposts and became *hiverants*. In fur trade parlance they were the "Northmen" who eventually became the contacts and traders the Indians dealt with, trusted, and lived with.

Whether Northmen or *mangeurs du lard*, all were voyageurs who willingly embraced a life of outdoor hardship and adventure.

By the nineteenth century, the trade routes from Montreal, Quebec, into the "upper country" of the West had been well established along the old Algonquian trails. These routes were annually traveled by brigades of canoes loaded with European goods chosen specifically for the Indian market. And while the greatest share of goods consisted of arms and ammunition (powder and lead) there were tons of dry goods, metal utensils, knives, hatchets, kettles, beads, pipes, tobacco, and an assortment of gewgaws.

The trade cycle began in the early spring when the ice left the St. Lawrence. Depending on where they departed, voyageurs paddled their canoes west against the current of the St. Lawrence to Montreal Island, where they turned north at the mouth of the Ottawa River and enjoyed clear paddling for 100 miles. Around the bends of the Ottawa there was always the shifting spectacle of scenery and wildlife: flocks of ducks rising off the water, blue heron rookeries in the tall white pines, whitetail deer wading and drinking the cold water, a black bear scampering off into the timber, or a great lordly moose standing knee-deep in the shallows rooting up water lilies.

One hundred ten water-miles up the Ottawa from Montreal Island they would encounter Claudière Falls above which lay 5 miles of rapids. The voyageurs, following the Indian example, might throw an offering of tobacco into the boiling cauldron below the falls to appease the dreaded Windigo, the huge, mysterious manlike creature that fed on human flesh. The Indians believed the Windigo could change its shape at will; its presence was felt when it hissed and howled in the black forest at night.

Votives performed, everyone would get a chance to stretch their legs by wading with heavy packs over and around the falls and rapids. Many of the voyageurs chose to use tumplines or head straps to carry their baggage, leaving their hands free to drive off the incessant blood-sucking mosquitoes, gnat columns, and biting deerflies.

Usually eight trips back and forth were required on each portage with a heavy pack over slippery rocks and cold water. It might take two or three days to complete the Claudière portage. Then there would be a 30-mile paddle over a beautiful lake, a restful relief from the backbreaking toil.

There were several more portages along the north shore past Chats Falls where the river rushed for a mile around dangerous rock islands. Then 20 more miles to the head of Lac des Chats where they detoured and followed a little river with short carries between little lakes that took them back to the Ottawa.

The next 95 miles was diversified by eight portages, some as long as 2 miles, before they left the Ottawa and followed the Mattawa westward with much poling and wading in swift, cold water.

There were many pleasant campsites along the way on sandy beaches along the shores of little, sparkling, spring-fed lakes. In a short while they reached Lake Nipissing, a great body of water that stretched out of sight beyond the western horizon. Broad, shallow, and quick to change moods, the Nipissing was believed to be bewitched by demons able to change its temperament from a smooth piece of glass to raging, churning, white-toothed fury. The Northmen anxiously skirted its southern shore arriving, at Claudière Falls at the head of the French River. Portaging a height of land around the falls, they dropped down and followed the French River, navigating 70 miles of rapids and cascades, deftly avoiding submerged boulders and logjams at racing speeds.

One last portage around a frothing cascade and the canoes now rose and fell with the swells of Lake Huron, the Mer Douce or freshwater sea the Indians called the Ottawa Kitchegawme.

West along Georgian Bay and into the North Channel were channels, islands, and inlets beyond number, and the newcomers quickly gained a respect for the memory of the old voyageurs who unerringly followed the routes passed down to them by the Ottawas and Ojibways. Occasionally a broad channel allowed a long view of a magnificent spangling of open water to the south. After 100 miles of threading island passages, the brigade rounded a headland and there in view, seated on a high lookout hill surrounded by great white pines, stood Fort Ste. Marie located near the Sault[2] or cascades of the Ojibeway Kitchegawme, which the French call Lake Superior, the upper lake. The voyageurs were now 700 miles from Montreal.

At the Sault, the western trade routes split. Some brigades made their way north and west along the north shore of Superior to the posts at Lake Nipigon, Kaministiquia, and the Grand Portage, then up the Rainy River to Lake of the Woods and the Red River country. Others veered to the south at the Sault to take the south shore of Lake Superior to Chequamagon and Fond du Lac, where they paddled up the Bois Brûlé (Burnt Wood) with a short portage to the St. Croix and then into the Mississippi. Still others entered through the straits of Mackinac and into Lake Michigan where they hugged the northwestern shore, paddling into the Green Bay or continuing south all the way to Fort Dearborn[3] at the mouth of the Chicago River.

The voyageurs who followed the Green Bay route ascended the Fox River, made the short portage over the divide into the Wisconsin River, and paddled downstream to the post at Prairie du Chien on the Mississippi and then south down the "Father of Waters." The voyageurs who went south by way of the Chicago River portaged over the low divide to the Des Plaines and Illinois Rivers, reaching the lower Mississippi just above the French Creole settlement of St. Louis. All the southern routes eventually took the voyageurs via the Mississippi to the established French trading settlements of St. Louis, Ste. Genevieve, and Kaskaskia.

These were the water highways that generations of French Canadians traveled to reach the interior of the continent. One of those voyageurs was Fred Dupuis. His story was typical of the young Frenchmen who chose to stay in the buffalo country and make the transition from voyageur to hide trader.

Depuis probably reached St. Louis in the late 1830s. And although it was nominally an American city, the language of the traders who moved in the circle of the Indians was still French. Dupuis probably started working for the American Fur Company and arrived at Fort Pierre in the spring of 1838, exactly 100 years after Louis-Joseph La Verendrye, the Chevalier, buried his lead plate on a hill 3 miles south of the new fort.

Dupuis was twenty, while the post was only six years old. One can easily imagine the feeling it must have evoked with its great log ramparts encircled by a host of smoke-stained tipis, throngs of Indians, and perhaps within a day's ride, great herds of bison.

Dupuis probably lived in the fort or its vicinity for the next eighteen years, working there until "the Company" sold it in 1855. Written accounts place Dupuis at a small fur post at the mouth of Cherry Creek on the Cheyenne River around 1860.

With the American Fur Company's abandonment of Fort Pierre along with the retreat of the bison herds farther west, smaller trading centers, farther from the Missouri, became necessary in attracting the business of the Indians, who were still doing most of the work of killing and skinning the bison.

Correspondence between Dupuis and Charles Primeau[4] suggests that he was still trading for buffalo robes while living in the midst of local Mnikoju and Sans Arc bands of the northern Lakota. In a letter written late in 1860, Dupuis noted to Primeau that the buffalo were becoming scarce and the Indians and their horses were becoming "poor." His underlying concern was that this situation would prove bad for Harvey, Primeau and Company's business.[5] In a subsequent letter dated March 1861, he apologized for not making a better trade after so much expense with the excuse that the demand for buffalo-hides had exceeded the local supply. It appears that the bison were gone from the area, and with them began a rapid decline of the local fur and robe trade.

Shortly after this letter, Dupuis seems to have left Cherry Creek in order to move over to Fort Sully on the east side of the Missouri. Details are sketchy but it is likely he took a position as a fort trader or agent for the American Fur Company there. At any rate, when Texas trail drivers began coming up to the post to deliver herds of cattle for military consumption, they gave him the calves, providing him with the nucleus of what would later become his famous blue-brindled, Circle D longhorns.

Dupuis eventually left Fort Sully and recrossed the Missouri to live on the newly created Great Sioux Reservation with his wife, a Mnikoju named Good Elk Woman whom he may have met earlier at Cherry Creek. In the fashion of the times, she became Mrs. Mary Dupuis. Fred and Mary relocated 35 miles up the Cheyenne River to a fine wooded flat near a prominent ford crossing. Here Fred constructed a hand-hewn log house 20 feet by 40 feet and pole barns and corrals for his longhorns, which he turned out to roam across the open range.

Dupuis's log house followed the general pattern of habitation that now began to proliferate across the buffalo country. Made of native cottonwood, the logs were cut and fitted together to create walls. The cracks between the logs were daubed and chinked with wet gumbo mud that held like plaster when dry. A heavy ridge log supported the roof logs, which were then covered with a 2-foot layer of gray dirt (Pierre shale). The deep dirt pack on the gently sloping roof was kept from sloughing by logs laid along the edge, notched to fit, and spiked to the wall logs. Once settled, the gumbo resisted penetration of rain and snow—in fact, moisture tightened its texture. These dwellings blended in perfectly with the country and proved comfortably cool in the summer, warm in the winter, and windproof if not insect- and rodent-proof.

Across the Cheyenne River a few miles below the Dupuis holdings, two creeks emptied into the river from the south. Though only a few miles apart, the creeks were separated by a high divide. In the early reservation days, each creek valley like this was inhabited by a *tiospaye*, or clan, of western Teton Lakotas. The creek farthest east was inhabited by a group of Mnikojus while the other was occupied by a group of Sans Arc.

At the time, Fred still appeared to have been acting as an agent for Harvey, Primeau and Company. He purchased pelts from both of these Indian groups and when he gathered a sufficient quantity, he delivered them to Fort Pierre. The frequency with which he took a load of furs to the river depended on the season and his abundance of pelts and hides. In any event, when he had fifteen or more pack loads, Dupuis and his wife loaded the pack horses for a trip to the river. The horses were tied "head to tail"; Mary led the first horse and Fred brought up the rear.[6]

Dupuis's old pack trail crossed the Cheyenne near his ranch and then headed south up the east side of Hermaphrodite Creek. Gaining the high plateau, it wound in a southeasterly direction, eventually picking up the "high line" or ridge on the west side of Frozen Man Creek. Somewhere near Hayes, South Dakota, it dropped down from the ridge, crossed Frozen Man, and picked up the main east-west Deadwood–Fort Pierre trail.[7]

As his livestock multiplied so did his family. The union of Fred and Mary proved a fertile one, producing ten children; nine of them reached adulthood, married, and produced offspring of their own. Of all their children, only one, Edward, attended a formal school in Virginia where he learned to speak and write English. The rest of the Dupuises spoke a patois of Lakota and English.

Following the marriage of each of his children, Fred built the new couple a small log home near his own. These cabins, like the main house, consisted of cottonwood logs with dirt floors and sod roofs. Perhaps remembering his many years at the fort, he lined up all the cabins in a long, neat row next to the main house.

In addition to this growing complex of cabins and family, a dozen or more tipis were pitched nearby where Mary's full-blood Sioux relatives encamped. This living arrangement grew into a large communal encampment/village in which the roles of the men and the women were strictly prescribed. The women of the Dupuis household tended a large vegetable garden while the men performed the heavy manual work and butchering of the livestock. One woman did all the baking, another cut and cooked all the meat, and another made the coffee and served all the food. Three times a day, every day, all the cooking and eating were done in the big cookhouse. By the 1880s about fifty people, mostly relatives plus a dozen drifters and friends who happened to be in the neighborhood, gathered daily in the cookhouse for meals.[8]

Along with the daily routines, there were dances and celebrations that rivaled anything of the kind in the territory. One event that drew the notice of territorial newspapers was the marriage of Dupuis's youngest daughter, Marcella, to Douglas F. Carlin, issue clerk at the Cheyenne River Sioux Agency and grandson of a former territorial governor of Illinois.

From the outset, local reporters made it clear that this was to be no ordinary "squawman wedding." It proved to be an unparalleled event done on a grand scale in the best, western-frontier style. People were invited from as far away as Pierre and Deadwood, the two main commercial centers at the time in western Dakota.[9]

The nuptials were held at the Dupuis home. According to the 1887 news reports, "70 important non-Indians," including the Pierre city council, were in attendance, along with 500 Sioux Indians. Forty fat steers and four buffalos were butchered and roasted during the event. While this served as the main menu fare, Dupuis was not to be out-classed. For his more refined guests he purchased four [wagon] freight loads of food, two 10-gallon kegs of whiskey, and imported wine for the ladies and delicate city guests. In addition, he had on tap many barrels of his homemade, wild grape wine, which seems to have been his personal favorite. The complete menu, printed in the Pierre, South Dakota, *Free Press*, reported that there were six kinds of meat and assorted pies, cakes, cookies, candies, crackers, and fruits "manufactured under the culinary art of the Indian women and was clean and palatable, or at least it was for men, who had ridden sixty miles through the pure Dakota ozone."[10]

After the feast, all the wedding gifts were brought into the cook-house and put on exhibition. One of the most impressive gifts, which could not be displayed, was the 500 head of cattle and 50 ponies Fred gave the couple, instantly making them one of the wealthier "west river" families of the time. It was reported that Marcella's sisters gave her a beautifully decorated buffalo robe.

Entertainment included fiddle music provided by two of the Dupuis boys. For the more robust guests there were contests of rop-ing, bronc-riding, and footraces while the less physically oriented

smoked, drank, and played marathon poker games. The Sioux dele-
gation stole the show by dancing continuously for three days, paus-
ing only every three hours for food.

The feasting, dancing, and celebrating went on for ten days. Not a
record perhaps in the annals of extended revelries, but impressive
nonetheless. Of the Carlin-Dupuis union it was reported that neither
one ever learned to speak the other's native tongue. Nonetheless the
union was long and prolific, producing ten children.

Dupuis's financial success was in large part due to his ranching
abilities and the access he had to thousands of acres of free Indian
reservation grass, which he was eligible to use thanks to the Sioux ancestry of his wife and children. By the late 1880s he was reputed to
own 3,000 to 4,000 longhorns and 500 horses. And although in the
later years of his life he had amassed a small fortune once estimated
at $25,000[11] in gold, he never passed up the chance to collect his
family's government issue of beef and supplies from the Cheyenne
River Agency.

By the time Fred reached his late sixties, he had managed to shape
a dynasty in which he reigned as the benign patriarch. He had successfully fused the feudal French trading system that he had learned
at Fort Pierre with his wife's Sioux matrilineal clan system, which by
custom entitled her relatives to share in all of her husband's wealth.
It all worked in part because of Fred's acumen as a trader and rancher
and his legendary hospitality and largesse. It also didn't hurt to be in
the right place, at the right time, with the right wife. Fred had the
understanding and ability to adapt as the country rapidly changed
from the domain of nomads, hunters, and wild animals to a land of
laws, leases, fences, and domestic cattle.

In 1898 this grand old man of the country died and true to the
Lakota ways of his wife, a great Sioux "give-away" was held to honor
his memory. Like the wedding of his daughter ten years earlier, it was
an event of unprecedented extravagance. It was reported that Fred's
children started giving away $20 gold pieces and livestock to all the
whites and Indians who were at the house at the time of his death until
Doug Carlin, Marcella's husband, put a stop to it. Later a "rigged-up,

extra good" saddle horse with saddlebags filled with 200 silver dollars, was brought out for a group of visiting Montana Crows. Each
Crow Indian passed the horse, taking a dollar until all the dollars
were gone; the last one received the horse and saddle.[12] In this and
other ways Fred Dupuis's wealth and property were shared with a
large group of people. No property, in keeping with old Lakota tradition, was inherited by his family.

During his long odyssey stretching from the shores of the St.
Lawrence to the western buffalo country, Fred Dupuis had managed
to change with the times. He founded a large, extended family who
by degrees themselves changed and drifted away, anglicizing their
surname to Dupris and Dupree. This by a man who by contemporary
accounts was described as being of "black" ancestry,[13] makes his
odyssey even more remarkable.

Fred Dupuis left a fascinating legacy of which almost nothing remains save a large extended family. Only a family cemetery plot with
a tall imposing headstone located on a high, windswept ridge not far
from the old one-room "Buffalo Church" commemorates his resting
place. The one-room church is weathered and open to the elements,
while the haunted cemetery overlooks a wide, desolate flat along the
Cheyenne River where no vestige of the frontier life of Fred and Mary
Dupuis remains.

FOURTEEN

Eyanpaha Wakan

When I started to build this house and began to study the stones, it be-came a regular obsession. I found that you had to turn a stone over and over and around, and look at it from all sides before you could cut it. If you didn't, you couldn't do one thing with it. Stones are a good deal like human beings in this respect. —Thomas L. Riggs

ON THE EAST END OF Oahe Dam stands a small, white, one-room, clapboard church of the kind once common at all the mission stations across the western plains of South Dakota. Inside are a dozen wooden pews that face a lectern and blackboards on all of the walls. Hymnal numbers and scripture quotations are written in white chalk on the front board.

The church is the only legacy left by a remarkable man the Indians called Eyanpaha Wakan, the Sacred Herald. The Oahe chapel, with its single steeple and bell, is one of the few that is still intact and in use as a church. It is part of the historical legacy the Rev. Thomas L. Riggs left of his lifelong ministry to the Lakotas of the western plains.

The old chapel was relocated to this imposing site in the late 1950s prior to the flooding of the upper Missouri River valley by Oahe Dam. Standing in the vestibule, I cannot resist a pull on the bell cord and am immensely pleased by the sweet, melodious chime of the old bell. It is a kind and gentle way to summon people to worship and an apt metaphor for the life of Thomas Riggs.

Riggs spent nearly all of his long, productive life on the northern plains buffalo country. He watched it pass from a wild frontier of bison trails, tipi camps, and curly grama grass to one of paved roads, wheat fields, fences, ranches, and small towns. Like Fred Dupuis's, his life was an interesting fusion of ideals that were both Christian and Lakota.

Riggs was born of missionary parents in 1847 on the upper Minnesota River at Lac Qui Parle. His father, Stephen R. Riggs, was a Congregational missionary who helped found the first permanent mission to the Dakota Indians in Minnesota. The elder Riggs is also credited for having preached the first documented sermon at old Fort Pierre in 1840 to a group of Yankton and Brûlé Sioux.[1]

Tom Riggs grew up among the Minnesota or Prairie Sioux,[2] early in life learning the rudiments of their language and culture as well as the sounds and rhythms of the wild prairies that surrounded him. In 1862 he fled with his family before the bloodshed and fighting that engulfed the upper Minnesota River country during the Sioux uprising. All of his experience as a youth would later provide him with a unique insight and knowledge for his future lifelong work of helping to uplift a dispossessed people whom he once described as an "infuriated race."

In 1872, at the age of twenty-five, the young Reverend Riggs began his mission work among the Saones[3] or northern Teton Sioux of western Dakota. He settled his home mission on a wide river bottom of the Missouri a few miles above the site of old Fort Pierre and began his work by constructing a log mission station, alone and by hand, on what was then known as Peoria Bottoms.[4] He worked alone because no other white man dared work for long in the open for fear of being attacked and murdered by the Sioux. This was a particularly lawless and unstable period of transition on the river. Old Fort Pierre, the once-famous outpost of the fur trade era, had disappeared seventeen years earlier, leaving a vacuum in what had been the old French-Indian order of things. Although Fort Sully was nearby to the north on the east side of the river, the surrounding area was an extremely dangerous no-man's-land.[5]

During this period of construction, Riggs subsisted on a poor diet of bacon, greasy fry bread, and coffee. At night he slept on the ground with his rifle at his side, and was often awakened at dawn by the ping of shots fired over his head by Sioux men hiding in the brush across the river.

The majority of the natives, however, were curious about the young man building a cabin by himself, and he often had friendly visitors and spectators. These visitors were Teton Lakota, most of whom belonged to one of the five main northern Teton subbands: Hunkpapa, Mnikoju, Sihasapa, Itazipcola, and Oohenumpa. At this time their population totaled between 3,000 and 4,000 people, most of whom were still living a roving, nomadic life in smoky tipis.

The Tetons lived in small family groups called *tiospayes*. These clans were loosely organized into larger camps that were scattered along both sides of the Missouri and around the Cheyenne River Agency, which at this time was located on the west side of the Missouri about 60 miles north of old Fort Pierre midway between the mouth of the Cheyenne and the Moreau. A good many of the northern Tetons were also scattered in small camps up the Cheyenne and Moreau Rivers and along their respective tributaries wherever wood and water were available.

It was the Lakota living closest to the Missouri who first began to attend the free mission school run by Riggs and later his first wife, Nina Foster Riggs, at the Oahe Mission. The church officially organized in 1876 with four members, one Indian and three whites. It was an inauspicious start but Riggs knew his work would take a lifetime. Progress in helping the Indians make the difficult transition from illiterate, nomadic hunter-gatherers whose knowledge was direct and intuitive to accepting the white man's abstract deductive paradigms of writing, mathematics, law, and logic was painstakingly slow. It required them to learn first how to speak, read, write, and think in an entirely new language and fashion.

This challenging work was undertaken primarily by Mrs. Riggs. To her credit and theirs, many native men and women persisted in learning the new ways. Eventually those who had known only a life of living in tipis, where clothes, utensils, and bodies were always grimy and greasy from the constant woodsmoke of fires, began to learn and grasp the new ways of bathing, eating with utensils, living in houses, dressing in store clothing, and occupying themselves in the everyday domestic activities of keeping a farm and a home.

By the late 1870s many native people had been won over by the kindness, patience, and example of the Riggs family. But the thorniest problem involved the question of Indian ownership of private parcels of land on the Cheyenne River Reservation. There were immense difficulties regarding the concept of land ownership since the Lakota were neither regarded as U.S. citizens at the time nor did they themselves possess an understanding of private individual land ownership. Further complicating matters was that no land surveys had yet been conducted on the reservation, which comprised a vast tract of the old buffalo country that lay between the Cheyenne and Moreau Rivers where most of them were now living. Nevertheless, Riggs earnestly persisted, and this problem too was solved. By the 1880s those who had adopted the civilized Christian ways promulgated by the Riggses were beginning to prosper on their small, river-bottom farms. These Indians who now spoke English and dressed as whites were colloquially termed "progressives" while those who resisted Anglo acculturation were called "traditionals" or "blankets."

While teaching them the ways of living in the new order, Riggs also shared with them his deeply held beliefs and teachings of Christianity. But his was not merely a religion of words and new symbols. It was one of living example, patience, compassion, tolerance, honest work, and character building. Riggs proved competent to the great task he had set for himself, and through his words and actions soon became a true friend of all the Lakota.

Riggs the teacher was also Riggs the student, and while he constantly prepared the Indians to receive and understand his message of the Spirit, he also prepared himself to better understand their life, language, and point of view. To that end, Thomas Riggs ministered unceasingly to his native followers, taking his message to them by horseback or with a buggy team often traveling an average of 200 miles a week crisscrossing the reservation and establishing a network of missions.

Throughout his travels Riggs was always dignified but never solemn, nor was he ever afraid to get his hands dirty or his clothes wet. During his fifty years of active mission work he traveled extensively across the grasslands and became an expert horseman and trainer as well as an adept frontiersman, farmer, builder, ethnographer, and naturalist.

He had an uncanny ability for remembering landforms, which allowed him to find his way across the vast landscape of the buffalo plains through pitch darkness and blinding snowstorms.

In addition to navigating through the fluctuating vagaries of an often hostile environment, Riggs constantly dealt with dangers more treacherous and immediate that lurked in the shadows and brush for a man who traveled alone or with a single companion across the plains. Although he was a man dedicated to the Spirit, he was also practical and took many precautions against the constant and real threat of attack and ambush.

In the early days of his circuit rides he traveled with a native guide who also acted as a soldier-companion. Their routine while traveling across the plains seldom varied. It included cooking their supper at a washout or waterhole just at sunset, always taking special precautions to see that their fire did not give off any smoke. Following supper they would ride on for several more miles in the direction of their destination until all light had faded from the western sky. Then they would bed down in tall grass a considerable distance apart from each other so that if a wandering band of Indians chanced to come upon one, the other might escape.

As a further precaution, Riggs always picketed his horse to his saddlehorn. He would then use the saddle as his pillow and sleep soundly, knowing his horse would come and wake him if there was any disturbance. And there were often several disturbances on every trip that alerted his faithful horse, Ralph.

Most intruders were prowling coyotes or small herds of pronghorns, but once, Riggs clearly discerned the sound of horse hooves traveling close by along with the voices of men talking as they rode through the darkness. Ralph seemed to possess an innate understanding of his job as sentry, for he never snorted or whinnied at a disturbance. He caught the reverend's attention by standing near Riggs's head as he slept and placing his nose down into his face.[6]

As the years progressed, the Oahe church grew from the founding four to 109, 80 of whom were Indians living near the church on Peoria Bottoms. Riggs had also established a long circuit of mission stations up both the Cheyenne and Moreau River valleys. These stations eventually had small churches for services and were cared for by native assistants personally trained by Riggs. Keeping in touch with his assistants and their needs required him to ride the circuit often.

Usually he began his circuit rides at his home mission of Oahe[7] on the east side of the Missouri. From there he headed west until he reached the head of Minniconjou Creek, where he turned to the north and followed the creek to its confluence with the Cheyenne. Near this point was the Elizabeth Memorial station, run by a trusted Mnikoju woman. From there he might travel up the Cheyenne past Fred Dupuis's place to the Buffalo church and then continue west to the Cherry Creek station.

On another occasion he might travel in a northerly direction from the Elizabeth Memorial station through a winding draw or gap known as the Okikse[8] that allowed access to the crest of the Fox Ridge divide.[9] Continuing north, he would drop down to the Moreau River and visit the Remington station near the mouth of Green Grass Creek.[10] From there he might proceed up the Moreau west to the Hope station at the mouth of Bear Creek and then west to the Thunder Butte station near the mouth of Thunder Butte Creek. The rides were long and strenuous and required perseverance, strength, and an intimate knowledge of the land and the people.

Periodically the Reverend's work required him to travel north to Fort Yates (North Dakota), south to the Santee Reservation in northeast Nebraska, or east to the Sisseton Reservation on the northeast side of the Prairie Coteau. The stories of his travels are redolent with anecdotes of native animals and people he met along the way. But beyond a doubt, his greatest singular adventure as a plainsman and friend of the Lakota people took place in the bitter cold winter of 1880–81 when he went on the last great winter buffalo hunt.

FIFTEEN

"They Run, They Run"

*I have been crying and praying, for I shall never again see this country as
I have seen it before.*   —Co-kan-tan-ka (1881)

NEAR THE END OF THE CIVIL WAR, bison, once a common sight
in the western Dakota buffalo country, had been pushed by hunting
pressure farther west into eastern Montana. By the early 1870s they
had became conspicuously absent from Dakota. When Custer's Black
Hills expedition, which originated in Fort Lincoln, crisscrossed the
heart of the old buffalo range of western Dakota during the summer
of 1874, his scouts were unable to find a single bison or detect any
sign of them.

The cause of this disappearance has been attributed to the work of
the Teton and their Cheyenne allies, who had at the end of the Civil
War devised a stratagem to contain what remained of the great northern herds in eastern Montana. They had managed to create a great
herdline or perimeter that effectively confined the bison to an area
of the northern plains about 350 miles long and 200 miles wide.[1]
This perimeter encompassed an area from about the Little Missouri
and Killdeer Mountains in North Dakota west to the Little Belt
Mountains in central Montana. The densest herd concentrations were
located in a huge triangular area sometimes referred to as the "flat-
iron" country, which lay between the Missouri and Yellowstone
Rivers.[2]

This herding action preserved the herds from the ruthless commercial
bison hunters who by 1873 had nearly completed the extermination

of the great southern bison herds. This protection afforded by the Indians allowed the northern herds to increase greatly in the years following the Civil War. It was also the reason why the Sioux and Cheyenne had been able to gather by the thousands and stay together in one last great encampment on the west bank of the "Greasy Grass" (Little Bighorn River) during the spring and early summer of 1876. It was this great Indian camp that Custer attacked on the morning of June 25, 1876. Following the Custer debacle, the great summer conclave on the Greasy Grass quickly broke up and the herd-line perimeter was abandoned.

Four years later in 1880, the railroad laid tracks into Glendive, Montana, which quickly became the hub for the last great bison kill in the northern plains. Buffalo hunters arrived by the hundreds and after outfitting themselves, moved down upon the herds from the north and east. This hunting pressure eventually pushed the herds south. During the fall of 1880, thousands of bison broke through a gap in the firing line and moved southeast in the direction of the Slim Buttes.

The Cheyenne River Sioux, many of whom had fought the Seventh Cavalry on the Greasy Grass, had quickly returned to their camps along the Cheyenne River after the fight and were now officially confined to their reservation. Their agency at this time had been moved to the mouth of Dry Creek on the Missouri between Fort Bennett on the west side of the river and Fort Sully downstream on the south.

It is probably safe to assume that few if any "progressives" in the northern Teton bands participated or were even present at the Custer fight, choosing instead to stay in close proximity to the agency and the mission stations in the river valleys. Although the "progressives" generally lived in close proximity to the agency along the Missouri, the "traditionals" maintained their camps 100 miles farther south and west near the mouth of Cherry Creek (Hump's camp) and at the mouth of Deep Creek (Big Foot's camp), both on the Cheyenne River.

Not surprisingly, many veterans of the Custer battle were living in these two camps in the late 1870s and 1880s. Half of the men in residence there were considered *watagla* (wild or hostile), according to Pete Dupuis, the oldest son of Fred and Mary Dupuis. Thomas Riggs also knew many of these men whom he described euphemistically as "being of the original type, and gentlemen uncontaminated."

Sometime in September 1880, far-ranging Lakota scouts were bringing back news to the reservation of the return of buffalo to the Chalky Buttes area of North Dakota and the Slim Buttes country of South Dakota. Their unexpected appearance after a long absence created a great deal of excitement on both the Standing Rock and Cheyenne River Reservations. The Lakota living in the Cheyenne and Moreau River camps quickly decided to organize what would become one of the last great traditional winter buffalo hunts on the northern plains.

Riggs made a request to participate in this hunt with the Cheyenne River Sioux and was invited to go with the Dupuis boys. What follows is his amazing account of the event. He began his narrative by justifying his participation in this great adventure as a cultural experience, which it certainly was, but he soon became a full and active participant and quickly warmed up to the excitement and passion of the chase.

Buffalo Hunt[3]

by Thomas L. Riggs

The last winter buffalo hunt of the Dakotas was in 1880–81. I was
the only white man who was a member of this party.[4] I went as one
of them, speaking their language and familiar with their customs;[5]
but this experience increased my vocabulary and my knowledge of
Indian customs and character not a little. Being the only white man
with them, I was able to study their habits and language; to learn
to think as an Indian and to understand his point of view. These
indeed were my chief objects in accompanying them. It also gave
me an intimate knowledge of the customs and laws that controlled
all hunting parties of the Dakotas when out for big game. ...

In the early fall of 1880, I had seen a stray buffalo near the
Cheyenne Agency and there were reports of others. In October the
Indians began talking of a winter hunt and one day Clarence Ward
(Roan or Gray-Haired Bear),[6] came to me and told me of their
plans, saying it would be a good chance for me to go along. His
wife was the daughter of Fred Dupuis [Dupris] and he said he would
find out from her family how they felt about it. He soon returned
and told me the Dupris boys and their mother were enthusiastic
over my going; that the mother and wife of Fred would go and
would be glad to have me share their tent. So that was settled.

We had snow early in October that did not disappear all winter.[7]
Towards Thanksgiving, the river froze over and just before it froze,

word came to me that they wanted to start just as soon as they could get their party together.

I took Sam as my riding or buffalo horse because of his speed and experience. Then I picked a pair of horses for my buckboard, one of which would do for a packhorse; got my "artillery," my clothes and bedding together with a sack of oats for the horses and crossed the river [over the ice] here at Oahe the day before Thanksgiving. I reached the Dupris' the second day.[8] They had a large establishment with several houses. We waited there a day before all were ready to start.

My buckboard team was a four-year-old mare (she had no name) and a raw-boned "clay bank" horse who was called just that. He was my packhorse, who, because of his orneriness and his hard mouth, was called by the Indians "the stiff-necked one." They were a poor team, but good enough in a way. My "artillery" consisted of a .50 calibre [Remington] rifle, a single shot with bolt action, a fairly handy gun with terrific power. I took as an extra, a lever-action single shot .45 calibre Sharps rifle and this, during the hunt, I loaned to Big Foot[9] for one of his henchmen to use during the hunt. ...

When we started north from the Dupris', there were twenty-five or thirty of us. Most of them went with their travois of tent poles, but the Dupris boys took a wagon. The first day we went only three or four miles up a deep ravine. The following days, going slowly, we worked out to a clump of brush on the northern slope of Fox Ridge where we rested for a day. We had snow almost every day, not much at a time, but enough to make us realize it was winter, and that real winter was on its way. Our move from that point over to the Moreau River was in a real storm. We waited on the Moreau for a day or two while two young men were sent to let the Moreau people, who were to join us, know where we were.[10]

When we started westward, we followed the valley of the Moreau slowly, some days not making more than three or four miles. In response to my impatience, the Indians said they did not want to

get their horses poor or tired out, so realizing their wisdom I
learned and practiced patience. The snow was getting deeper and
deeper all the time. Traveling in this slow way, we finally came in
sight of Slim Buttes (Paha-zibzi-pila) which was our goal.[11] When
we were well in sight of these buttes, the old hunters began to plan
on sending out scouts to find out where the buffalo were.

There were a hundred and one in our party.[12] I suppose I was the
"one-th." About half of these were women. It was said we had three
hundred horses and, I was told five hundred dogs. I asked why in the
world they had brought so many dogs, and the reply was that it was
to fatten them up. They were very thin when we started, but on the
hunt they got good and fat. This was so they could be used for food.
The process for preparing them to eat was a very swift one. The dog
was killed and the hair singed off and he was ready for the pot.

One evening Roan Bear and I had turned out our horses with
the bunch in the breaks, where they would paw away the snow
and feed during the night. He proposed that we go to the "soldier
lodge"—Tiyotipi, or council tent, and learn what was to be done.
There had been talk of sending men "to the hills," for we were
now not far from where big game might be found. The soldier
lodge was like other tents, though larger than most, and stood
in a sheltered spot not far from the middle of the camp, which
was pitched on the south side of a fringe of trees and brush. In
one respect, however, this tent was quite different from the others.
There were none of the usual trappings of travel around the door,
nor any ordinary signs of cooking and home life inside. No woman
is ever allowed to enter it. Food is brought from other tents by the
women and set down outside. This lodge is the heart of the camp
and levies on all for voluntary contributions. Here all general matters
are discussed and plans made which are announced in due time
by the "eyanpaha" (crier, or herald) who makes proclamation
through the camp.[13]

I was invited to take part in the selection of the scouts to be sent
out. The circle in the tent was pretty well filled with men. Probably

the "slate" had been made up beforehand. At any rate, two men
were selected and their instructions given in much detail—just
where they should go, what they should do. They were to go to
certain well known landmarks.[14] The two selected were sworn to
this service; each with one or both hands placed palm down flat
on the earth, received the instructions and made silent pledges.
There is no fixed form for this oath, nor is it given aloud. The
solemnity of the occasion and its serious purpose is felt and
responded to by those selected. Many others also joined in this
vow and prayer. I sat next to "Touch-the-Cloud" (Mahpiyaiyapato)
and noticed that he rubbed away the grass and leaves at his side
and sat with one hand flat on the earth. Seeing that I was noticing
this, he said: "I am offering prayer with one hand and I now do
so with both." I did the same. The earth is the mother of all and
prayer is offered in this way as the oath is administered, lest the
all-mother give alarm to the buffalo and carry to their ears
knowledge of the presence and purpose of men.[15]

Life in camp next day was dull and anxious. The "scouts" had
gone, as was evidenced by the absence of their second best horses,
not their buffalo runners. Going out to scout for buffalo is known
as "going to the hills"; if returning with good news, the scouts would
be the "runners," making their report from the top of the first
convenient hill at some distance but in sight of the camp. "What do
you call them if they have no message; if they come back and say
there are no buffalo?" I asked. "We shall not see them if they have
nothing to tell. They will not come back till after dark and even
then the dogs of their own tents will not know when they return."
I thought this rather hard on the poor fellows, but it occurred
several times during our hunt, in which case even the next day
the scouts had little to say except in answer to questioning.

It was just before sunset that our "runners" came into view and
the entire camp went wild.[16] The returning scouts appeared on a
ridge about a mile from the camp and there separately and from
opposite directions ran their horses several times at right angles to

our view. "That is good," said Charger. From there our runners
came full tilt to a second rise nearer by and repeated the maneuver.
"We shall have plenty of meat by this time tomorrow," said Yellow
Owl. A third time the runners gave the signal when but a short
distance from camp and then rode with all the speed their tired
horses had left, to a little knoll where the camp crier and others
had gone to receive the report. We gathered, facing the west, for
the runners were coming from that direction. Each man brushed
aside the snow before him and kneeled on one knee placing one
hand on the bare ground. The old crier had gathered a few dry
"buffalo chips" and piled them before them. Straight to him the
runners came. Jumping from their horses, the leader kicked the
little pile aside and both knelt opposite the crier and facing us.
The crier lighted a pipe, took a whiff himself, and after reverently
touching the earth with the bowl and lifting the stem to Heaven
above, he presented it to the leader and said: "You have grown
up amidst these hills and valleys—tell me, I pray, if you have seen
anything of prowling wolf or flying buzzard and feeding animal
(buffalo) beyond the hills whence you come; tell me truly and
make me glad." The runner who received the pipe took a mouthful
of smoke, in turn offering it to earth and sky, passed the pipe to
his comrade and answered, "Yes." The crier from camp then cried
a shrill "Hai-ee! Hai-ee!" The crier then asked for particulars and
answer was given in detail. Again more is asked for "from beyond
that." Even a third time a call is made for "beyond that." The official
report having been made, all rose and hurried back to camp to
prepare for the run to be made the next day. Men, women and
children were making as much noise as they possibly could.

The report came in on Saturday night and they all wanted to
move. Sunday was a beautiful day and they all got up and broke
camp early in the morning. I told them I wasn't going to hurry
off—I would stay there and let them make a road for me. They
objected, saying, "It may storm and you can't get there." I said,
"Well, if it starts to storm, I will follow you up even if it is Sunday."[17]

I was very much surprised and pleased to find that Roan Bear, with whom I was bunking, didn't go with the rest. We sat down together by the fire and talked and told stories and read the Bible. The deserted camp was a desolate-looking place and along towards evening the sky began to look very forbidding, so we started out and overtook the others. The camp had been made in a very protected place—an amphitheater on the southwest corner of Slim Buttes where there was a little wood and some water, though we used melted snow for water. About the camp were two or three hundred acres of beautiful grass, only it was covered by two or three feet of snow. The horses, however, went to work pawing, for they knew their business, too.

Next morning we were out early—fifty-six men of us—leading the horses we were to ride during the buffalo run and taking with us a number of extra packhorses. Soon after daybreak we neared the place where buffalo had been seen on Saturday. When we could see each other more clearly, I noticed the blackened faces of those who had been appointed "soldiers" for this run. This was the sign of authority and it was their duty to keep the party together and to stop any ambitious hunter from starting away and alarming the game before all could take part on even terms.

The morning was gray and chilly[18]—the day before Christmas. The snow was deeper than the older men liked and many falls were predicted, but several remarked that there would be fewer broken bones because of this. The buffalo were not far away and some were soon seen, but the herd was very small and there was considerable talk before it was finally decided to run these. We were tired of venison, porcupine, skunk and badger meat, and every man longed for the food of former days—buffalo meat, "the meat that satisfies and has 'ping' to it."[19]

We changed mounts, taking our running horses—the pampered ones that had run loose all the way out and at every opportunity had been fed the strength-giving shavings of the inner bark and the twigs of young cottonwood trees. These were the horses on which

we now depended and about which we had bragged mightily
night after night. A few of these were experienced buffalo runners
of known speed and staying power, but there were many untried
horses. My own (Sam) was an old hand and knew all that a horse
could know about running buffalo, besides being very fast. Every
man in camp knew him, for he was the horse that Can-pta-ye
(Wood Pile) had on the Little Big Horn against Custer in '76.[20]
Some men rode bareback, but most of them used a convenient,
lightly stuffed running pad. I had added stirrups to the Indian-made
pad I used.

While changing to our running horses, a consultation was held
and as this was going on, one of the quieter men led his horse to
one side and with covered head seated himself on a slight rise of
ground. Joining us again he said, "I have been praying that we
may have a successful run and that no one may be hurt; my heart
tells me we shall soon eat fresh meat." There had been excitement
before but now it was intense, affecting horses as well as men.
Some rode along quietly, making no show of their eagerness,
while some of the men rode like demons, recklessly using the
heel and quirt to tune their horses up to the rush they would
soon have to make. A few of the horses were equally wild.

There is nothing which changes the appearance of a human
being quite like the expression on an Indian's face when he starts
to run and shoot buffalo. I have heard the Indians themselves
speak of it, but I never really understood it until I saw it myself.
They look fearful—like demons. When they get into the hunt,
their faces look like fiends.

For weapons we had magazine and single-shot rifles, though
Little Bear, who rode a famous Pinto horse [an old-time hunter],
carried his bow and arrows. To prevent losing one's horse, in case
of a fall, each man had a small line, about twenty feet long tightly
tucked under his belt; one end of the line was fastened to the bridle
bit and the other tied to the belt itself.[21] My own hands on this first
run, were very full. I, of course, was excited as any and it was all I

could do to control my horse who would first carom against
the horse on one side and then against one on the other, much
to my discomfort and deep anguish of soul, for in the midst of
this [running], my line slipped from my belt and dropped behind,
[providing] a most tempting loop—horse on one end and I on
the other—for someone to step into and I be jerked off and
covered with snow! To pull in, recoil and tuck away my line was
nerve-splitting work at the moment. My heavy rifle was extra
trouble. I could easily have used another pair of hands!

One of our "soldiers" who had been left with the main party
was very suspicious of those who were doing scout duty above us.
He declared that they were deceiving us, and as we could see nothing
whatever, he finally started off in a hurry to see for himself, running
his horse over a little rise and down into an open draw leading out
of the valley. Suddenly there was a cloud of snow and both man
and horse disappeared. The man rose unhurt and after much effort
helped his horse from the snow-covered washout into which he
had ridden. As he turned back, shaking the snow from inside his
clothing and clearing it from his gun, Roan Bear whispered loudly:
"He's cooled off now," and we trotted up the valley with a better
hold on ourselves.

The head of the valley brought us out on a bit of level country.[22]
We turned to the left and hardly eighty rods [400 yards] away the
already startled buffalo closed up and began to move giving their
stumpy twists of tails an upward flirt as they broke into a lumbering
gallop. I hardly saw them except to note that they suddenly vanished
as if swallowed up in the earth. The first wild burst of the chase left
me off to the right and for a moment I thought a trick had been
played on me. In a flash my horse was running like the wind in
the rear of the silent, hard-whipping riders. These disappeared as
unexpectedly as had the game a second before and now I reached
the edge of a steep-sided, flat-bottomed water course, to see the
buffalo climbing out the opposite side and scampering away, while
in the gully before me my comrades were strung out in a most

disorganized style. Under the snow there was a wide sheet of ice
and probably twenty horses were down, with their riders in all
positions of falling and quick recovery. A few were across the ice
or were slowly making their way over, while others were picking
themselves up out of the snow, helping their horses and taking
stock of damage. It was a most impossible sort of drop-off and
I would have given all I had to be able to pull up on the brink.
My horse [however] would not have it so, and with my heart well
up in my throat we went over and were across with the fortunate
ones before I had time to think of the next thing to be scared at.
What a horse I had! Indeed, I had now drunk deep of the wine
of the mad chase and would not stop at anything!

The run was well on and the leading hunters began to shoot.[23]
Those on slower horses far in the rear also began to shoot, much
to the disgust of those in front, where man, horse or buffalo stood
an even chance of being hit!

This first run of ours allowed but one lone buffalo to escape.
We packed back to camp the meat from fifty carcasses. One of these
was killed by Little Bear with his bow, in the way of his fathers.
The arrow was driven entirely through the body, entering the right
flank with its steel point sticking out low down on the opposite side.
In former days this was often done, but it requires great strength
of both bow and arm. Usually several arrows were necessary and
often the game would run for miles after being hit in a vital spot.
[When the buffalo falls, the hunter, if on a swift horse, does not
stop but passes on in pursuit.] Those on slower horses, especially
the relatives of the owners of the swift one[s], follow and soon
skin and cut up the animals, selecting dainty morsels of liver or
the belly fat [for quick consumption] as they work.

On one of our later runs, I was through and on my way back,
looking for others of the party when I came upon five or six men
cutting up a buffalo and lunching at the same time. It was late
in the day and I remarked that I was very hungry. I had not eaten
for twenty-two hours. Charger said, "Here, take this," and cut off

a great chunk of raw liver and passed it up to me. Most of the
men had blood marks from ear to ear. I cut off as small a piece
as I thought was respectable and put it in my mouth, but it was
an awful job for me to chew and swallow it. When my host
offered me a second cutting, I declined with thanks. I was just
as hungry as I had been before, while the rest of them were fed,
fit for another day.

By long established hunting customs, there was a strict law of
division of the kill which was never questioned, though disputes
often occurred as to who had killed the animal. The division varied
only with the number helping to skin and butcher; the hide, one
side and the hind quarter belonged to the man who had shot the
animal. His first assistant had the other side and a hind quarter,
and the second assistant came in for the brisket and the two front
quarters.[24] On most hunts there was more or less stealing of game.
The relatives of a prominent man were quite likely to claim the kill
as his and the rightful owner would lose it unless the size of the
bullet or some special marking gave conclusive evidence. This
practice was fully recognized by the Indians themselves and a
saying often heard in buffalo camp was: "The slow horses get all
the buffalo!" and "Lucky is the man that has many relations!"
Another joke was, "A shot buffalo has no tongue!" and it was
a fact that if a hunter killed one animal and went on after another,
when he returned to his first kill, the beast's tongue would be gone.
The taking of the tongue was not considered as a theft, for it was
the custom after the hunt for those who had appropriated the
tongue to give a feast, taking the credit of the entertainment,
but in a way returning the tongue![25]

One night after dark, six of us were bringing an overloaded bunch
of pack horses through deep snow towards the temporary camp
when an immense herd of buffalo came up from the southwest
and diagonally crossed our front. One of the most reckless acts I
ever knew of on a hunt took place at this time, when even the stars
themselves had gone to sleep.

Co-kan-tan-ka rode up to me and said, "I make a night run—
come!" I was riding my pack horse and had no wish to get into
a herd of buffalo and have him fall down with me, so I declined
the honor and Co-kan-tan-ka disappeared, going right over
towards the buffalo. I heard the report of his gun, then almost
immediately another flash and report and a little later another.
One of the men said, "Does he want to kill them all?" We did
not see him for a long while but kept on our way. After a bit
he hailed us from the southeast and everyone but Clarence Ward
and myself went off to help him. He finally had shot a buffalo
and they went to help skin it and bring in the robe. When he
caught up with us, he told us what happened. The first shot
was a miss and suddenly he found he was right in the midst
of the buffalo. They were running on all sides of him, bumping
against his legs, and in his excitement he threw the lever of his
gun so quickly and so hard that the hammer was jarred down
and the shot went off in the air. This didn't steady his nerves any,
you may be sure, with the result that he did exactly the same thing
again! That exhausted all the shells there were in the magazine
and realizing what a big fool he was to be so scared and nervous,
he started more cooly to hunt in his belt for cartridges. He found
he had only three left, and as his belt had slipped around, they
were in the middle of his back, so he had to throw off his blanket
to reach them! When he got out one cartridge, he very carefully
pushed it into the chamber of his gun and although the buffalo
were still bumping against him, he kept his wits about him and
his eyes open and finally managed to work out of the running
herd and get his buffalo.

This man was one of those in the Custer fight. His "Agency
name" was Lazy White Bull, but the proper translation of the
name—Ptesanhunka—would be "White Buffalo Cow Leader."
His nickname was Co-kan-tan-ka and he was usually addressed
by that name.[26] His real name was only for state occasions. He
told me a great many things about the Custer fight. He was one

of Sitting Bull's active lieutenants, but before the fight Sitting Bull ran away, and Co-kan-tan-ka had to work under the counsel of others who were handling affairs.

After we all came together in our temporary camp, we spent a comfortable night. The following night in the main camp, Touch-the-Cloud, as he came in, said that he believed he was the most unfortunate man in the whole party. Someone asked him how that was. He said he had not been able to tie the meat on his packhorse so that it would stay put, but kept falling off into the snow every few steps, and he had been busy all evening hunting it up and fixing his pack. After listening to his statement, I said I could go him one better and I was called on to prove my statement. I had killed an enormous animal, and, after skinning it, I threw the green hide over the horse and sat on it. The hide froze stiff as marble and in passing through a deep drift I was lifted clear off my horse, "the stiff-necked one," which passed out from under me and left me straddling the frozen hide on top of nothing. I was promptly awarded the distinction I had claimed, the absurd helplessness appealing to all—and to this day, fifty years later—the story of the time I rode on a buffalo hide without any horse under it, is still told and laughed over by the Indians.

And so after each day's run we would make our way back to camp with an abundance. The fires crackled, the pots boiled and all were smiling and happy. No one was injured and the hides would make the finest of robes. To be sure, there were some disappointments. Some of the horses turned out poorly. Charger rode a big, blaze-faced brown that ran splendidly until he saw the strange-looking woolly beasts with their wagging chin whiskers and then he bolted and ran away in the opposite direction for two miles [with its unwilling rider].[27] [Some horses of which much was expected turned out poorly.] Roan Bear had a little black [horse from which he expected great things, but which failed to do well. And so the talk of the camp came and went. The dogs that came from home, lean and scrawny, grew sleek and fat. ...]

Epilogue

By early February the active part of the buffalo hunt was over and a weary Riggs set out for home. After he had come far enough east, he stopped at a stage ranch[28] on the Moreau River, wrote a letter, and sent it home from there. The letter, dated February 4, 1881, stated that he had been gone for six weeks during which time the party had accumulated more meat than the ponies could pack. On the way out, he wrote, they took 200 deerskins and ate 148 porcupines.

Riggs noted that the snow on average was 2 feet deep and crusted, making travel difficult. He added that the "ponies' legs are badly cut."

Riggs had garnered seven robes but had had two from the first run stolen, which, he wrote, "put a damper on me." Because he could not wrangle for his game, he satisfied himself with taking only a single animal on each of the last two runs. His horse, he wrote, was "very fast and an old hand at the business or I would have got nothing save the experience," adding that they had all been eating nothing but meat for the last four weeks.[29] "I would," he finally wrote, "like some clean clothes and clean food."

There were many other anecdotes regarding the stubbornness of overloaded mules and the heroic efforts of the hunters in trying to haul back huge amounts of venison and bison meat. Riggs also noted that the game of "plumstone-shooting" was very popular and went on to praise his buffalo horse, which had been impeccably trained for the art of bison hunting.

Summing up his narrative and true to the original point of his quest, Riggs wrote that "one part of my education, perhaps the most valuable, was in learning to see life from their point of view, to understand their mental reactions and, in short, to think as they did, no longer a stranger or outsider but as one of them. I rejoice in the knowledge that I was so accepted."

On the way home when the party reached the Moreau River and were about 50 miles from Dupuis's place on the Cheyenne, Riggs and Clarence Ward left the main group and "corkscrewed" around and over the ridges. On the second night they made camp at the head of a ravine on the Fox Ridge divide. They were very tired and thirsty and stopped to melt snow for drinking. By the time they finished, it was nearly midnight and both men were "so used-up" that they spread their blankets on top of the hard, crusted snow and lay down. "Fortunately for us," Riggs recalled, "there was no wind. As it was, this was the coldest camp I can remember."

They followed the crest of the Fox Ridge divide eastward to "the Gap,"[30] and turning down and south they reached the Dupuis ranch where they received a warm welcome. Riggs wrote that Dupuis and another old Frenchman (Canadian) greeted him in true "early-day manner with tears, laughing, curses, and prayers curiously intermingled. Fred called to one of the boys, 'take Tom's hawse; put de hawse on de stabe; put hay on de hawse; and Tom come in de house and put your feet on de stove!'"

The main body of the hunt separated later on the Moreau. Those from the Cheyenne River area arrived home four or five days after Riggs and Ward.[31]

Forty years later, accompanied in an automobile by his son, Theodore Riggs, Thomas Riggs revisited the Slim Buttes. Overlooking the expanse of grass and winding draws where he had participated in the last great winter buffalo hunt, he eloquently recalled that experience and the poignant words of Co-kan-tan-ka for his son:

> Co-kan-tan-ka was really quite a man, and I well remember one day in
> January 1881, when he and I climbed the southern end of Slim Butte.
> It was a wonderful view, looking down to the east, down the valley of
> the Moreau River, clear beyond the Missouri to the divide or coteau;
> the great river valley from north to south not showing at all; a full
> hundred and fifty miles of snow-covered hills and valleys lying
> nearly flat. There was nearly two feet of snow, brilliant, glittering,
> hostile; and not a bush, tree or bare hilltop to break the expanse.
> Co-kan-tan-ka seated himself on a boulder and drawing his blanket
> over his head, covering all but his face, looked eastward down the
> valley of the Moreau. After fully half an hour of silence, as the sun
> began to go down, Co-kan (we often left off the last syllables) turned
> to me, and rising from the stone, said: "I have been crying and praying,
> for I shall never again see this country as I have seen it before."[32]

SIXTEEN

Dreaming Back the Old Days

And this is the tragedy and the irony of our struggle to hold on: not only is it impossible, but it brings us the very pain we are seeking to avoid.

—Sogyal Rinpoche

AFTER OVER A CENTURY, a pall still seems to hang over the valley of Wounded Knee, South Dakota, or so it felt the gray and blustery November day I tarried there.

The 1880s were a crucible for the Teton Lakota. It was a period marked by profound change resulting in a great emotional struggle to maintain their identity and culture in the face of unrelenting waves of foreign intrusion. Technologically primitive but proud, the western Lakota were being cast from their position as uncontested masters of the northern plains into the uncomfortable and unaccustomed role of the vanquished. It was a change that came with a host of restrictions many were loathe to accept.

Throughout the nineteenth century, mercantile American society continued to covet and aggressively exploit the resources of the northern plains. The subjugation of the western Lakota as a people, however, was more a function of business than of inherent evil. Native peoples were simply in the way of "progress," specifically agrarian, mineral, and commercial development.

For the federal government, far removed on the east coast of the continent, the question of how to deal with the northern plains Indians who subsisted in the rugged interior of the buffalo country had many facets, which included mercantile expansion, the legality of treaty claims, and Christian morality. The emphasis of how the American Indians should be dealt with often shifted depending on the president, Congress, the federal budget, and the tenor of public opinion at any given time. The Indians never knew what to expect nor, to be fair, did the U.S. military. Subjugation and order, however, were givens. Typically, the closer Indian Affairs bureaucrats and military officers got to the place, the time, and the people, the more immediate and personal their responses.

Co-kan-tan-ka, like many Lakota, fully realized that the disappearance of the buffalo and confinement to the reservation clearly signaled the end of their traditional lifestyle, which focused on the chase, raiding, and war. Their fate in the new order of the buffalo country was to walk the "white man's road." That metaphorical road in many respects was being carefully laid out by men like the Sacred Herald and many others much less capable in various governmental and religious bureaucracies. Their philosophy was a paradigm shift emphasizing nonviolence, farming, and ranching. Yet the old nomadic life of movement, hunting, and warfare had yet to be dissolved.

The four bands (excluding the Hunkpapa) who comprised the majority of the 3,000 Sioux living on the Cheyenne River Reservation in the late 1880s were slowly adjusting to the white man's road in large measure because of the work of missionaries, both white and native. Reservation life was changing the people in many ways, apparent in both the new look of the people and the Indian settlements. Although the settlements were still referred to as "camps," they were actually communities of log cabins scattered along the creeks where the various chiefs had settled their bands. Most of these communities had a store, a school, a church, and often a post office, and all the communities were becoming better connected by a network of wagon roads that followed the old trails. Many of the small cabins, although sparsely furnished, were neatly kept. Near the cabins were horse corrals, sheds, a garden plot, flocks of free-ranging chickens, and puppies being fattened up for the stew pot. Every two weeks, families would take their wagons to the Cheyenne River Agency located on the Missouri River and collect their rations.

While appearances were promising, most of the Sioux were still living in a difficult limbo of transition. Many wore a mixture of clothing from both cultures, symbolic perhaps of their thoughts, which in part consisted of the old traditional concepts and the new alien forms. The old world traditions of bison hunting, raiding, and fighting were now either gone or taboo, and yet they still haunted the people's collective memory. The new world order centered on a circumspect, sedentary lifestyle based on Christian morality, gardening, ciphering, reading, and writing. Although useful, these new methods of thought and activities were foreign and derived from sources not their own. The Lakota had no stories for them, no way to incorporate them in a sacred way as they had for everything else in their lives. Unable any longer to live in the old ways, they were yet incapable of living entirely in the new. This situation created tension and frustration, which every Indian had to grapple with in his or her own way. How each chief viewed it, and how each man and woman solved it, would seal their collective fate.

As grief for the loss of their old freedoms and lifestyle mixed with the frustration and tensions created by the new, words of hope arose to soothe the broken and weary spirits of the northern plains Indians. These words would come from Wovoka, the Paiute "prophet" from western Nevada, a man well versed in the missionary teachings of the Mormons. In 1886, Wovoka claimed, he heard the voice of God, who gave him a simple message for all Indians: "Be good, behave always. It will give you satisfaction in your life."

Wovoka proclaimed that he had seen heaven and it was a beautiful, level, green country filled with abundant game and fish that awaited them and that "they must not fight, that there must be peace all over the world; that they must not steal from one another, but be good to each other, for they were all brothers."[1] In a second revelatory vision occurring in January 1889, which Wovoka called the "Great Revelation," he claimed to have "died" for two days before spontaneously reviving.[2] From this trip to heaven Wovoka prophesied that the "earth shall die" and that the northern Paiutes "must not be afraid" because "the earth will come alive again." He also added that the animals would return while non-Indians would be destroyed.

To usher in this new world order the Indians would need to believe and to faithfully perform a sacred dance if they were not to be buried under the new green sod. Wovoka himself would have more power to control the elements of nature and to bring rain. "Jesus is now on earth," he told them. "He appears like a cloud. The dead are all alive again. I do not know when they will be here; maybe this fall or in the spring. When the time comes, there will be no more sickness and everyone will be young again."[3]

Furthermore, he instructed them not to tell lies and "not to fight with the white man or with each other, nor were they to lie around in idleness, but to work, and that for five days every three months after first purifying themselves they must dance the Ghost Dance, which he would teach them."[4] Finally, when Wovoka was satisfied that all the Indians had received his teachings and had properly prepared themselves, he would destroy their old, sad world and create for them a new, happy one.

Wovoka had few believers in his new "religion." However, a fortuitous coincidence in which he successfully predicted a great rainstorm that broke a drought and saved the crops in western Nevada in the spring of 1889 gave him some measure of credibility with the local Paiutes. Predictably, the whites scoffed at his "power" and his "latest news of heaven" while Indians began to embrace his message with enthusiasm. Wovoka's comforting prophecy, a mixture of Mormonism and Christianity, was nonetheless Indian in origin and concept. His message and reputation slowly drifted east, taking root in the psyche of Indians who were starved for any message of salvation and deliverance from their desperate predicament.

During this period in the buffalo country a new bitter enmity was brewing between the Lakota who had signed the 1889 Land Agreement opening the reservation for white settlement and those who had adamantly opposed it. The earth and its anima were a fundamental concept and a profound philosophical tenet of the Lakota identity as a people and a nation. To divide it and sell it constituted a violation of their homeland, their culture, and their identity. It was one more devastating crack in their old world reality.

Most of the Lakota leaders, like Short Bull, who heard the words of the Paiute immediately used his message as a means to vent their own frustration and rage at the whites and their authority while dwelling on the demise of their oppressors.

Short Bull immediately began dancing and teaching new dances to the Indians at the Pine Ridge Agency, with several ceremonies of his own invention. Soon many men were devoting a great deal of time to dancing fervently until they dropped from exhaustion and experienced strange hallucinations. After months of dancing, Short Bull was arrested in the late summer of 1890 and held for a short time. Emboldened upon his release, he proclaimed himself the Messiah and declared that because of the white man's interference he would hasten the fulfillment of his prophecy and resurrect the dead at once.[5] In the late fall hundreds of his Indian followers fled the reservation with him to the badlands to dance and escape the nervous officers who were trying to maintain order and stop the dancing.

That same summer, Kicking Bear, a Mnikoju living in Big Foot's camp on the Cheyenne River, returned from Nevada with Wovoka's message and reported it to Big Foot and Hump. Kicking Bear, at forty-one, was a tall, big-boned, heavy-featured warrior who had been a good friend of Crazy Horse and had fought beside him in the battles of the Rosebud and the Little Bighorn. He was tough-looking and tough-talking and, like Short Bull, had no fondness for white men and their works.[6]

An Oglala by birth, Kicking Bear had married Big Foot's niece, Woodpecker Woman, and was living with his wife's people, the Mnikoju. He was undoubtedly intelligent and imaginative. Thomas Riggs, who knew him "tolerably well," wrote in his memoir that "he [Kicking Bear] would have been abundantly able to manufacture and publish the message said to have come from far away out of his own imagination without assistance. Every word of it was in full accord with his past and present hopes for the future."[7]

Kicking Bear was also counted as one of the most militant of the Lakota delegates to bring the Ghost Dance message back to the Sioux. Upon his return to South Dakota, he and his codelegates discarded

Wovoka's explicit instructions "to farm, to work willingly for the whites in cooperation, and to send their children to school."[8] Except for the Lakota, all the delegates from the other thirty-some odd tribes who had also heard Wovoka's teachings seemed to understand that they were to keep the peace with the whites until the new millennium appeared and rolled over them.[9]

When Kicking Bear returned to the Mnikojus on the Cheyenne River, he was initially met with indifference. Few of them took interest in the new predictions partly because the spring had been a good one. Regular rains had come at the right time to freshen the parched winter prairies, turning the grass sweet and green while their crops were thick and flourishing.

By July, however, as is common in buffalo country, the rains abruptly ceased and the earth baked and cracked in the summer heat. The sun became a blazing copper disk suspended in a hard, pewter sky, while the corn that had looked so promising a few weeks earlier withered in the searing winds that blew up from the southwest. On the political scene the situation was also deteriorating. Government beef rations for the Indians on Pine Ridge had been reduced by nearly 50 percent and the Sioux were once again on the brink of starvation.[10] The time, the season, and the place had been set as if by fate to test the patience and forbearance of the Teton Lakota.

Little Wound, an Oglala chief who began to Ghost Dance fervently on the Pine Ridge Reservation, described one of his vision trips to heaven as going back before the time of the whites when the Lakotas still lived in skin tipis and used the bow and arrow, and the land was wide and green in every direction. Little Wound said that the great Messiah took him to see all his deceased friends and relatives, who embraced him with tears of joy.

On a long walk, the Great Holy told him that the earth was "bad" and "worn out" and that he and his people needed a new place to live where the "rascally whites" could not bother them. Near the end of his trance, Little Wound added that if the holy men could make medicine shirts for the dancers and pray over them, no harm could come to the wearers; the "bullets of any whites that wanted to stop the Messiah Dance would fall to the ground without hurting any-body, and the person who fired the shots would drop dead. The Great Holy had said He had made a hole in the ground and filled it with hot water to put all the white men and the nonbelievers in."[11]

The Ghost Dance, or more accurately, *Wanagi Wacipi*, the "Spirit Dance Ceremony," of the Sioux had now been fully formed to order for the confused, the angry, the hopeless, and the dispossessed. While it was rapidly gathering adherents on the Rosebud and Pine Ridge Reservations, Kicking Bear took it up to Sitting Bull, who was living on the Grand River on the Standing Rock Reservation. Sitting Bull embraced it immediately. However, when Kicking Bear set out to spread the news again to the Cheyenne River Sioux, the majority of whom were now Christianized and living on the east side of the reservation, he was ignored.

There were two notable exceptions, though: Big Foot (Spotted Elk) and Hump, both of whom led large Mnikoju camps of nearly 400 in-dividuals, most of whom were "traditionals." Hump's camp was lo-cated near the mouth of Cherry Creek while Big Foot's camp was 40 miles farther up the Cheyenne near the mouth of Deep Creek. Like their discontented southern relatives, the Sicangu (Brûlé) of Rosebud and the Oglala of Pine Ridge, the Mnikojus on the Cheyenne River now adopted the Ghost Dance with zealous passion.

Hump was a well-known and respected warrior chief who had led the charge that annihilated the hapless Lieutenant Fetterman and his command at Fort Kearney in Wyoming in the winter of 1866. Hump had also refused to sign the Laramie Treaty of 1868 and, in the sum-mer of 1889, had sent his club-wielding braves to break up the lines of Indians waiting to sign the Land Agreement.

Big Foot, in direct contrast to Hump, was regarded as a diplomat, peacemaker, and friend of the whites. His band, however, was con-sidered unruly by the U.S. military even before the Ghost Dance, and his camp was the home of Kicking Bear.

Big Foot's predicament was further complicated by a medicine man in his camp named Yellow Bird, who was anti-white and deeply dedicated to the old ways. He was an adept and skilled agitator orator who was able to keep Big Foot's people in such a frenzied state over the *Wanagi Wacipi* ceremony that they danced day and night for as long as they were able to move and stay awake.

Mary Traversie Dupree Talks, an educated woman of French and Lakota ancestry, was teaching during the fall of 1890 at the Cherry Creek school. She had recently married Edward Dupree, the only literate son of Fred and Mary Dupuis. Mary, who was twenty at the time, wrote a vivid description of the Ghost Dances she witnessed at Cherry Creek:

> They danced across the creek west of the present [mission] station on a large flat. It was late fall, the air was very crisp with heavy frost on the ground. Quite some distance away, one could hear the shuffling of many moccasined feet on the frost covered earth. Much wailing, shouting and burst of song could be heard at frequent intervals. ... People would hold hands shuffling forward and sideways, hour after hour without food or water until finally they fell from sheer exhaustion. Others who were not dancing carried them away and placed them in their tipis where they slept and had their visions.[12]

Mary added that many had visions of going to heaven and seeing the huge carpet of grass that Wovoka had described. Others, however, envisioned nightmares. One dancer told of seeing his children deceased, walking about aimlessly and crying. "This vision," Mary recalled, "upset the entire group of people."[13] She also reported that the crying and wailing of the dancers could be heard for miles up and down the Cheyenne River valley. On clear, still evenings the sounds were "particularly terrifying and unnerving."

Big Foot's people, like those of Hump, had become so thoroughly caught up in the hysteria and the dream of the beautiful new world that throughout the fall of 1890 stretching into mid-December, they did little else but dance and wail. Slowly coming to believe that danger lurked in this millennial frenzy, nervous, inexperienced Indian agents both at Rosebud and Pine Ridge called upon the military to come in, stop the dancing, and restore order. Military orders were soon issued to arrest and remove the most disruptive elements of the movement and to relocate all the bands temporarily to the nearest military installation. With the cavalry on the move, tensions rose among the Lakota and rumors quickly spread that the Indians were to be rounded up and shot.[14]

In mid-December of 1890, Hump had been cajoled at the behest of his old friend, Captain Ewers, into moving his band to the Cheyenne River Agency near Fort Bennett on the Missouri River. Gen. Nelson Miles wanted Big Foot and his people escorted west to Fort Meade in the Black Hills. The general's intention was to locate all the bands to nearby forts where they could be watched until their frenzy died down. He gave the job to Captain Sumner, who had already developed a good working relationship with Big Foot. However, through a series of mistakes, miscommunication, and trickery, Big Foot and his band eluded Sumner's grasp and surreptitiously traveled south across the badlands to the Pine Ridge Reservation.[15] Miles now considered Big Foot's Mnikojus armed and dangerous.

Seriously ill with pneumonia, Big Foot and his band were eventually apprehended near Wounded Knee Creek on the evening of December 28, 1890, and placed under tight military guard during the night. The next morning, shortly after 8 A.M., Big Foot's 100-plus warriors were ordered out of their tipis. The warriors came forward and seated themselves on the ground in front of the troops and were then ordered to retrieve any weapons. The first twenty left and returned a short time later with two guns. After a brief consultation with the officers, the soldiers were ordered to stand within 10 yards of the seated warriors while another detachment was ordered to search the tipis. After a rough and thorough search, the soldiers returned with about forty rifles, most of which were old and useless.

According to Mooney's report: "The search had taken considerable time and created a good deal of excitement among the women and children as the soldiers had in the process overturned the beds and other furnishings of the tepees, and in some instances driven out the inmates. All this had a bad effect on their husbands and brothers, already wrought up to a high nervous tension."[16]

To make matters worse, Big Foot was confined to his tipi, too sick to take charge of his restive camp, while Yellow Bird was "walking among the warriors, blowing on an eagle bone whistle, and urging them to resist. He told them that the soldiers had become weak and powerless, and that their bullets would not injure the Indians, dressed as they were in their sacred ghost shirts, which nearly all of the Indian warriors wore."[17] As he spoke in Lakota, the officers were unaware that he was preparing and inciting them for battle.

Alice Ghost Horse, a thirteen-year-old Lakota girl who witnessed the unfolding scene on horseback at a distance, later wrote that Yellow Bird stood facing the east with his hands up to say a prayer to the spotted eagle asking that he die instead of his people.[18] All accounts agree that Yellow Bird then stooped down, picked up a handful of dust, and threw it into the air.

Accounts of what happened next differ. Historical reports indicate that at that moment, a young Mnikoju identified as Black Fox dropped his blanket from his shoulder and shot an army officer at point-blank range. Other warriors then dropped their blankets and sprang to their feet armed with revolvers, knives, and warclubs.

The Lakota version states that two sergeants roughly grabbed a deaf man identified as Black Coyote (Fox) with the intent of disarming him and that in the ensuing scuffle, Black Coyote raised his rifle above his head to keep it away from the soldiers and it discharged into the air.[19] Either way, the tensions of the morning were finally ignited by a gunshot. A young, nervous army officer shouted, "Fire! Fire on them!"[20] and within moments Hotchkiss guns positioned on the surrounding ridges and trained on the camp were unleashed, sending a hail of lead from the heights into all the combatants as well as the women and children bystanders. It has been estimated that half the warriors were killed in the first deadly volley. The survivors sprang to their feet, casting off their blankets as they rose. Most of the warriors had hidden revolvers and knives in their belts, while a few carried warclubs.[21] For a few minutes it was a bloody, close-quarters, desperate hand-to-hand fight.

Meanwhile, from the surrounding ridges guns poured in 2-pound explosive shells at the rate of nearly fifty per minute, mowing down everything alive and reducing tipis to little more than shreds hanging on splintered sticks. In a matter of minutes nearly 180 Indian men, women, and children, some still lying in their burning tipis, along with 60 soldiers lay dead or wounded.

Following the initial barrage, the Hotchkiss guns were trained to rake the ravines where survivors, mostly women and children, ran for their lives. Strict orders had been issued to the soldiers that women and children were not to be hurt, but the terrible butchery continued, the work of mostly young, raw recruits from the East who were incensed and infuriated by the death of their comrades. And though most of the warriors had been killed in the encampment, the bodies of women and children were scattered along a distance of 2 miles from the gory scene of the encounter. Yellow Bird was reported to have fought furiously and was later found shot and burned in his own tipi still fiercely clutching his Winchester.

At the time of the battle, Kicking Bear[22] was in the badlands preparing for a final Ghost Dance and thus missed the fight along with Short Bull and his followers. After learning of the butchery, Short Bull and his warriors attacked a party of soldiers between Wounded Knee and Pine Ridge but were repulsed. A thousand warriors and their families, camped farther south on White Clay Creek during the Wounded Knee debacle, were all now thoroughly hostile to the army. But General Miles, who arrived a few days later, urged the leaders to bring their bands in and surrender, giving his word that their rights and needs would receive attention from the government while warning them that to resist any longer was useless because their retreat was cut off by his soldiers. Friendly chiefs were also instrumental in persuading the hostile Indians to ask for peace.[23]

Kicking Bear and a handful of his followers held out for two weeks on the Stronghold Table in the White River Badlands before symbolically laying his rifle down at the feet of General Miles. It was now over. Historians later marked the Wounded Knee massacre as the final chapter of Indian resistance on the northern plains.

As for Kicking Bear, in an odd twist of fate peculiar perhaps only to America where agitators often become celebrities, he was invited and allowed to join Buffalo Bill Cody's Wild West Show and toured Europe for a number of years, rather than being banished to a forlorn military post.

When news of the Wounded Knee massacre reached Wovoka in the Nevada desert, he quietly pulled his blanket over his head in mourning. Later he spoke these poetic words to his believers: "In days behind, many times I called you to travel the hunting trail or to follow the war trail. Now those trails are choked with sand; they are covered with grass, the young men cannot find them. My children, today I call upon you to travel a new trail, the only trail now open—the White Man's Road."[24]

SEVENTEEN

Roundup Years

*The old boys and the old times ought to be remembered. I went across
from Rapid [City] to Pierre in 1900, and what a country it was then!
I often say that I don't regret my age in the least, for I was born early
enough to enjoy a sort of freedom that no Americans will ever know again.*
—Badger Clark

IN THE SUMMER OF 1881, "boss cowman" G. E. "Ed" Lemmon was
headed southwest out of Fort Yates, Dakota Territory, on his way back
to the Black Hills when he encountered a herd of buffalo between the
forks of the Grand River. He estimated the herd size at 5,000 animals,
which he described as "swarming" across a long tableland. "We didn't
bother them," he wrote later in his biography, *Boss Cowman*, "except
to rope a few, earmark them and play with them awhile."

As cowboys, Lemmon and his crew were more interested in how
bison responded to a rope than to a rifle. At the time, Lemmon was
filling U.S. government Indian contracts for beef and knew that he
was on reservation land that since the Laramie Treaty of 1868 was
legally off limits to market hunters and white men. The bison herd
Lemmon and his men encountered was part of the same group that
had only recently escaped the Montana killing grounds. They would
be annihilated that winter by Sioux from the Standing Rock and
Cheyenne River Reservations.

With the demise of the last free-roaming bison herds across the
Grand, Moreau, and Cheyenne River valleys, the plains were now open
for the longhorns. Herds were already slowly being built up by old
French-Canadian traders and scouts like Basil Clement (Claymore)
and Paul Narcelle who, as former trappers, traders, and employees of

158

the American Fur Company, got their start in the cattle business as old Fred Dupuis did: with calves and leftover livestock from the early cowmen who drove herds up from south Texas to feed the reservation Indians and the soldiers at Fort Sully.

Basil Claymore had led a particularly adventurous life. He had trapped with the legendary Jim Bridger, guided numerous government survey expeditions, and knew all the military officers as well as the prominent Sioux leaders of his time. He served as an interpreter at Fort Sully and, like Narcelle and Dupuis, had fathered a large family of mixed-blood children who, like their fathers, intermarried with members of the Cheyenne River Sioux tribe. Descendents of these families were becoming prominent ranchers on the east side of the Cheyenne River Reservation.

Beginning about 1882 and continuing through the decade, southern cattle outfits drove stock up from the southern plains to the northern ranges, which had only recently been cleared of bison. Most of these cowmen spread their herds out on the rich grasslands west of the Cheyenne River and Standing Rock Reservations and beyond the Little Missouri River into eastern Wyoming and Montana on what was then open government rangeland.

As the cattle boom of the early 1880s continued, huge herds built up and more cattlemen moved in. With no fences to hinder movement, cows were often pushed east across the imaginary line of the 102d meridian, which separated the free government ranges from the reservation grasslands.

It did not take long before homesteaders and cowmen, looking for farmland and more grass, turned a covetous eye toward the forbidden grasslands dedicated to the Standing Rock and Cheyenne River Sioux. Cattlemen wanted in, homesteaders wanted in, and so did the railroads. Pressure was slowly being applied to state and federal government officials to open the land up for settlement.

John R. Brennan, a cattleman and promoter, stated bluntly that "the Great Sioux reservation is not only useless to the Indians, but [since it remains closed,] useless to the white man." Other proponents of opening the reservation further argued that closing the reservations strangled trade and traffic to the Black Hills and denied "thousands of citizens" a chance to work on these "rich and fertile lands that now lie dormant and unproductive."[1]

While the political debate heated up, a disaster awaited the cattle outfits as the winter of 1886–87 got under way. The previous winter had been a particularly mild one with little snow—an "open winter" in the parlance of the cowman. What grass did sprout during the ensuing dry spring of 1886 was quickly seared by hot winds that started early in the summer. Streams dried up quickly, and because most of the beaver had been trapped out earlier, there were few intact beaver dams with their attendant natural standing pools of water.

Superstitious old-timers remembered that during the fall of 1886, there had been "ominous signs" of what lay ahead. What beavers remained had piled up more saplings than usual; native birds "showed a marked uneasiness," flocking together earlier than usual; prairie animals grew heavier coats; and it was reported that northern white owls were in evidence.

By the late fall of 1886 the overstocked ranges were completely grazed out. Furthermore, the cattle market was glutted, creating low demand and low prices for beef and leaving little incentive for cowmen to reduce the size of their livestock herds. In early November the first blizzards roared in, followed by bitter subzero temperatures in the −30° to −40° F range. The snow and cold held on all winter and long into the spring. When the cold finally abated late in the spring of 1887, thousands of cow carcasses lay frozen under great drifts of snow. Cattle losses were heavy and ranged from 10 to as high as 90 percent for some outfits. For a while the pressure was off to open the reservations. Yet investors proved resilient, and before long the biggest outfits were moving thousands of cattle up from the Southwest and Mexico to restock all the open ranges again.

In 1889, the same year South Dakota entered the Union, three quarters of the male Indian population had finally been induced by incentives and a host of operatives, both white and Indian, into ceding a large portion of their reservation lands to the government. Across the entire state, 9 million acres of land was thrown open to settlement and treaties were signed with the railroads to allow them access. Six smaller reservations were created in South Dakota in 1889, one of which became the Cheyenne River Sioux Reservation, which encompassed the eastern half of the Fox Ridge divide as its backbone along with the lower reaches of the Cheyenne and Moreau Rivers.

Four major bands of northern Tetons occupied specific districts of the Cheyenne River Sioux Reservation. Generally speaking, the Mnikoju, the most numerous, occupied the Cheyenne River and located their main camps near the mouth of Cherry Creek and Deep Creek; the Sans Arc occupied the Moreau valley; and the Blackfeet and the Two Kettles generally lived along the Missouri River. Farther north, the Hunkpapas were settled on the Standing Rock Reservation. As part of the land settlement, each adult Indian male over the age of eighteen received an allotment of 320 acres along with two milk cows and a pair of work oxen. They could also apply for an additional allotment of grazing land held in common. In addition, the treaty provided the tribes with herds of breeding cows and a complement of bulls.

In 1903 the Bureau of Indian Affairs, serving as trustee for the tribe and its members, began leasing out the vast domain of the Cheyenne River Sioux Reservation. It was a boon opportunity for the big southwestern cattle outfits that had been searching for more good range for their expanding herds. What had once been buffalo country west of the Cheyenne River Reservation line (102d meridian) was occupied by the Three Vs (VVV) and the Sheidley Cattle Company (Flying V), which was partially owned and managed at the time by Ed Lemmon. Since the early 1880s, both of these cattle outfits had been occupying open rangeland west of the reservation line.

The first outfits to pick up the new reservation leases included the Matador Land and Cattle Company, the HOs, and the 73, all of which based their main cow camps along the Moreau River. The outfits that occupied the southern half of the reservation stretching down to the Cheyenne River were the Turkey Track, the Sword and Dagger, the Mississippi Cattle Company, and numerous Indian outfits whose stock ranged on the cattle company leases. The larger, prominent French-

Indian outfits who ran roundup wagons of their own included
Benoists (ben-WAY), LaPlant, Narcelles, Herbert (aye-BEAR), LeBeau,
Claymore, Rousseau, Traversie, and Dupris along with many others
possessing reservation grazing rights. These big cattle outfits employed
scores of men to handle and process the huge herds that were spreading out across the grasslands. In the process they were importing and
creating a cowboy lifestyle and an empire of cattle and horses.

The Matador Land and Cattle Company arrived in the spring of
1904. It was a large Scot concern managed by Murdo Mackenzie.
Based in Trinidad, Colorado, the Matador had huge land and cattle
holdings in Wyoming and Texas and was reputed to own more than
124,000 head of cattle when Mackenzie assumed the position of general manager in 1890.

In the spring of 1904, trainloads of cattle came north from the
Matador's Texas ranges and detrained at Evarts, South Dakota, on the
east side of the Missouri directly across the river from what was then
known as "the Strip." The Strip was a 6-mile-wide, 87-mile-long
"right-of-way" that stretched along the entire northern border of the
Cheyenne River Reservation. Fenced on both sides with watering
areas spaced about every 10 or 12 miles, it was a grassland superhigh-
way for moving cows back and forth to the railhead shipping yards
at Evarts.

Along with the cattle came a large complement of Texas cowboys,
all dressed in traditional fashion: pants; boots; leather chaps; a vest
with pockets for matches, tobacco, and a notebook; a silk scarf; and
a wide-brimmed Stetson hat.

Murdo Mackenzie had managed to secure a huge lease of 530,000
acres for the Matador that encompassed the northeast section, or
about one sixth of the Cheyenne River Reservation's 3 million acres.
Upon seeing it in the spring of 1904, he dryly observed: "I must say
this pasture pleased me exceedingly. ... The country is rolling, with
deep depressions without any stretch of country being high or level.
The grass is what they call gumbo grass and buffalo with grama
mixed. The grass is very fine and the sod is as good as anything we
ever saw."[2]

Ike Blasingame, a young cow puncher who came up with the Matador cowboys from Texas in 1905, was delighted by what he saw after working the dry scrub of southern Texas. He glowingly described the country as "an almost untouched world of wild, fresh forage."

It was a splendid range scattered with long draws and a fine growth of grass stirrup-high in some areas. The draws held cottonwoods, ash, and elms that provided cool shade in the summer and shelter from blizzards in the winter. Spread out in the draws and across the country were thickets of juneberry, chokecherry, and wild plum, which filled the air with a sweet fragrance in the spring and provided a nutritional, edible fruit in the summer.

Wild animals were also abundant and included wolves, coyotes, wildcats, and lynx as well as beaver, mink, and muskrat. All of these lived down along the river valleys and draws, some of which still held old beaver dams with backed-up pools of pure, clear water. It was a cattleman's paradise, and before the end of the year, Mackenzie had stocked his range with 30,000 to 40,000 head of cattle.

South of the Matador lease was the Turkey Track lease, managed by Capt. Burton C. "Cap" Mossman. The Turkey Track was headquartered along the Pecos River in southern New Mexico. Mackenzie and Mossman agreed to split the cost of erecting a four-strand barbed-wire fence 40 miles long down the spine of the Fox Ridge divide to separate the two grazing leases. Other cattle outfits, including the VVV and the Flying V, also brought their steers to the reservation ranges, taking up the western sections.

The general cattle cycle for all the large stock outfits generally went something like this: The southern ranches would ship their young steers by train up to Evarts in the spring, allowing them to graze or "finish" for a year or so. Following the fall roundup and sorting, the finished steers were herded back east via "the Strip" to Evarts, or LeBeau, South Dakota, where they were shipped to the big stockyards in Chicago and sold, depending on grade, for 25 to 35 cents a hundredweight on the hoof, with the average steer weighing about 1,200 pounds.[3] When prices were low, Mackenzie held steers back a second year, further fattening them and usually getting a higher price.

Mackenzie later told Ed Lemmon that his policy was to market only enough mature beeves each year to declare an 8 percent dividend for the stockholders, sometimes carrying the stock to five years of age in order to do it.[4]

Before the first year was over, some 60,000 cattle had entered the Matador range. With steady cattle prices and grass leased at a mere 3 cents per acre, the Matador showed a tidy profit for its investors after expenses.

But weather on the northern plains can scatter the best-laid business schemes like leaves in the wind. The bottleneck for any cattle outfit lies in getting the cows through the winter, and winter in the northern buffalo country can often mean deep snow, blizzards, and severe cold as part of the regular natural cycle.

One of the worst winters on record in the early twentieth century set in with a howling blizzard in early November 1906. It followed the late fall pattern typical in this country. A wind usually blows in from the northwest, bringing rain, which turns to sleet. This is followed by wet flakes and finally powdery snow. In a matter of minutes the ground becomes slick and icy, then white. The wind then picks up to a gale force, twisting and whirling great clouds of blinding snow into massive, suffocating drifts. This might go on for two or even three days.

During the long winter of 1906–7, one howling blizzard accompanied by subzero temperatures followed in the wake of another. The blizzards began in November and roared through December and into January, burying fences and forage and driving longhorns into drifted-over draws. Foundering in these drifts, cattle suffocated when their nostrils froze shut. Cowboys rode the range to move cattle to sheltered areas, but with little or no forage the animals simply died of starvation in a sheltered location.

When the snowdrifts finally melted away in May, the creeks were choked with loads of longhorn carcasses. Where they had huddled together on the Missouri River bottoms, the bodies lay so thick that a man could hop from one to another for a quarter of a mile at a time.[5] Along the mouths of the Moreau and Cheyenne Rivers, longhorn carcasses piled up like driftwood waiting for the spring rise of the Missouri to dislodge them and float their bloated bodies south. Ike Blasingame noted in his classic book, *Dakota Cowboy*, that the stench of death on the river bottoms drove everyone up to higher ground.[6]

Great bovine die-offs in the northern buffalo country during particularly severe winters were nothing new. One had occurred twenty years earlier during the severe winter of 1886–87. Trappers and mountain men in their time recalled long flotillas of bison carcasses that floated down the Missouri in the spring following severe winters.

After the winter of 1906–7, cattle from points far to the west were spread out across the Cheyenne River Reservation, necessitating one of the biggest roundups ever staged across the northern plains. Roundup bosses and their wagon and cowboy reps from numerous outfits from as far west as Wyoming and Montana started out at the southwestern edge of the Cheyenne River Reservation near Bridger and slowly swept out in a wide arc to the northeast, gathering longhorns into huge herds. These great herds, numbering in the thousands, were first sorted by plains area of origin and later by specific brands. The final tally of cattle losses was staggering, and a number of large cattle outfits, including the Turkey Track and the Sword and Dagger, closed their northern operations after the 1907 spring roundup and gave up their leases.

Seeing an opportunity in the devastation, Cap Mossman quickly picked up the Turkey Track's lease, bought out the Sword and Dagger, and in the spring of 1907 formed a partnership with Frank Bloom and Mahlon Thatcher to create the Diamond A Cattle Company, with headquarters in Eagle Butte, South Dakota.

Mossman's style was an interesting contrast to that of the staid and conservative Scot businessman, Murdo Mackenzie. Mossman was a flamboyant cowboy character with an eccentric flair who took delight in lighting his cigars with a tightly folded and creased $100 bill. Before coming to Dakota he had organized the Arizona Rangers in 1901, building a reputation as a fearless manhunter by tracking down Mexican rustlers and bandits who were then infesting the border country of the Southwest. Mossman was also a well-respected businessman and an astute cattle manager who operated on a scale that approached the stature and ability of the great cattle baron himself, Murdo Mackenzie.

The Diamond A's leases took in two thirds of the Cheyenne River Reservation encompassing some 2 million acres from the middle of the Fox Ridge divide south to the Cheyenne River and west from the Missouri to the reservation line. The Diamond A soon became the largest cattle outfit in the state. In a matter of months, Mossman had built a grass and cattle empire of epic proportion.

In 1914 the Matador closed out its operations on the northern plains and returned to its home ranges in Texas. Thirty-six years later in 1950, when the Matador liquidated all of its assets, an English company bought its holdings for the staggering sum of $19 million, returning to its stockholders more than thirty times their original investment. Mackenzie, who had died eleven years earlier in Denver, missed the great windfall of cash he had been so instrumental in building.[7]

Mossman went on to acquire the Turkey Track Ranch in New Mexico and continued to move cattle from his Pecos River headquarters to the Cheyenne River Reservation. Following World War I and during the boom of the 1920s, the Diamond A prospered. But its days were numbered. In 1934 the Indian Reorganization Act, better known as the Wheeler Act, allowed the Cheyenne River Sioux to organize their own tribal government and to ultimately exercise more control over their land and leases. Slowly the tribe began closing out Diamond A leases.

The great decade of drought that began in the 1930s continued to reduce the size of the Diamond A's operation and herds. Despite these setbacks, the Diamond A continued to operate during the 1940s in the old traditional way, with a chuckwagon and a cook who served up the standard fare of bacon, beans, biscuits, prunes, and dried apples to a cadre of men who lived a life in the saddle during the day and slept under canvas tarps at night. The only difference was that cattle were now being shipped more frequently by truck.

In 1947, Mossman sold out his interest in the Diamond A and retired to Roswell, New Mexico. Leon Williams, the new owner, continued to operate the Diamond A, but on a reduced scale, until his death in 1959. On October 14, 1959, a dispersal sale of all the Diamond A Cattle Company's personal property and holdings was held in Eagle Butte. The last cattle empire consortium that had once been the great Diamond A was now nothing more than miles of old barbed-wire fence, broken-down corrals, and fading memories.[8]

EIGHTEEN

"The Last Best Homestead Country"

*The plains are not forgiving. Anything that is shallow—the easy optimism
of a homesteader; the false hope that denies geography, climate, history;
the tree whose roots don't reach ground water—will dry up and blow away.*
　　　　　　　　　　　　　　　　　　　—Kathleen Norris

ON A GRAVEL ROAD a mile north of the abandoned hamlet of Ordway, South Dakota, a large, glacial boulder with a bronze plaque marks
the site of the Richard Garland homestead where the young prairie
writer Hamlin Garland[1] lived with his parents from 1881 to 1884.

The site where the small frame house stood is nothing more than an
unremarkable slight depression in the earth outlined with a few chunks
of rough stone. What was the backyard is now a thistle patch with a
long, neatly stacked row of large, round hay bales, and beyond that, a
patchwork of scraggly tree belts, overgrazed pastures, and fields of soy-
bean stubble and dry cornstalks rustling in the cold October wind.

This landscape tableau, altogether impersonal, coarse, and dreary,
marks the struggle of one pioneer family who came to Dakota too
early to farm successfully and, like so many others, it has dried up
and blown away. The cold wind and the immovable boulder are ap-
propriate symbols of this difficult country that tried and broke so
many lives and spirits.

In May 1908, nearly a quarter of a century after Garland left the
family's east Dakota homestead, Congress opened up one of the last
homestead areas in the lower forty-eight states, the Cheyenne River
Sioux Indian Reservation. The Chicago, Milwaukee, St. Paul and Pacific
(C, M, SP & P) railroad quickly purchased a right-of-way through the
center of the reservation that followed the Fox Ridge divide between

the Moreau and Cheyenne Rivers. The railroad's plan for making money consisted of hauling immigrants and supplies west, selling them land claims, and shipping their agricultural produce east. It would profit from their labor on both sides of the equation.

Even before the tracks were laid, the railroad began printing and distributing illustrated sale bills that read:

You Need a Farm
in
The Heart of the Famous Fox Ridge,
The Last Best Homestead Country,
A Land of Fertile Prairies,
Pure Water & Untold Opportunities

Other brochures printed by real estate brokers and speculators amplified the virtues of the Fox Ridge country and western Dakota, boasting:

> No state in the Union can offer the advantages for a home that does
> South Dakota. We have a mild and healthful climate and millions
> of acres of fertile soil awaiting the care and cultivation that soon will
> be given to it by the people who are flocking to its borders. We have
> numerous lines of railroads, affording market for produce. We have
> ample rainfall, assuring good crops. We have energetic and intelligent
> people, assuring the best conveniences, such as schools and churches,
> telephones and government. ... The broad fields await your coming,
> and in them lies hidden, boundless wealth and an independent
> existence.[2]

Following this enticement was a list of descriptions of the soil, climate, and crops being grown, along with testimonials from farmers already there. It was the promise of America. Here was the land that would fulfill one's dream of "boundless wealth and an independent existence."

Railroad brochures told the reader how to buy train tickets for an idyllic excursion into this cornucopia. And why not become a farmer? The land was practically free and you could be your own boss. All you had to do was buy a train ticket to western Dakota, file on a claim of 160 acres, farm part of it for a little over a year, make some improvements, and pay it off with the profits.

Things had changed in the forty-six-year interval since the Homestead Act of 1862 was passed by Congress. The initial act gave 160 acres of land to anyone twenty-one or older, so long as one improved it and lived on it for five years. Stipulations since then had been modified numerous times so that by 1908, homesteaders in the last big Dakota land rush had to pay down a substantial amount of the price of the land at filing and the balance when final proof was made. Government land wasn't free anymore, just cheap.[3]

Land prices in the Fox Ridge country in 1910 varied from $2.50 to $4.50 per acre depending on the government land assayers' opinion of the value of the property. Generally, land closest to the railroad tracks went for the highest price, whether it was better farmland or not.[4] Other stipulations to the 1908 act were that the homesteader must reside on his/or her property for a period of fourteen months and make improvements that included a house, a dug well, and 10 acres of plowed ground. Getting something to grow on that 10 acres of plowed ground was another matter.

In March 1910 the Milwaukee Railroad (C, M, SP & P) announced it had finally finished its survey for a branch line south and west of Mobridge, South Dakota, to the Fox Ridge country. The end of its line would be called Faith, where it now owned three quarter sections of land (480 acres).

In the meantime the railroad, which had started laying track south out of Mobridge in 1909, had reached its terminus at Isabel, South Dakota, and was now intent on constructing its junction off the main track south to the Fox Ridge divide. This track crossed the Moreau River at Promise, South Dakota, and then followed the course of Virgin Creek south to LaPlant. From LaPlant the tracks climbed the Fox Ridge divide and headed west along its crest. Along the way the railroad built a series of sidings about every 10 to 12 miles where the steam locomotives could take on coal and water.

The proposed sidings on Fox Ridge from east to west were named La Plant, Ridgeview, Mossman, Parade (Paradis), Eagle Butte, Lantry, Dupree (Dupris), and Red Elm, terminating at the new railhead town-site of Faith. (Faith was named after the president of the Milwaukee Land Company's daughter, not for the virtue it would take to come there and homestead.) The iron road, with its steaming, puffing iron horse spitting grit and cinders, had finally penetrated one of the last major grassland domains of the old buffalo country.

Upon the railroad's announcement of sidings, people struck out overnight for clusters of survey stakes hammered into the ridge at the proposed railroad townsites. Loads of lumber, tents, sheep wagons, and shacks began converging on Faith from all directions. One day word came that three buildings were up, the next day it was reported that there were five, and on the following day there were seven. On May 23, 1910, the premier issue of the *Faith Gazette* reported that there were "twenty-five well built buildings in town." While the paper was vague about the definition of "well built," its exuberant, exaggerated boosterism continued to draw people, who came on foot pushing wheelbarrows, on horseback, and in wagons to file and literally "stake a claim."

A chronicler who was present at the founding of Faith wrote:

> The noise of the hammer makes a din that equals the noise of the streets of a good size city; tents, beds, bedding, loads of merchandise, automobiles, light rigs, and saddle horses are strung in an endless string around the town and the residents remind one of a colony of busy bees intent upon getting their places of business into running order, and in becoming established. ... Everybody is as buoyant and hopeful and enthusiastic as at a county fair, or the rush of a new gold diggings. They welcome the new arrivals, dozens of whom are coming in every day, with the glad hand, and his first wonder is if all the town are politicians and the next is a fear that they have all gone crazy.[5]

Crazy indeed. All of the new arrivals were in fact squatters since the railroad owned all the land and the town had not been platted nor had the track been laid. Nevertheless, if a man wanted to hold a building site for a few days, he bought a bunch of shingles and placed them on "his lot." In the meantime, the spring of 1910 had been a cold, backward affair. Because there was only one heating stove in the whole town and no fuel except the blocks and scraps the carpenters left around the new buildings during the course of their construction, people often gathered together just to get warm.

"We used to hover over this one [stove]," one chronicler recalled, "with our overcoats on and try to imagine we were comfortable and when a newcomer arrived he was not admitted to the circle unless he produced his quota of fuel. Creature comforts were at a premium; there was no fresh meat and the restaurant dished up bacon three times a day until a man got so that the smell of bacon, when he came in the door, made him sick at the stomach."[6]

On July 7, 1910, the town company was assuring everyone that the tracks would be laid in ample time to ship in a winter supply of coal. Meanwhile, real estate continued to boom. The best corner lots on Main Street sold for $1,300, while inside lots went for $800 to $1,000. On one day the company sold $50,000 worth of property based on nothing more than fervid hope, blue sky, and speculation.

After the town had been legally platted on the proposed south side of the tracks, everyone who had squatted on the north side— the majority—had to move. This task had been expected, and after several moving outfits (horse-drawn wagons) had been prepared for action, the scramble to see who could get over the still-nonexistent tracks began. For a few days everything was up on wheels, and within a couple of weeks the whole town had literally picked itself up and moved.

With the approach of winter, local citizens became apprehensive about the train's arrival. The town raised a purse of $600, which was to be paid to the contractor if the rails were in Faith by January 15. Fortunately it was a mild fall followed by an open winter, and on Friday, January 6, 1911, the work train pulled into Faith, which the *Gazette* boasted was now a town of 300 people already in business. Three days later a passenger/freight train hauled in the first train depot along with a carload of immigrants.

A photograph taken on that unusually mild January day of 1911 shows a group of some two dozen men standing by the tracks. The majority of them have their coats open, revealing buttoned-up, heavy, wool cardigans. Most are wearing black wool billed caps and look ill at ease waiting for the camera shutter to click. Standing somewhat apart from the immigrants are two gentlemen, dapper and at ease in their suits, vests, white shirts with ties, and derby hats. Their hands are stuck in their pockets holding their suit jackets open. They are the only two talking in the photo tableau—probably speculators who had already acquired large tracts of land at bargain prices and were now about to unload them for tidy profits.

What the immigrants saw in Faith when they walked south of the tracks that warm January day of 1911 was a bustling little business community that included a doctor, a newspaper, two barbers, two restaurants, a bakery, a department store/pharmacy, a post office, a pool hall, a hardware and furniture store, a meat market, an icehouse, two livery and feed barns, a woodworker/wainwright shop, three hotels, a drugstore, a grocery, a law and loan office, two banks, a land office, a dry goods, a harness shop, a lumber yard, a blacksmith, a flour and feed store, and a farm machinery and implement house. Goodwill, optimism, and boosterism must have flowed through the streets like runoff from a summer thunderstorm.

If the list of new businesses in Faith was impressive, the business district wasn't. It consisted of one wide main street 2 blocks long running perpendicularly south of the tracks. This main dirt thoroughfare was flanked on both sides by raw, narrow, one-story buildings that were no more than small, flimsy shells with a frame constructed of rough lumber and covered on the outside with unpainted shiplap or common boards. A good many of the merchants had erected only a shell and were conducting business under a canvas tarp. With nary a tree in sight, the town must have appeared frail and puny against a backdrop that was nothing but blue sky, tan grass, and distant horizons.

Nearly a century removed, it is difficult to imagine what it felt like arriving in a new, open country by freight car or immigrant car, or being a merchant or a tradesman who had helped found and build a new town in less than twelve months. Early Faith must have resembled the Dakota boomtown of Ordway[7] Hamlin Garland wrote about so eloquently in *A Son of the Middle Border*: "I found a hamlet six months old, and the flock of shining yellow pine shanties strewn upon the sod gave me an illogical delight, but then I was twenty-one—and it was sunset in the Land of the Dakotas! All around me that night the talk was all of land, land ... and each voice was acquiver with hope, each eye alight with anticipation of certain success."

Garland continued: "Hour by hour as the sun sank, prospectors returned to the hotel from their trips into the unclaimed territory, hungry and tired but jubilant," while in town, "hearty, boastful citizens talked almost deliriously of 'corner lots' and 'boulevards' and their chantings were timed to the sound of hammers."[8]

The railroad's extensive advertisements, along with realtors who had traveled to Europe earlier lecturing and handing out glowing literature, had attracted well over a million immigrants, a large majority of whom would ride the trains into central and western Dakota. Colonizing organizations in the states had also been busy in the large cities luring people from all walks of life and all races and creeds to the great rainbow that was now arching over the Fox Ridge country.

In his novel *The Moccasin Ranch*, Hamlin Garland again described a "boomtown" on the Dakota Prairie in language sensual, romantic, and deeply evocative. "The town lay behind them on the level, treeless plain like a handful of blocks pitched upon a russet robe. Its houses were mainly shanties of pine, one-story in height, while here and there actual tents gleamed in the half-light with infinite suggestion of America's restless pioneers. ... There was a poignant charm in the air—a smell of freshly uncovered sod, a width and splendor in the view which exalted the movers beyond words."[9]

With each arriving train more homesteaders poured in from the big cities of Minnesota, Illinois, and Iowa on special excursion rates with various intents. Many had trades and skills but wanted to try something entirely different, something rural and free that had the taste of adventure and freedom, in an entirely different setting. Foreigners, most of whom came from central and eastern Europe, were escaping oppression, overcrowding, and military conscription while seeking an opportunity for more land and a place to grow and raise a large family. The chronicles of their struggles are amazing, heroic, and frightening. Nothing had prepared them for this new arid land where the wind regularly scoured the landscape, the sun had a searing edge, and every living creature tended to come with sharp teeth, a prickly spine, or a sting.

Josef Kindwall, a Swedish-American immigrant, wrote an incisive eyewitness account of the three years he spent in western Dakota, first briefly on a ranch, and later on a homestead with his father in Dewey County on the Cheyenne River Reservation near Timber Lake, South Dakota.

Kindwall arrived in the spring of 1910 at the age of fifteen just in time to experience the newly built town of Timber Lake, which he described as "a small aggregation of tents and shacks fragrant with new lumber and canvas, spiced with the windborne scent of the surrounding sage." He went on to relate how he quickly "explored the one, short grassy street" that comprised the settlement and noticed the various businesses and hostelries located in tents and shacks that were in operation: "At noon a loud banging on a suspended plowshare summoned everyone to dinner in a huge tent where a stew of meat and potatoes was copiously ladled out, at what seemed to me an exorbitant charge—50 cents. It was horse country, so we plied our fork and spoon with one hand while we whisked off the flies with the other."[10]

Kindwall was searching for a rancher named Benoist who had earlier promised to hire him. He caught a ride on a wagon and traveled east a few miles from town, reaching Dog Butte late in the afternoon.

I clambered up the steep side of the butte, my eyes and ears alert for rattlesnakes, [and] somewhat breathless, the altitude of the region being above 2,000 feet. Peering along the horizon, I finally located

what seemed to be buildings near a ravine or "draw," looking like
miniature dollhouses in the slanting rays of the late sun. I had no
compass, but tried to take landmarks until I found what looked like
a dim trail in the right direction.

As I marched along, hoping to arrive before dark, my heart was in
my mouth; for every time a grasshopper whirred I imagined it could
be a rattlesnake, which were fairly numerous but, as I learned, not
aggressive. I had not walked far before I suddenly found myself
surrounded by a herd of wild cattle (the word wild is actually
redundant, all cattle out there being wild). It was tremendously
upsetting, and though I tried to move quietly through them, I was
further disturbed by the sight of a tall man on the far side of the
herd, in a "draw" or gully.[11]

The man proved to be a Texas cowboy who worked for Benoist.
The cowboy took the young man to the main house, where Kindwall
was fed and met a host of other cowboys. He described the foreman,
named Seelye, as "a real cattleman" who had been a bookkeeper in
Chicago and had come west for reasons of health. Kindwall said that
"he [Seelye] slept outdoors on a sturdy box like cot and kept his six-
shooter under his pillow."

Kindwall was hired by Benoist and started riding herd on a small
group of pregnant mares. He rose at 4 A.M. to keep track of them
during the day and soon learned their habits. Often he had a good
deal of time to lie down in the shortgrass while the horses grazed. He
would loop the bridle reins over his arm and "gaze dreamily at the
sky or if possible find a draw where a few cottonwood trees would
whisper with their leaves in the wind. A buzzard[12] might be wheel-
ing in the sky, or a coyote would be patiently loping along on the trail
of a jack rabbit. Grasshoppers whirred, but no longer simulated
rattlesnakes. There were very few of the latter, but occasionally I killed
one by beating it with my 'throw rope' or lariat, which I could coil
into long loops, beyond the snake's striking range."

Kindwall was absorbing the lore and skills of the cowboys that
spring until a summer grass fire destroyed the range, forcing Benoist
to lay off some ranch hands, including Kindwall. He returned to

Minneapolis where his parents were living and undoubtedly shared the stories of his adventures with them.

Later that summer of 1910, Benoist died in a horse accident. Kindwall's mother also passed away that summer, and though it was decided that Kindwall would stay in the city to finish his schooling, his father, bitten by the "bug" of adventure himself, decided to homestead on the Cheyenne River Indian Reservation west of Timber Lake.

For the move west, Kindwall's father, Alfred, rented a railroad boxcar in partnership with another man, a Mr. Gundstrom, who was to follow later with his wife on a passenger train. Alfred bought "an old horse, a spring wagon and a harness for $45 which he loaded in the car with his old kitchen stove ... two chairs, a bed spring and mattress and some lumber for the house-to-be." On the trip Alfred shared the boxcar with his horse.

Alfred Kindwall arrived on the prairie near Isabel, South Dakota,[13] in mid-September 1910 and with some assistance built a 12 × 24–foot shack (288 square feet). Josef, desperately wishing to return west, persuaded his father to let him join him and he arrived on the homestead near Isabel on the last day of October 1910.

That winter, Josef hunted jackrabbits, shot an occasional crane, and trapped muskrats for their hides and extra meat. He helped his father build a 10 × 12–foot sod barn with 2-foot-thick walls. During the construction, Alfred, who was in his late forties, suffered a horrible accident. While standing on a ladder he fell headfirst into a nail keg, cutting a long gash into his head. Fortunately he recovered without any serious complications.

Water was always a problem for most of the homesteaders, and a well soon had to be dug on the Kindwall place. Josef found an anthill at the edge of a draw near the house, noting that "it was said that ants always found water." The Kindwalls obtained a hand posthole auger and started the laborious task of boring through 20 feet of hardpan soil before reaching a small trickle of water. They installed a second hand pump and, as Josef wrote, "felt lucky."

Because of all the roaming range cattle the next order of business was a fence around their quarter section. "It happened," he wrote, "that the government was getting rid of miles of fence on a strip to the south of us and was selling it very cheap. We got some of it and spent days, I guess weeks, of painful work, pulling staples, coiling wire, and lifting out fence posts—most of them rather slender branches of ash or cottonwood. Putting up the fence was another long job, and winter was upon us before we finished."[14]

As the following spring progressed into summer, their well water gradually became undrinkable and unusable for any purpose, and they were forced to dig deeper by hand with a pick and a shovel, using a bucket at the end of a rope to hoist the dirt up and out of the hole. After a great deal of hard labor they were able to excavate a hole 3 to 4 feet wide and 30 feet deep with about 5 feet of water in it good enough to use. "But," Kindwall wrote, "the water level varied with the season, and we could never be sure; it was constant worry."

Josef, young and always enthusiastic to try new things, read in *The Dakota Farmer* that a steam tractor would give them the edge they needed to succeed in farming and make money. His father decided to take the gamble and tried to purchase one. Unsuccessful in securing a loan, he managed to pick up a one-cylinder, 25-horsepower International Harvester, which a salesman assured them could pull six plows. It turned out to be a primitive, clumsy, heavy piece of equipment that never pulled its quota of six plows and often only managed two when the sod was especially dry and hard.

The tractor venture was a fiasco. The machinery company repossessed it and saddled the Kindwalls with a large debt. That summer they managed to raise some flax, but as Kindwall grimly summed up their efforts, "the wind blew away much after it was cut, and the yield was small, price low." They were now in their third summer on the homestead and it was plain they would have to pull out. His father had "proved up" on the homestead and had hoped to sell it, but that too failed. "We were broke," Josef wrote.

They had endured three years of privation, taking baths only in the summer when it rained, fighting bedbug infestations in their shack, suffering through blazing summer heat, and enduring winters with deep windpacked snowdrifts and temperatures of −48°. Yet, Josef was reluctant to leave. "It is," he would write years later, "contrast that gives life to pictures and zest to living."

In the last summer on the place, Josef's horse kicked Alfred, breaking the tibia in his right leg, which he then fell on, creating a compound fracture. Fortunate in being able to find the sole local doctor in that country and bringing him to the shack, Josef pulled his father's leg one way while the doctor pulled it the other, and the two of them managed to set the leg bone. Recuperation was a painful ordeal for Alfred, leaving him with a limp and a cane for the remainder of his life.

That October 1913, Josef Kindwall left the homestead on horseback and headed for his uncle's home in Iowa, 530 miles to the southeast. When he reached the old Cheyenne River Sioux Agency on the Missouri River, he tarried briefly to recall his adventures, realizing that the river was to be "a rubicon," ending a life of hardship and adventure he knew he would miss.

"Never again," he later wrote, would he know "the wide horizons, the sweep of the rolling plains, adventure, and the 'wilderness'" for which he had "hankered so long. Three years of much hardship and anxiety, but also of hope, of youthful exuberance, of the stuff that dreams are made of." He was eighteen years old, and would go on to become a successful physician and live a long, productive life in the Midwest.

When Hamlin Garland in his later years recalled the ultimate futility of the dryland homestead where he and his parents had struggled, he was less sanguine in his memoirs than the young Kindwall and wrote of it gloomily:

> Another dry year was upon the land and the settlers were deeply
> disheartened. The holiday spirit of … before had entirely vanished.
> In its place was a sullen rebellion against the government and against
> God. The stress of misfortune had not only destroyed hope, it had
> brought out the evil side of many men. … Two of my father's

neighbors had gone insane over the failure of their crops. Several
had slipped away "between two days" to escape their debts.

The trees which my father had planted, the flowers which my
mother had so faithfully watered, had withered in the heat. The
lawn was burned brown. No green thing was in sight, and no shade
offered save that made by the little cabin. On every side stretched
scanty yellowing fields of grain. ....[15]

By 1915 a good many of the early homesteaders on the Fox Ridge
had "proved up," went broke, sold out if they were lucky, or simply
abandoned the country. For the majority of the early homesteaders
on the Fox Ridge farming proved a heroically dismal failure. Garland,
in his later years as a successful writer living comfortably in southern
California, regarded his family's homestead and the entire experience
in the darkest of terms:

> It seems an immeasurable distance from me now and yet it is so
> near that the thought of its passing brings an illogical feeling of loss.
> It meant so much to me at the time; I hated it, and yet, as it was the
> only shelter my mother had, I dared not say so. From it my sister
> was married and in it she died. Flimsy as a pine box, it rested on the
> ridge, an ugly fungus of the plain. It floated for a time like a chip
> on the edge of a silent landswell and then—it sank, as the village of
> Ordway had sunk. Nothing on that inexorable plain is built to last.
> Dozens of other towns as vociferous as ours have found the same
> grave. One can hardly find on the sward the spot which they once
> polluted. This is the genius of our Middle West. Confident, ready,
> boastful, it is for a time only. It is tragic or it is humorous (according
> to the observer) when a people so hopeful and so vigorous dies out
> upon a plain as a river loses itself in the sand.[16]

And yet, regardless of whether they stuck it out or went broke and
left, the majority of homesteaders would later recall that some of the
happiest days of their lives were spent out on their homesteads. It was
a chance, an opportunity, a risk, but most of all it was an experience—an adventure to be recalled and savored in later life.

Kindwall, like many other young homesteaders, retained his exhilarating memories of riding horseback and walking miles to attend a dance or social gathering and along the way experiencing the multitude of sights, sounds, and smells that were pure prairie: the delicate scent of blooming pasque flowers; the trill and chortle of meadowlarks in the early spring; the pungence of crushed sage after a hailstorm; flaming sunsets followed by cool, sweet evenings; and a ride under a vast dome of spiraling stars. Elemental and austere, living under the big sky of the buffalo country could be sublime and unforgettable.

NINETEEN

The Missouri Plateau

Dusk and Western Star, you gather what glittering sunrise scattered far.
—Sappho

THE MISSOURI PLATEAU ECOREGION lies south and west of the Missouri River, stretching west across Dakota into northeastern Wyoming and eastern Montana. It is classic northern plains scenery marked by windswept buttes and long tables that shade into blue and purple as the sun sets. Its sagebrush plains and solitary landforms were made famous by Charles M. Russell and Frederic Remington, who incorporated them as backdrops for many of their dramatic western scenes.

The crevices and pinnacles of the lone buttes were once favored nesting sites for golden eagles, falcons, prairie hawks, and ravens. Below the buttes and escarpments, shortgrass plains roll out in all directions, breaking into fissured badlands and rough-cut draws. The atmosphere is usually sharp and clear and dry. In the summer it tastes of dust and sage, while the silence and emptiness hint of the grandeur of infinity.

Over the years I have poked around many of these tables and buttes searching for, among other things, old battlefields, petroglyphs, caves, fossils, rattlesnakes, falcon nests, dinosaur bones, and ripening wild fruit. I have encountered gale-force wind, torrential rain, greasy mud holes, lightning-ignited grass fires, searing heat, and a host of wildlife. When I reflect back on these trips, my spirit soars like a hawk on the wind.

One late-summer trip took me to Ekalaka, Montana, on a hunt for the old Miles City cutoff route. Even with excellent maps I ended up in a ranch yard with a frantic barking dog the first try; in the middle of a dry, desolate alfalfa field the second try; and a locked gate at the bottom of a rough draw the third time. After two more attempts I gave up, frustrated by the intense heat, and the rough, dusty roads. I hit the Ekalaka highway and headed north for Baker, Montana. My destination was the Chalk Butte country of southwestern North Dakota, and I had to move quickly if I was going to get there in the daylight.

I had wanted to poke around White Butte, the highest point in the state, for years, and now was the time to see if I could salvage something out of this daylong trip. White Butte is actually part of a large complex of chalky ridges and hills that cover a good deal of Slope, Hettinger, and Stark Counties. These white hills are composed of thick layers of chalky, white clay that melts into classic badlands topography when it rains.

The butte itself is privately owned, and I have to get permission to climb it from a small, white-haired woman with flushed cheeks and beery breath who demands that I give her $20 for the privilege. What a day, and now I have to deal with a troll. I balk at the price and we compromise with 10. By 6:00 I am finally driving south down a soft, sandy, white section-line trail that takes me within easy walking distance of the foot of White Butte.

The immediate area around the north side of White Butte is hard-packed, white clay as smooth and pleasant to the touch as a hardwood dance floor. Above this surface, at odd intervals pouring out of the clay walls and onto the floor, are streams of sorted river pebbles and cobbles composed mostly of colored feldspars, including pink granite, snowy quartz, petrified wood, and hematite. The pebbles dribble down from the walls and form outwash tongues that look like spilled treasure—the polished mountain detritus of 40 million–year–old Eocene streams. I want to fill my pockets.

I pick up a deer trail freshly marked with coyote scat that winds along a rough gully through creeping ground juniper, chokecherry thickets, and a thin, spindly grove of stunted ash. Higher up, I reach a ridge-line littered with quartzite rubble commemorating another ancient streambed that now caps and preserves the soft white clay that lies beneath it. The ridgeline runs south, and I follow it to another game trail that zigs up to the top of the butte, where I am refreshed by a soft, dry, southerly breeze. I relax in a bed of sedge surrounded by ground juniper and drink in the wide-sweeping landscape.

Barely discernible to the northwest is the small, singular hump shape of Sentinel Butte near the Montana–North Dakota line; to the northeast and closer in lie the two long tables known as East and West Rainy Butte, with the hump of little Baldy in the middle separating them. To the near west lie the Chalky Buttes, a 1.5-mile-long, north-south ridge that parallels the White Butte ridge I'm on. Directly south and below me lie a jumble of bald hills and breaks, with more buttes and tables on the horizon 40 miles in the distance. Directly below me on the north, a steep, sheltered draw yawns at me. It has a remarkably fine, healthy grove of ash. Well protected and difficult to access, it presents an attractive, deeply hidden green oasis in a country that is raw with wind blowouts, hardpans, and bare white-knuckle ridges.

Sitting cross-legged and gazing quietly into the fading deep, blue firmament, I think I can feel the earth spin. Maybe it's the potency of the wind and the long shifting shadows of twilight that bring on this pleasing sense of harmonic convergence.

Riding a roller coaster of wind above me are five Merlin falcons. They sit on the wind for a while, then drop like stone darts, stooping, gliding, veering off to pitch and roll and chase one another. As the moon appears in the southeast, its wide, dusty rose face waking up to watch the sunset, I recognize it as Sappho's "rosey-fingered moon." "Startling is the fecundity of sea, field and memory," she wrote, "which appear to flow from this uncanny moon and fill the nightworld."

The falcons spin out more dazzling aerial acrobatics in the deepening magenta gloam, proving that they own the sky and this evening they are going to play in it. Just after sundown the wind calms and they all disappear into the north.

For obvious reasons my trip to White Butte is special, but there are many other buttes and tables, each unique in its own subtle manner. About 20 miles west of Faith is an elegant, eight-mile-long table known as Fox Ridge, which rises 250 to 300 feet above the surrounding Hell Creek formation. It is devoid of trees except in the lower draws that support ash.

Fox Ridge was formed during the Paleocene, the first epoch of the Cenozoic, and is composed mostly of dark clay with a narrow crest of pale sands. A thin layer of limestone on top protects its soft clay underbelly from erosion. Within the cracks of the limestone are moss agates made up of translucent pieces of chalcedony flecked with iron and manganese oxide that give it a dark green, mossy shade.

North of Fox Ridge, the Hell Creek formation has been extensively carved into deeply eroded draws and canyons, some of which have thick, white, fossilized tyrannosaurus femurs and hadrosaur skeletons protruding from them. One particularly scenic canyon is fringed with groves of juniper (cedar) that gave it its name, Cedar Canyon. In the fall on the smooth, dark floor of Cedar Canyon are deer-scraped cedars and wildcat tracks hardened in the mud. In the summer, Mountain bluebirds flit through the cedar groves along with small flocks of curious, dun-colored Say's Phoebes, which like to perch on the clay pinnacles.

The Missouri Plateau country has fine herds of pronghorn that glide over grassy ridges as well as herds of mule deer bounding and bouncing over sagging barbed-wire fences. Before the devastating winter of 1996–97, I counted a herd of 100 pronghorns gathered together northeast of Fox Ridge near Signal Butte. During that brutal winter the herd was completely eradicated.

Because of low rainfall and the roughness of the Missouri Plateau, a good deal of the country, particularly along its breaks, remains unscarred by the plowshare. It is here that a prophet might walk or a madman might wander in profound solitude. Out beyond the isolated gravel roads, the horizon line, like linear time, is thin and easily lost when one is down deep in a rugged draw or a badlands maze where odd bits and pieces of the distant past may appear in various stages of dissolution and decay.

A few years back, I took a trip up a typical plateau country creek with the unassuming name of Rabbit. An old gentleman who had spent his entire life in the plateau country of western South Dakota and grew up on the banks of Rabbit Creek acted as my guide. Rabbit Creek empties into the Moreau River not far from a little old store, now defunct but still standing, called Usta. The name is obscure but is said to mean "cripple" in Lakota. A Texan named it after old Ed Lemmon, who walked with a cane all of his adult life because of a horse injury he sustained in his adolescence.

Near the mouth of Rabbit Creek below a high cutbank, Ben Ash, a person of some historical note, had a horse ranch in the late 1890s when it was all still open-range cattle country. Ash was born in 1851 in Indiana and was working as a deputy marshal in Yankton, Dakota Territory, when he hired out as a teamster in 1873 with the Seventh Cavalry and moved with Col. George Armstrong Custer up to Fort Lincoln, south of Bismarck. He served as wagonmaster for Custer's Yellowstone Expedition that same year.

The following summer, 1874, he accompanied Custer's exploratory "vacation" expedition with the Seventh into the Black Hills.[1] After his return, Ash was petitioned by a group of prominent people in Bismarck to return to the Black Hills and authenticate the rumors of gold reported there. Ash knew the Black Hills were on restricted Indian treaty lands and that to go there would mean trespassing. Nonetheless, as an experienced plainsman, he was able to slip out of Fort Lincoln in the dead of a mid-December night. He spent the next few days riding up the ice of the frozen Heart River to avoid detection by both the army and the Indians. Eventually he turned southwest and on Christmas night 1874, reached the Moreau River near the future site of Bixby, South Dakota, and made camp. The following day he reached the high divide between the Moreau and Sulphur Creek and sighted the Black Hills some 60 miles away,[2] blazing a new, and considerably shorter, route than Custer took.

Four days later his party struck Custer's old trail at Bear Butte and made their way up to the vicinity of present-day Hill City, South Dakota, where Ash found twenty miners from Cheyenne working in their shirtsleeves in an unfrozen stream recovering placer gold with a sluice box. He bought $150 worth of placer and made his way back via Gordon's Stockade near present-day Custer, South Dakota, meeting the Gordon party and exiting the Black Hills via the Rapid Creek gap at the present site of Rapid City. He received a warm welcome from the citizenry of Bismarck upon his return, and his route to the Black Hills later became the Bismarck-Deadwood Trail.

In the early 1890s, Ash bought the Quarter Circle W Horse Ranch on the Moreau River at the mouth of Rabbit Creek. It was located about 30 miles downstream on the Moreau River from where he had camped at Bixby that cold December night of 1874. Later, Ash moved his cattle to the ranch and built it into a "big outfit" called the C Cross that took in the ranges from upper Rabbit Creek all the way to present-day Faith, South Dakota, 20 miles to the southeast.

For a while Ash prospered until his operation was hit hard by the severe winter of 1903–4, after which he switched from cattle to sheep. During the winter of 1916–17, one of his sons was thrown from a horse far from the ranch and froze to death. Their grief prompted Ash and his wife to sell out, and he quit the ranch that spring and headed east. The fences and corrals gradually deteriorated, the big frame house he had built was moved away, and the logs of his old headquarters eventually disappeared. Today absolutely nothing remains of the once-spacious and prosperous C Cross Ranch. The only indication of a habitation site is a round depression choked with buckbrush on the edge of Rabbit Creek.

Another interesting life story unfolded about a half dozen miles farther up Rabbit Creek from Ash's place along a particularly beautiful creek bend fringed with great cottonwoods. Near the bend stands a small, white frame house with boarded-up windows. It is riddled with woodpecker holes, and only the addition of a new green metal roof has staved off its inevitable collapse.

The house was built by John Jackson about 1904 of native milled cottonwood. When a nearby homesteader named Earl Jones saw the place, "he fell in love with it," according to his son, Gilbert, declaring that if he could get it, he "would stay here and never move." Jones bought the place from Jackson in 1909 and quit his nearby dugout.

Inside the old house a calendar features a picture of JFK looking saintly and angelic. The year is 1965, the same year Gertrude Jones, Earl's widow, looked at the place for the last time and moved into Faith. Her old cutting board, embellished with a painted cherry on one corner, still hangs on the wall over the sink bowl.

As he shows me "the home place," Gilbert recounts that his mother was from North Dakota and his father from Red Oak, Iowa. The house interior consists of a small kitchen attached to a parlor and a tiny downstairs bedroom. "This is the room I was born in in 1923," he says, peering into the small bedroom. "All of us kids were born here and a lot of the neighbors, too."

The focal point of the parlor is still there: a great potbelly stove adorned with a shiny, tin, filigreed grate. Arranged around it are an old rocking chair and assorted wooden chairs. The parlor is dark and smells of dry rot and mold. Little light manages to leak in through the front window with its heavy shade and plywood covering. It reminds me of a museum; a shrine that Gilbert maintains in memory of his pioneer parents and his upbringing. He loves this place as much as his dad did. His roots are here and they run deep.

A narrow staircase off the kitchen leads to two upstairs bedrooms above the parlor where a total of five children once slept. Gilbert refers to the back bedroom as "the cold room"; the other bedroom over the parlor was heated through a floor vent above the stove. The girls slept in the latter room. It's not hard to imagine what the "cold room" felt like in the depths of a Dakota winter, with thick frost encrusted on the inside of the lone window, piles of quilts on the bed, and a floor with the touch of an icehouse.

Outside it's a typical late October afternoon. The cottonwoods stand stark, leafless, and dignified. In the small front yard an old rusty hand pump still gushes cold, hard water when primed and prodded. East of the house and next to the creek, Gilbert points to the place where his dad's 1920 Overland caught fire when Gilbert tried to start it up to go to a dance. "We all had to push it over the bank and it rolled over and into the creek. It landed on its roof and the creek eventually buried it." Like a lot of plains history, not a vestige of it remains, fodder for archaeologists in the far future when the creek changes course again and decides to dig it out.

As we ford the creek, a big catfish stirs itself from the bottom. We head downstream a short distance to a small grassy flat where four Ree earthlodges once stood. Like the Ben Ash site, there are only hints of shallow depressions. Gilbert claws at the low bank with a three-prong rake, eventually producing a dun-colored dart point. "We found a lot of pottery pieces and arrowheads here when I was a kid," he remarks.

Walking down through the gallery grove of immense, gnarled cotton-woods along Rabbit Creek, I spook two mule deer. After a while I find a pleasant spot in a small grove of ash trees and sit in the golden leaves. It is the spot, Gilbert later recalls, that the Jones family used as a picnic ground.

In an hour it will be dark. The moon will be full and bright and the trees will cast their long, dark shadows into the silvery light. If I stay, I will see deer and horses walking through the cold stillness, along with the spirits I am sure haunt this quiet and peaceful place in the heart of the Missouri Plateau country.

TWENTY

The Buffalo Return

The end is always the beginning.

FOUR YEARS AFTER LEWIS AND CLARK returned to St. Louis, the naturalist John Bradbury traveled up the Missouri via keelboat with a group of traders. He was intent on describing life in the upper Missouri country, and his journal is replete with remarkable descriptions of the immense buffalo herds he frequently encountered along the river. None, perhaps, is more descriptive than the following:

> We landed, ascended the bank, and entered a small skirting of trees and shrubs, that separated the river from an extensive plain. On gaining a view of it, such a scene opened to us as will fall to the lot of few travelers to witness. This plain was literally covered with buffaloes as far as we could see, and we soon discovered that it consisted in part of females. The males were fighting in every direction, with a fury which I have never seen paralleled, each having singled out his antagonist. We judged that the number must have amounted to some thousands, and that there were many hundred of these battles going on at the same time, ... I shall only observe farther, that the noise occasioned by the trampling and bellowing was far beyond description. In the evening, before we encamped, another immense herd made its appearance, running along the bluffs at full speed, and although at least a mile from us, we could distinctly hear the sound of their feet, which resembled distant thunder.[1]

How many animals were spread out over that plain nearly two centuries ago Bradbury could not fathom. He was constantly astonished by their numbers and behavior. Up until recently, the prehistoric numbers of bison on the Great Plains were pretty much subjective speculation. The naturalist Ernest Thompson Seton, writing in the early twentieth century, estimated prehistoric herd size for the entire Great Plains ecoregion at 60 million. More recent studies that have examined the environmental limitation factors of the northern plains, however, indicate that the Great Plains could have supported no more than about 30 million bison.

A range of statistical studies indicate that it would have taken about 25 acres of grassland to support one bison per year, which would be a density of twenty-six bison per square mile. Allowing for the competition of other grazers such as elk and horses in the historical period, this number could be 27 to 30 million buffalo for the entire Great Plains province.[2]

Bison herd numbers, of course, were never static and fluctuated yearly depending on the season and the severity of summer droughts and winter blizzards. Droughts that might last for a few years or extend for as many as fifteen could be particularly devastating. During a severe, long-term drought, 70 to 90 percent of the native vegetation could die back, starving the herds.

Buffalo also had wolf packs to contend with. It has been estimated that gray or buffalo wolf numbers approached a population of nearly 1.5 million. Early eyewitness accounts by plains travelers often remarked on the size of the wolf packs that followed herds, noting groups of animals in the hundreds.[3]

And then there was the ultimate predator—man, who over the two decades that followed the Civil War, nearly managed to perform what contemporary observers of the time assumed unthinkable: the extinction of all the bison on the North American continent.

Many years ago a professional acquaintance told me an intriguing story about a pronghorn hunting trip he took in a remote area of Butte County, South Dakota. He was out walking some rough country when he stumbled across an amazing tableau. Before him, etched into a shallow cutbank, was the complete outline of a bleached buffalo skeleton pressed into the dark Pierre shale. Lodged inside the ribcage area was a piece of splattered lead. For years the story and the image haunted me.

In the late 1980s, I made it a point to visit the rancher who owned the land to verify the story and see the tableau for myself. Kenneth Hanify grew up on the family homestead and lived in Butte County all of his adult life. Old and infirm at the time I met him, he confirmed the story, and because of my interest produced a blacksmithed picket pin he had found nearby of the type used by the old buffalo hunters to picket their horse while they made "a stand." Hanify found it about a quarter of a mile from the bison-bones tableau when his shod horse kicked it one afternoon.

On a late spring morning he drove me out to the site to see if any relics remained. It was a rough, twenty-minute bounce over a roadless, badlands landscape. To my disappointment nothing remained at the site except for a handful of small splintered bone fragments and a bison tooth. "This was it," he said. "When I first came out here there was a bison-horn sheath lying on this little sodded outcrop, but it was all the way John said it was twenty years ago."

The morning was unusually windless and calm, with the sun high and bright in the sky. We both leaned up against the side of his battered pickup bed and looked north without speaking. Stretched out all around us was a vast, broken country of sagebrush flats and shallow draws with a handful of stunted trees and dark badlands buttes on the far horizon. There were no other signs of life or of the twentieth century.

Given the backdrop, it was easy to conjure up the image of a buffalo hunter making a deadly long-range "stand" from somewhere behind me on one of the low clay hills to the west not far from where his horse was picketed. The landscape was perfect for a good stand.

The hunter would have walked a ways from his picketed horse to the low butte and stuck his forked shooting stick into the soft clay before sitting down and propping his large-bore, heavy rifle barrel in the fork. He would ideally be downwind from the herd. Having determined the range to be 400 or 500 yards, he would have flipped up his fancy windage sight and then opened a box of long shells.

The rifle he carried would have been a monster. The typical buffalo gun was a single-shot with a long, heavy, octagonal barrel chambered for large-bore, long cartridges—44-77, 45-70, 45-120, and 50-90—the first number referring to the caliber size of the barrel and bullet, the second number referring to the weight of gunpowder in grains.

The long-range shots required a heavy slug of lead in the 470- to 550-grain category and 70 to 120 grains of gunpowder to push it. The heat generated by the successive explosions of the large-capacity, self-contained cartridges quickly warmed the barrel of the rifle. And as the heat increased, the barrel expanded inversely, decreasing the accuracy of every succeeding shot. So the optimum gun barrel needed to be as heavy and as long as possible to lower the coefficient of heat expansion before the gun lost all accuracy and had to be cooled.

After everything was prepared, the hunter would have settled himself down, either sitting or prone, behind his rifle sight and started firing shots methodically and as quickly as possible working the periphery of the herd as the animals instinctively closed in for protection. It was imperative to continue shooting them before the wind shifted and they discovered where the danger lurked and ran.

To keep the deadly action going, some of the hunters carried a second buffalo gun for use while the first one was cooling. A good hunter, if he shot well, might kill thirty to fifty buffalo at a stand. As for the buffalo, they would have heard an odd muted bang in the distance that matched a puff of powder smoke, followed by a distinct "wump" as another one fell over.

One of the last wild buffalo hunts of any consequence took place in this vicinity in the summer of 1883, when the remnants of the northern bison herd, some 10,000 animals, broke through the lines of buffalo hunters on the eastern Montana killing field. The herd headed southeast away from the firing line and onto the plains northeast of the Black Hills.

When word got out about the approaching herd, it was mostly miners from Deadwood and hide hunters from Rapid City along with Indians from the Standing Rock and Cheyenne River Reservations who surrounded them. In a couple of weeks they took 9,000

hides. The last 1,000 bison were annihilated in a grand, two-day hunt
staged by several hundred Sioux led by Sitting Bull and joined by a
crowd of white sport hunters.[4] When the hunters finished their work
here and in eastern Montana and southwestern North Dakota that
fall, only a few hundred plains bison remained scattered about in
small bands of five to ten animals huddled in the remote badlands
of eastern Montana.

The hide hunters, however, were oblivious of what they had accomplished and outfitted themselves again in the summer of 1884
for the next season's hunt. In the early fall of 1884, they left Glendive
and Miles City and moved west across the rugged terrain of the "flat-
iron" expecting to find buffalo at any time. After a couple of months,
they reached the foot of the Little Belts in central Montana and knew
the worst. The buffalo were gone. The vast northern plains herd that
had roamed the country from the foot of the northern Rockies east to
the James River, north to the Saskatchewan, and south to the Nebraska
Sand Hills no longer existed.[5]

Two years later in the spring of 1886, William Hornaday, chief taxi-
dermist for the U.S. National Museum in Washington, D.C., realizing that the days of the wild buffalo were numbered, left for eastern
Montana to acquire some bison skins to mount for a national exhibit. He established his base camp on the old buffalo-hunting
grounds along the Big Sheep Mountains[6] and after many weeks of
persistent searching found and shot four bison.

He returned again later that September, employing cowboy guides
to hunt the same area, rumored to harbor a remnant herd. He reported that "day after day the men ranged back and forth across country 'scored by intricate systems of great yawning ravines and hollows,
steep-sided and very deep, and badlands of the worst descriptions.'"

During this fall hunt, Hornaday and his men spent two and a half
weeks before they were finally able to bring down eight animals.
After a total of two months in the field that year they shot twenty-five
animals, the largest being a stub-horned bull that weighed 1,600
pounds. Hornaday was delighted with this great prize bull, noting
that "nearly every adult male we took carried old bullets in his body,

and from this one we took four of various sizes. ... One [bullet]" he reported, "was found sticking fast in one of the lumbar vertebrae."

Hornaday completed his exhibit that winter, receiving such rave reviews from the press that the American Museum of Natural History was immediately prompted to create their own bison display. They outfitted their own hunting party in the fall of 1887, dispatching Dr. D. G. Elliott to the Montana flat-iron. Elliott combed the country for three months and found not a one. The revelation came as a complete shock to everyone—naturalists, hunters, and the public.

Two years later in 1889, Hornaday conducted a survey of free-ranging, unprotected bison in the United States. He counted 85, with another 200 surviving under very lax federal protection in Yellowstone National Park, 550 in the vicinity of Great Slave Lake, Canada, and 256 scattered about in zoos and private herds.[7]

The unregulated, unrelenting slaughter of bison that had been carried on for a decade on the northern plains had nearly consigned a masterpiece of evolution, exquisitely adapted to its environment, to the dustbin of natural history. During this period, plains ecologist and historian Daniel Licht noted in his book, *Ecology and Economics of the Great Plains*,

> Many bison were killed for profit, and perhaps a few to eliminate
> the food source of the Native Americans, but the journals of early
> explorers provide insights into other possible reasons. John James
> Audubon noted in his observations that most of the men were
> "too lazy ... to cut out even the tongues," and William Hornaday
> suggested a moral sickness when he wrote, "It would be an
> interesting psychological study to determine the exact workings
> of the mind of a man who is capable of deliberately slaying a noble
> animal, in the full knowledge that he can make no earthly use of it,
> but must leave its magnificent skin, its beautiful head, and several
> hundred pounds of fine flesh to the miserable coyotes and the
> destroying elements. If such an act is not deliberate murder, in
> heaven's name, what is it?" Barsh pointed out that as many as five
> dead bison were abandoned on the plains for each one shipped
> back east.[8]

The wanton waste and destruction of bison on the Great Plains stand as an ugly, unprecedented hallmark of human disrespect, greed, and ignorance. Only the Romans during the reign of Emperor Tiberius and his sons, who built the Coliseum to kill animals as sport (as well as men), approach anything comparable to this kind of wanton, mass destruction of native animal life.

The end of the great wild bison herds, countless beyond number, was writ here in the relic tableau once etched in the dark shale before me, and now that too was only a faded memory, dissolved back into the earth.

During the late 1980s I had occasion to wander extensively over the old buffalo country north of the Belle Fourche River and south of the Slim Buttes. I watched jackrabbits make their broken runs and admired golden eagles perched on shale outcrops. I delighted in the sight of pronghorn herds and the graceful bounding of mule deer. And of course there were the herds of sheep and cattle. Yet somehow I felt the country still belonged to the bison. It was still theirs in the earth their blood had enriched.

Then, in the early 1990s, amazingly or miraculously the bison started to return to this country. In 1994, Greg Smeenk and a handful of other ranchers around the Black Hills began putting up miles of new heavy-duty fence and restocked bison on their old ranges. For Smeenk, who grew up in Butte County, it was, as he put it, "the best thing I ever did."[9]

Smeenk and his wife, Sherrie, own and operate Thunder Canyon Bison Ranch just south of Deer's Ears Butte. On a morning in late May near the end of the twentieth century and the beginning of a new millennium, we watched and admired his large, handsome bison herd as they moved and grazed in their instinctual way as one gregarious group, en masse, over the grassland. It revived my memories of a variety of encounters with bison over the past twenty years and I blurted out to Greg, "They're not like cows at all, not for a minute. They move differently, act differently, think differently, graze differently." Greg nodded and added, "They also leave the prairie in better shape than the cows did. I just like coming out here and watching them. I could come out here and watch them every day."

In fact, bison are more efficient grazers than domestic cattle, which is to say their rumens convert more grass to protein.[10] They require about 30 pounds of forage per day whereas beef need 35 to 38 pounds. And when bison graze, they often do so together, maintaining a compact herd formation and grazing everything before moving on. When not grazing, bison lie down and "don't walk off grass," metabolically conserving energy, unlike cattle who tend to walk continually. This grazing rhythm creates a natural rotational pattern that allows grasses to recover faster.

Having evolved on the arid plains, bison are able to travel much farther than cattle to a water source and can go for longer periods without drinking. This enables them to graze the highlands. In the winter with a little snowcover, they can graze for a few days without coming to water.

The popular shorthorn breeds of cattle that replaced the bison on the northern plains, notably red and black Angus, Shorthorns, and Herefords, are very different kinds of bovines. As their names imply, they evolved in the wet, temperate climate of the British Isles. Bred since the early nineteenth century to be docile and fattened quickly on corn, they tend to be overweight, sluggish, slow-witted creatures. Having evolved soft, fleshy bodies grazing lush grasses and forbs in a damp climate, they still retain an instinctual tendency to bunch up near water, along river bottoms and stream banks, where they are most likely to find shade and the green, succulent vegetation they crave.[11] This habit of standing in and bunching up near water on the arid plains for long periods in the dry season denudes ecologically fragile ponds and riparian areas of vegetation, notably tree saplings, littoral zone plants, and shrubs, all of which stabilize a bank. Destabilization affects a bank's ability to hold soil and slow the flow of water, which in turn affects the stream's water quality, and thereby the birds, fish, and a wide host of invertebrates that live near and in it. All this results in a continually degrading grassland ecosystem.

Standing outside of Greg's pickup, I was exhilarated to be in their midst again: a large, wild herd of bison in its natural habitat moving in an age-old instinctual rhythm with the grassland, the birds, and the morning breeze. It felt right and true and enormously satisfying.

The yearlings stopped and lingered, sniffing the air and staring at me curiously before moving on at their own pace, yet always in sync with the herd flow. The big bulls walked purposefully in the rear behind the cow/calf pairs in the lead. Each animal was an individual marked by its own unique coloring and shading of red to black to gray. Yet their power was unmistakably as one, as a herd. It was all seamlessly bound together, not just ecologically but spiritually: The sky, the sunlight, the grass, the sage, and the bison fully completed the harmonic expression of a life force that animates the northern plains. It was apparent that this herd of free-roaming bison was a vital, healing presence to a tired, exhausted land.

American Indians who know bison claim that they have a power about them that the old shamans could share. Perhaps. Twenty-five years ago I sat downwind from a bachelor herd of four old bulls one summer afternoon in Wind Cave National Park. While they ruminated in a shallow draw, I sat cross-legged some 30 feet away to observe them. We were comfortable together through the late afternoon when suddenly one of the great bulls raised himself to stand, and for an instant I saw a shaman standing in buckskin wearing a great buffalo hat. I blinked in astonishment and disbelief at the buffalo staring at me.

After spending an hour with the herd, Smeenk and I drove up to Deer's Ears Butte and climbed up to the saddle that separates the "ears." I looked north to the Slim Buttes. At this point I stood midway between the site of the old relic bison tableau to the southwest and the south end of the Slim Buttes to the northeast where the Rev. Riggs and Co-kan-tan-ka gazed out over the buffalo country that cold winter day of 1881. It had been nearly 120 years since that last hunt, and I decided to travel that afternoon to the Slim Buttes and retrace Riggs's final visit there near the end of his life.

The main part of the Slim Buttes consists of a long table of white rock cloaked in pine that rises a few hundred feet above the surrounding plains. This table stretches for about 30 miles in a north-south direction. Edges of the long escarpment terminate in a variety of small handsome buttes, pinnacles, carved fingers, and vertexes. Thanks to their rugged remoteness in the heart of the Missouri Plateau, the Slim Buttes still harbor a great deal of wildlife, solitude, and peace.

I drove north up to Divide Pass and then turned off the highway and followed a rough, deeply rutted trail southeast down the spine of the table. From the crests on top the views from the pine forests to the south and west were wide and tranquil.

I wandered deeper in, up and around the heads of rugged canyons, until late in the afternoon when I felt the need to stop and find my own spot to rest and reflect. I turned off the trail and followed my instincts down a grassy track that led to a small pine-sheltered spot beyond which a dramatic panorama of plains and buttes lay under a tapestry of clouds, light, and shadow. It corresponded well both by sight and by feeling to the description Riggs and his son, Theodore, gave on his last visit by car to the south end of the Slim Buttes.

Near the edge of the pines I found a campfire ring, neither recent nor old. The fire ring had been neatly filled in with jagged native stones the size of my fist. On top of the stones lay a couple of dried sprigs of sage. It appeared that someone had built a small fire of pine, burned sage, and prayed. Gazing out across the vastness of a golden afternoon I remembered Co-kan-tan-ka's words: "I have been crying and praying, for I shall never again see this country as I have seen it before."

Northwest, some 20 miles beyond the Slim Buttes, I recalled an archaeological site located near the foot of the "Jumpoff" country, which is a high ridge that forms the headwaters divide for the Grand and Moreau Rivers to the east and the Little Missouri to the west. Recently excavated, the site was dated as at least 500 years old and was an area where bison had been herded into a small natural enclosure and killed.

Adjacent to the kill site, a complete circle of bison skulls was unearthed with the horn cores touching. It resembled the kind of power
circle the old Mandans built to "call the buffalo" and is unique in the
fact that nothing like it, to my knowledge, has ever been unearthed
on the northern plains. Its discovery also roughly coincided with the
reintroduction of bison in this part of the Missouri Plateau country.

Some American Indians believe that the sign of their redemption
will be the return of bison and elk to the old buffalo country of the
northern plains. It's a good start, but it will take more than that. It
will take a conscious and determined change of spirit and heart in
how we share the earth with all its creatures and an understanding
and appreciation for the healing power and beauty of natural biodiverse ecosystems.

The old order will never be again, but the reintroduction of bison
to the northern plains may be an indication that the healing has
begun. And perhaps all the old prayers calling back the buffalo are
finally being answered.

> *They say a herd of buffalo is coming;*
> *It is here now!*
> *Their blessing will come to us.*
> *It is with us now!*[12]

When I spoke the words aloud to the earth, it seemed an old sense
of peace and well-being settled into the land. And I knew it was good.

Notes

Chapter 1

1. The Woodrow Vore family owned the property where the site is located from 1888 to 1989. At that time the family donated the site to the University of Wyoming with the stipulation that it be developed for the purpose of scientific research, education, and economic development.

The Vore site, like so many archaeological discoveries, was uncovered by accident in 1970 when Wyoming highway engineers took core samples out of it in anticipation of possibly running Interstate 90 over it. Four feet down through overlying stratified sediments they discovered a plethora of bone chips, beads, projectile points, and stone tools.

Principal investigator Dr. Chuck Reher, then an archaeology graduate student at the University of Wyoming, began the research that led to what he now believes is one of the most significant and well-preserved bison jump sites in North America.

In the fall of 1991 a group of citizens from the region who were interested in the project formed the Vore Buffalo Jump Foundation, based in Sundance, Wyoming, with the long-range goal of developing and constructing an interpretive museum and research laboratory on the site. The jump site is now marked and easily accessible from the interstate service road (old U.S. Highway 14). It lies between the old highway and the interstate about 6 miles west of Beulah, Wyoming.

2. The last layer holds metal arrow points, clearly ushering in the historic period.

Chapter 2

1. W. H. Hamilton, *Dakota*. p. 16. Hamilton further stated that "mud would roll up until it began to rub the sides of the wagon bed, and when all four wheels got to rubbing, the team couldn't pull it, even if it was downhill." (pp. 66–67).

2. However, though the crust may harden and appear solid, it often belies a slick surface just underneath it. This "mud" contains bentonite, used in a variety of industrial and household products.

3. Good examples still remain of a couple of the largest sand dunes that were petrified over the ensuing eons. Thunder Butte, in northwestern Ziebach County, South Dakota, is perhaps the most spectacular. Another is Rattlesnake Butte, about 30 miles south of Thunder Butte.

4. One of the finest examples of an oyster (*Inoceramus*) shell concretion lies at the top of Dog Butte a few miles east of Timber Lake, South Dakota. *Inoceramus* were bivalve mollusks, including giant species with shells 3 feet wide.

5. Edward O. Wilson, *The Diversity of Life*, p. 27.

Chapter 3

1. The form of this mammalian ancestral dinosaur still exists in the kangaroos and wallabies of Australia. These marsupials are interesting examples of the mammalian link to the reptiles of the Cretaceous.

2. Ludlow sandstone became a perfect medium for prehistoric Indian carvers who left fine examples of carved petroglyphs on the smooth walls. The best cave, known as Ludlow, is a natural declivity in the sandstone on the southeast side of the North Cave Hills. It was first documented by the Custer expedition, who passed through here in 1874. Named in honor of Custer's geologist, William Ludlow, it was a treasure trove of American Indian artifacts left by generations of vision seekers.

Across the ravine from Ludlow Cave and deeply etched into the soft sandstone is one of the finest carvings of a bison I have ever seen in stone. It features a deeply incised bas-relief of a horned bison and looks remarkably like the bison cave paintings in southern France. This petroglyph has a smaller bison carved inside the larger one. Undoubtedly this was once a powerful place for buffalo magic.

3. This formation takes its name from the Tongue River, which rises in the northern Bighorns before turning north to flow into the Yellowstone in eastern Montana. The Crow Indians named it after a rock formation on a nearby crest of limestone in the Bighorns that resembles a long, white tongue. The "tongue" is on the eastern crest of the Bighorns west of Dayton, Wyoming, and is visible from U.S. Highway 14.

4. North Dakota geologists recognize five Paleocene sedimentary formations that are visible in the southwestern part of the state. All are characterized by silt, clay, and sand interspersed with thin lignite lenses. These formations are classified, oldest to youngest, as the Ludlow, Cannonball, and Slope (undifferentiated); the Ludlow and Slope are composed of delta and river sediments and the Cannonball is composed of tidal flat, estuary, shore, and offshore marine sediments. They also identify two later Paleocene formations made up of the same materials as the Bullion Creek and the Sentinel Butte.

In eastern Montana the Paleocene is composed of the Fort Union formation and broken down as "members," classified from oldest to youngest as the Tulloch, made up of thinly bedded sandstone and mudstone; the soft Lebo shale, which erodes into vast plains; and the Tongue River, with a thick bed of sandstone that takes the form of cliffs and rims. All members contain seams of lignite.

In South Dakota the Fort Union group, from oldest to youngest, is classified as the Ludlow and Tongue River formations.

5. North Dakota geologists describe another deposition at these buttes, recognizing an Eocene deposit they classify as the Golden Valley formation, consisting of brightly colored, yellowish clay and sand layers deposited by lakes and river sediment, and then the Oligocene White River group on top. Curiously, the North Dakota "chalk" buttes (Oligocene formations) lack the ponderosa groves common in the Montana and South Dakota formations.

Chapter 4

1. In 1997, Maureen Raymo, a geochemist, theorized that the uplifting and subsequent chemical and mechanical weathering of such massive mountain ranges as the Himalayas over eons of time created global cooling. She believes that rising mountain ranges and the chemical processes inherent in weathering acted as a huge sponge to absorb great amounts of carbon dioxide, which in turn created a reverse of the greenhouse effect (lowering the ambient climatic temperature of the earth). Taking into consideration the obvious climatic effects of mountain building on wind direction, orographic uplift, and the resultant moisture-squeezing in the form of snow at high elevations makes Raymo's theory on the Ice Age and global cooling over the last 40 million years plausible.

The standard theory for global cooling and the Ice Age is based on the work of Yugoslavian mathematician Milutin Milandovic, who proposed that the irregularities in the earth's movement and their influence on the amount of solar radiation received by the earth accounted for glaciation and inter-glacial stages of the Pleistocene.

2. During the 2 million years of the Ice Age, there were four major ice advances: the Nebraskan, Kansan, Illinoian, and Wisconsin. New evidence (most notably the many different lake levels of glacial Lake Missoula) suggests that there were numerous ice advances and retreats during this period.

3. A magnificent mural in the Smithsonian Museum of Natural History depicts this Ice Age migration.

4. Most of the information on bison evolution is taken from Valerius Geist's excellent book on the subject, *Buffalo Nation: History and Legend of the North American Bison.*

Chapter 5

1. In fact, Toussaint Charbonneau was probably still living there when Catlin visited it. Overshadowed in history by his famous wife, Charbonneau was an amazing character in his own right who had a long and interesting life on the northern plains.

History first finds him spending the winter of 1793–94 in Canada on the Assiniboine River at Pine Fort trading house. The following year, at the age of about thirty-six, he moved south to live and trade with Hidatsas on the Knife River where he acquired a Shoshone wife, probably a captive. He soon adopted Hidatsa ways and language and was taken in by the tribe where he honed his talents as a trader, trapper, and interpreter.

In the early 1800s he won a captive Shoshone teenage girl named Sakakawea (Sakajawea) in a wager and left with her and Lewis and Clark for the Pacific and a place in history. After the Corps of Discovery returned to St. Louis, at the behest of Capt. William Clark, Charbonneau bought a farm in Missouri and moved his family there. But the northern plains called him back, and in 1811 he, Sakakawea, and his children returned to the newly established Fort Manuel, named after Manuel Lisa on the upper Missouri and located just above present-day Kenel, South Dakota. Most historians believe that it was here in December 1812 that Sakakawea succumbed to a "putrid fever" and died. She left two children who would be raised by Indian Agent

William Clark on his estate outside of St. Louis. Fort Manuel was burned that winter, probably by Indian allies of the British, in conjunction with the War of 1812.

Charbonneau moved back in with the Hidatsas on the Knife River and went to work as a trader for the American Fur Company (Pierre Chouteau et al.) and later for its successor, Pratte & Chouteau. He was still living and working as a trader in March 1838 (aged about eighty) when he hailed a canoe approximately 70 miles upriver from Fort Clark, North Dakota, headed down the Missouri en route to St. Louis. In this encounter he was described by Charles Larpenteur, a clerk at Fort Union, as "an aged white man" in the midst of his Hidatsa friends, "wearing a red flannel shirt and trousers" and looking as "old as Methuselah" (Robertson, p. 260).

The following August, the trader Joshua Pilcher met Charbonneau on the upper Missouri and described him as "tottering under the infirmities of his advanced age" (Robertson, p. 287). Soon thereafter, the remarkable old French-Canadian trader who had managed to survive an astounding eight decades amidst the vicissitudes of trapping, hunting, disease, and war disappeared from the annals of history and the northern plains. What a memoir he might have written.

2. Virginia Bergman Peters, *Women of the Earth Lodges*, p. 24.

3. Ibid., p. 25.

4. This six-day creation format and comparison of buffalo and cattle suggest that these elements are historical-era additions to their creation myth.

5. Ibid., p. 26.

6. Ibid., p. 33.

7. John Bradbury, *Travels in the Interior of North America*, p. 141.

8. Peters, p. 38.

9. Ibid., p. 54.

10. Ibid., pp. 141–142.

Chapter 6

1. The original Ree were probably a branch split off from the Skiri (Wolf) Pawnee who in very early times lived in the Republican River country of present-day northern Kansas and southern Nebraska. In the 1870s, Pawnee scout Luther North found the ruins of a large Pawnee village near Columbus, Nebraska. He recalled standing in the center of an outline that had once

been a great ceremonial lodge measuring 70 feet in diameter. Eagle Chief, chief of the Skiri, replied that "the Skiri had lived at that place a long time ago and that the big lodge was probably a general meeting place and was used for all public gatherings, councils and religious ceremonies. He said also that it was while living at that village that the Skiri became separated" (Grinnell, *Two Great Scouts*, p. 235).

In the spring of 1874, while Luther North was waiting for a steamboat in Bismarck, North Dakota, a group of Custer's scouts nearby began talking amongst themselves. North wrote that "they were speaking a language that sounded like Pawnee." North started conversing with them, noting that they were "A-rik-a-ras, speaking the language used by the Skiri band of Pawnees." He added that they could understand him very well, but their dialect differed from that of the Skiri, so that he could not always readily make out what they were saying (Grinnell, *Two Great Scouts*, pp. 239–240).

The historical Skiri, or Skidi, eventually located their villages on the Loup (Wolf) River near its confluence with the Platte in central Nebraska.

2. Population estimates for the prehistoric Ree/Arikara are difficult to determine. Estimates run as high as 30,000 and as low as 5,000. Robertson (p. 158) estimates their combined population at 7,500, and Lehmer at 8,800, both of which seem a bit conservative. I believe they were closer to 10,000 before the smallpox epidemics.

3. Annie Eloise Abel, *Tabeau's Narrative of Loisel's Expedition to the Upper Missouri*, p. 198.

4. Ed Lemmon later wrote in his biography, *Boss Cowman*, that though he considered the Musselshell country of central Montana better cow country, he nonetheless chose to settle his vast cow herds in western Dakota.

5. All the plains village Indians—Mandans, Hidatsas, and Arikaras—relished rancid meat.

6. Douglas Parks, "Arikara," in *Handbook of North American Indians*, ed. Raymond J. DeMallie, *Plains* vol. 13, pt. 1, p. 366.

7. Abel, p. 139.

Chapter 7

1. Hoita, a minor mythological figure also known as Speckled Eagle, had, according to legend, once imprisoned all living things in Dogden Butte. The *Okipa* lodge represented Dogden Butte, which put Hoita in charge of super-

vising this important dance. This is the only time Hoita gained such importance in the Mandan cosmology (Peters, p. 45).

2. R. G. Robertson, *Rotting Face*, p. 104.

3. "North Canoe" refers to a particular style and type of Northwoods
cargo canoe.

4. Nellis M. Crouse, *La Verendrye*, pp. 44–45.

5. Martin Kavanagh, *La Verendrye*, p.100.

6. The decision over who received advanced armaments and technology
in the Indian world was not new to the French and one Verendrye should
have been aware of, for he suffered the consequences of Samuel de Champlain's actions of a century earlier: The French, after maintaining friendly
terms for years with both the Huron and the fierce and powerful Iroquois
League of western New York, supported a Huron attack on the Iroquois near
Lake Champlain in 1609. Thereafter, the implacable Iroquois counted the
French among their enemies, creating untold future misery for their traders
and priests. The Iroquois hunted down and all but exterminated their hereditary enemies, the Huron and their allies.

7. Kavanagh, p. 126. See also Bernard DeVoto, *The Course of Empire*, p. 205.

8. Kavanagh, p. 140.

9. Ibid., p. 142.

10. Ibid., p. 144.

11. "Stoneys" is a nickname derived from their habit of dropping hot
stones into a buffalo paunch of stew to boil it.

12. G. Herbert Smith, *The Explorations of the La Verendryes in the Northern
Plains, 1738–43*, p. 50.

13. What exactly constituted a "league" is in doubt. DeVoto believes it
was 2.5 miles, Crouse 2.42 miles, and Hubert and Kavanagh 3 miles. I use
DeVoto's 2.5 measurement.

14. Kavanagh refers to a hill called the "Calf Head" (*Tête la boeuf*), which
he places 1 mile south of Darlingford, Manitoba, as the site of the first
mountain (p. 149). Smith discusses the landmark in some detail, describing Calf Mountain as a "small hill rising slightly above the surrounding
prairie and the site of an Indian mound about ten feet high" (p. 80). He also
suggests other higher, more prominent sites along the Pembina escarpment
as good possibilities for the first mountain, including Medicine (or Signal
Hill) and Pilot Mound. Crouse prefers Star Mound.

15. This interesting reference DeVoto noted in *The Course of Empire* is tantalizingly obscure. He wrote that Verendrye heard there was a mountain that

shone night and day (*"La montagne dont la pierre luit jour et nuit"*) while he was at Lake Nipigon (p. 196).

16. G. Hubert Smith, p. 48.

17. Ibid., p. 63. By today's standards this act must appear ironic, but then everyone's lands and rights in the early eighteenth century were subject to the whim of an all-powerful monarch.

18. *Journals of the La Verendrye Trips to the Mandan Villages on the Missouri River in 1738–39 and to the Foothills of the Rocky Mountains in 1742–43*, translated by Douglas Brymner, from a Report on Canadian Archives being an appendix to Report of the Minister of Agriculture, Ottawa, 1889; reprinted by *The Quarterly of the Oregon Historical Society* 26(2) (June 1925): 47.

19. G. Hubert Smith, p. 65.

Chapter 8

1. Elliot Coues, ed., *History of the Expedition Under the Command of Lewis and Clark*, p. 236.

2. Ruben Gold Thwaites, *France in America, 1497–1763*, pp. 57–58.

3. Nellis M. Crouse, *La Verendrye*, p. 162.

4. These Indians were probably Kiowas or Cheyennes, both of whom were living at that time near the Black Hills.

5. The Snakes were probably the Eastern Shoshones or Comanches. They were a particularly fierce and hostile group of mounted nomads who were known to range from the northern plains to the Pueblos of the Rio Grande and deep into Mexico on their raiding forays. They were "the lords of the plains" and by the middle of the eighteenth century blocked all traffic across them.

6. Anne H. Blegen, *The Verendrye Explorations*, p. 53.

7. Most of the Horse Indians were probably Plains Apaches, once numerous along with the Kiowa in the area of the Black Hills. The Plains Apaches, Kiowas, and Kiowa-Apaches, being closest to the Spanish settlements in the south, would have obtained horses before the northern tribes. The Comanches would drive them all from the Black Hills and usher in an era of terror across the Great Plains.

8. Noted plains historian George Hyde believes these people were the Chaui Pawnee. They may have been on their winter bison hunt in the area south of the Black Hills. Their main summer villages were to the southeast in the vicinity of the Platte River.

The Pawnee were composed of four large allied groups that occupied separate villages in prehistoric times along the Platte and Republican Rivers. They were the Chaui or Chawi (Grand Pawnees), the Kitkahahki (Republican Pawnees), and the Pitahawirata (Tappage Pawnees). These three groups were commonly designated as the South Band Pawnees and comprised the "east villages," namely, east of the Skiri (Panimahas or Wolf Pawnees). The Skiri lived west of the South Bands and hunted the central plains north and west of the Platte. All were superb warriors and would have been mounted and armed with bows and possibly guns. They had summarily defeated a brigade of some twenty mounted Spanish conquistadors who had come to the Platte country to chastise them for allying with the French in 1720.

9. These were probably another group of Pawnee who may have been camped along the North Platte River (Belle Rivière). All these groups would have been far from their main villages and out on their annual fall buffalo hunt. Hence, the Chevalier encountered an unusually large group of people on the western plains at this time of the year.

10. Blegen, p. 55.

11. I believe the mountains they had been marching toward in late November and all of December were either the southern Bighorns or the northern Laramies. Their route would have been west of the Black Hills across the Thunder Basin, which is a high, dry windswept plain often devoid of snow in the winter.

12. I believe the Snake camp was along the North Platte in the vicinity of the northern Laramies, possibly near present Casper, Wyoming.

13. Blegen, p. 57. The river island where the Frenchmen grazed their horses during their retreat from the Snake camp was likely on the North Platte (La Belle Rivière).

14. The "Chokecherry People" are commonly identified as a small village band of Arikara living on the Missouri River.

15. The ease in learning this language (Arikara) suggests it was a related one (Pawnee).

16. The Verendrye lead plate is about the size of a rectangular western belt buckle. Inscribed on it are their names, the date, and a claim on the land for France. The plate was discovered in 1913 on a hill above the mouth of the Bad River. It is housed in the South Dakota State Historical Museum in Pierre.

17. That it took them six weeks (forty-two days) to cover 200 miles is unexplainable. Were they walking again? Even at that pace, it's only an average of 5 miles per day. Perhaps the spring weather was wet and snowy, making

the earth a gumbo quagmire and the flooded rivers too treacherous to ford. This would have created delays and miserable travel conditions, but the Chevalier made no mention of it or any other explanation for why it took them so long to reach the Mandans.

18. The search for an overland/river route across North America beguiled English and French traders and explorers for well over two centuries. The Chevalier would later turn his attention to the Saskatchewan River, but never follow it up to the northern Rockies. Lewis and Clark finally blazed a route in 1805 over the mountains, twelve years after Alexander Mackenzie followed a tortuous Canadian route using the Fraser River. Neither course proved even remotely feasible as a trade route to the Pacific.

Chapter 9

1. John K. Townsend, *Journey Across the Rocky Mountains to the Columbia River*, vol. 21, p. 161.

2. J. R. Mead, *Hunting and Trading on the Great Plains, 1859–1875*, p. 57.

3. Annie Heloise Abel, *Tabeau's Narrative of Loisel's Expedition to the Upper Missouri*, pp. 195–196.

4. Andrew C. Isenberg, *The Destruction of the Bison*, p. 38.

5. The Cheyenne occupation of the Missouri River trench was relatively brief. Bits and pieces of evidence suggest they lived in earthlodge villages along the river stretching from the area around present Mobridge, South Dakota, north to Fort Yates, North Dakota. The time of this occupation was probably the late seventeenth and early eighteenth centuries. Interestingly, an old Milwaukee Road railroad map printed about 1900 names a long ridge about 10 miles west of the Missouri near Kenel, South Dakota, the "Cheyenne Hills."

6. For more information on the seven principles of the Cheyenne see my *Island in the Plains: A Black Hills Natural History*.

7. Abel, pp. 154–155.

8. Isenberg, p. 41.

9. Tom McHugh, *The Time of the Buffalo*, p. 74.

10. The old hunters considered it extremely important that no bison be allowed to escape the surround because it was believed that an escapee would communicate to other animals the tactics Indians used to hunt and kill them.

Chapter 10

1. The present-day James River. *Cansunsun* is a Sioux word meaning "river of the white woods," which according to Peter Carrels referred to the bleached-white dead tree trunks found along the river (p. 65). Carrels believes these trees were killed by prairie fires, but if that were the case, the stumps would have been charred black.

I believe the trees were drowned and the bark simply peeled off a year or two later, revealing the white skeletons. This was the case when the James River flooded for a number of years in a row in the late 1980s and early 1990s. The floodwaters covered the floodplains for months and virtually drowned all the big groves of trees, which later peeled and exposed their bleached trunks. The Rev. Stephen Riggs, who crossed the James in 1840, was told by his Dakota guides that the river was called the Tituhu Oju (Full of Oaks). The name of this stream seems relative to whom you were with and where. (*South Dakota Historical Collections*, vol. 13, p. 335.)

In 1794, Jean-Baptiste Truteau, a French trader, named the Cansunsun "Rivière aux Jacques." The name was later anglicized to "James River." An early Dakota Territory legislature tried to rename it "Dakota River," but it never stuck and the name "James" was made official in 1907 (Carrels, p. 65).

The James is the longest tributary of the Missouri as well as the slowest and most crooked, taking 700 miles to run 300 miles as the crow flies to the big muddy. A large oak grove on the river southeast of Aberdeen, South Dakota, which the Sioux called Otuuhu-oju (place where the oaks spring up) was the site of their big trade fair and a meeting place for thousands of Sioux in the late eighteenth and early nineteenth centuries. It is likely that plans for conquest of the Missouri and beyond were laid here.

2. George Hyde, *Red Cloud's Folk*, pp. 15–16.

3. Royal B. Hassrick, *The Sioux*, p. 65.

4. Ibid., p. 71.

5. Andrew Isenburg, *The Destruction of the Bison*, p. 79.

6. *Hunkpapa* translates as "Those Who Camp at the Entrance," *Itazipcola* as "No Bow" or "Sans Arc" in French, *Oohenumpa* as "Two Boilings" or "Two Kettles," *Sihasapa* as "Blackfoot," and *Hohwoju* or *Mnikoju* as "Plants by the Water." Of the southern Tetons, *Sicangu* translates as "Burnt Thighs" or "Brûlés" in French, and *Oglala* as "Scatter One's Own."

7. Isenburg, p. 70.

8. Annie Heloise Abel, *Tabeau's Narrative of Loisel's Expedition to the Upper Missouri*, pp. 104–105.

9. Effie Florence Putney, *In the South Dakota Country*, p. 23.

10. Isenburg, p. 42.

11. This important river ford was later called The Sioux Passage or Three Rivers of the Sioux. It now lies submerged under the waters of Lake Francis Case backed up by the Fort Randall Dam.

12. According to Bernard DeVoto, "in the sign language a gesture which pantomimed decapitation meant 'Sioux'" (*The Course of Empire*, p. 205). There is some debate over when and which group carried out this attack. Historical anecdotal evidence clearly points to a Sioux attack. In 1937, George Hyde wrote that as late as 1760, "below the Great Bend, on the east bank near the mouth of Crow Creek, [there] was a very large and heavily fortified village, a kind of southern outpost city" (*Red Cloud's Folk*, p. 16). He added that this "strong Arikara village on the east bank below the Great Bend was destroyed by these Minnesota Sioux" (p. 19).

South Dakota state historian Doane Robinson wrote in 1948: "Although the [Crow Creek] site has not [yet] been excavated scientifically, an early Arikara culture is suspected." He further noted that "among local people [i.e., the Crow Creek Sioux] it is referred to as 'the last battle-ground of the Sioux and the Rees'" (Bice and LaCroix Interviews). "Historic Sites in the Fort Randall Area," *South Dakota Historical Collections*, vol. 24, p. 549.

See also Royal B. Hassrick's *The Sioux* (p. 66) for motives and acts of Sioux hostility/warfare against the Arikara.

When the Crow Creek site was excavated in 1978, skeletal remains were discovered eroding from a cutback overlooking the Missouri. The actual number of individuals slaughtered here, based on the remains, was 486. The preponderance of the skulls were adult, suggesting the young women and children were taken as prisoners (slaves).

One of the excavators working on the site, Larry Zimmerman, later hypothesized that this massacre was carried out in A.D. 1325. He based this date on one carbon-dated fragment of charcoal buried at the site (personal interview with Bob Alex, former director of the Archaeological Research Center for the South Dakota State Historical Society, 1985).

Zimmerman theorized that this attack was carried out by members of the same tribal group or another group of plains village horticulturalists who were starving and intent on seeking food and space. There is absolutely no evidence, anecdotal or otherwise, to support this theory of internecine warfare. To the contrary, Verendrye, who visited the Mandans in 1738, was told that they had long been at peace with the Arikaras and only recently had troubles developed between the two tribal groups. In light of all the specific ethnographic and historical evidence as well as motives, the Sioux, probably the Yanktons, were the most likely perpetrators of this heinous massacre.

13. Cortez invaded the Valley of Mexico in the summer of 1521. Just prior to the invasion, an imported black slave from Cuba had contracted smallpox, and the disease spread like wildfire among the natives, both allies of Cortez and the Aztecs. Estimates of the dead range from 2 to 15 million Indians all across Mexico. With the streets of Tenochtitlán littered with the stench of thousands of rotting bodies, Cortez was able to handily subdue the Aztec capital and plunder the empire.

A century later, European diseases, mainly smallpox, had reduced the native population of Mexico by a staggering 85 percent, from about 10 million to 1.4 million (Robertson, p. 102).

14. Isenburg, pp. 55–56.

15. Ibid., p. 56.

16. R. G. Robertson, *Rotting Face*, p. 126. Waves of smallpox continued to ravage the three Missouri River tribes so that sixty years later, at the end of the 1830s, 17,000 to 20,000 Arikaras, Mandans, and Hidatsas had succumbed to it, a death toll in excess of 85 percent of the combined tribes. The remnants of these three tribes banded together in 1839 into one village for mutual protection and benefit at a place called Fishhook Bend on the Missouri River.

17. Hyde believes these were Saones, but a good case could be made for the Yanktons and/or Brûlé Tetons. Tabeau refers to the Brûlés as a fierce band of southern Tetons who were in control of the Missouri River from Loisel's post on the Missouri at Cedar Island some 30 miles south of present-day Pierre to the Arikara villages on the Grand River. These same Brûlés would push Lewis and Clark to the brink of battle in 1804 at the mouth of the Bad River. Hyde, *Red Cloud's Folk*, p. 13.

18. *South Dakota Historical Collections*, vol. 7, p. 455.

19. Bragging that the Arikaras took "the place of women," Yankton warriors lorded it over their neighbors, pillaging their cornfields and gardens, stealing their horses, and beating their wives and daughters.

Such trade that existed between the Yankton and Arikaras following the debacle of smallpox has been described as "formalized coercion," the Sioux imposing the terms of exchange. Seeking to escape their persecutors, the Arikara survivors moved up to the Grand River. But the move did little to halt their tormentors. Relishing their role as pirates of the plains, the Sioux continued their outrage (Robertson, pp. 187–188).

20. The Good River is now called the Cheyenne, probably a shortened version of "Where the Cheyenne Plant," a reference to the corn and pumpkin plantings they kept for many years at the mouth of Cherry Creek on the Cheyenne River. The French traders referred to the Cheyenne River as the Belle Fourche (Beautiful Fork of the Missouri). This name was later given to the North Fork of the Cheyenne.

21. "Earth Smoke" probably refers to a number of coal seams clustered around the mouth of the White River. These seams periodically smoulder and smoke for months at a time. It may also refer to the fog, which on cold mornings in the spring and fall, often rises up from the warmer shallow water of the river.

Chapter 11

1. Tabeau noted in his narrative "that this nation [Cheyennes] was for a few years established on the Missouri; but, having neither the patience nor the weakness of the Ricaras to endure the insults and the vexations of the Sioux, it had to resort to open war ... they abandoned agriculture and their hearths and became a nomadic people" (Abel, p. 152).

2. Trudeau, a French Canadian trader to the Arikaras during the 1790s, noted that hostilities were going on between the Tetons and the Cheyenne as late as 1795. This is also suggested by a Brûlé Sioux winter count notation. See George Hyde, *Red Cloud's Folk*, p. 24.

3. The basis for this account is an early pioneer story in the *Faith Country Book*.

4. In battles waged by the Cheyenne and Sioux, no one gave orders per se that would have been obeyed. Plains Indians did not practice military discipline. The individual Indian usually fought in his own way, and for this reason Indians were seldom able to best the disciplined American troops.

5. Spook Creek heads in the vicinity of Faith, South Dakota.

6. Another battle arose over the possession of the hot springs in the southern Black Hills. The Sioux sought to take possession of the springs from unwilling Cheyenne, which precipitated a fierce battle in 1869. The Cheyenne were eventually besieged by the Sioux and driven out. The place-name "Battle Mountain" to the east of Hot Springs, South Dakota, survives as testament to this encounter.

Chapter 12

1. The American Fur Company, founded by John Jacob Astor, established its western branch in St. Louis in 1822. So great was this organization's ruthless success over all rival opposition that a mere mention of "the Company" was sufficient to identify it. Pierre Chouteau, Jr., was closely linked with the American Fur Company and eventually purchased its Western Department from Astor when the latter retired in 1834.

2. Fort Pierre was larger than Fort Union, which was built in 1828. The latter post also lacked the refinements of Fort Pierre and, according to Robert Athearn, "suffered by comparison made by passersby." *Forts of the Upper Missouri*, p. 24.

3. Effie Florence Putney, *In the South Dakota Country*, p. 28.

4. Athearn, p. 25.

5. John E. Sunder, *The Fur Trade on the Upper Missouri, 1840–1865*, p. 119.

6. Ibid., p. 134.

7. Ibid., p. 135.

8. As early as 1802, President Jefferson ordered Meriwether Lewis and William Clark to take a measure of cowpox vaccine (which protected against smallpox) with their Corps of Discovery to vaccinate the Indians (Robertson, p. 220). In 1818 the federal government again attempted to vaccinate the Indians of the upper Missouri, directing Col. Henry Atkinson to vaccinate Indians while on his two-year Yellowstone Expedition.

In 1837, Joshua Pilcher, trader and Indian agent to the river Indians, begged William Clark for the funds and personnel to vaccinate the northern Plains Indians against a raging smallpox epidemic. Clark agreed, but what eventually was accomplished was too little and too late.

The intentional infection of Indians with smallpox was the exception, not the norm. The only documented instance of intentional infection of Indians with smallpox that I know of took place during the French and Indian War by the British at Fort Pitt. In the spring of 1763 the fort was under siege by a large group of Delawares. The British in the fort had smallpox and intentionally gave an infected blanket and a handkerchief to the Indians as a gift. By July the Delawares had been decimated by the disease and the fort remained in English hands. That same year, British general Sir Jeffrey Amherst urged Col. Henry Bouquet to determine some way to infect more of France's Indian allies, but they had neither the knowledge nor the expertise to carry out such a sophisticated plan (Robertson, p. 124).

9. Andrew Isenberg, *The Destruction of the Bison*, p. 103.

10. Athearn, p. 31.

11. Ibid.

12. Ibid., p. 43.

13. Ibid., p. 48.

14. *South Dakota Historical Collections*, vol. 1, 1902, p. 290.

15. Ibid., p. 291.

Chapter 13

1. An *engagé* was a legally apprenticed servant bound to a fur company by the advancement of an outfit (personal equipment, including clothing necessary to undertake a trip into the wilderness) and some trade goods.

2. "Sault" is an old French word that means "to jump" and refers to the fact that voyageurs had to jump from rock to rock to portage the falls and cascades in the St. Mary's River, which separates Lake Superior from Lake Huron.

3. Old Fort Dearborn, the site of present-day Chicago, was built at the mouth of the Chicago River at the southwestern end of Lake Michigan in 1803. It was burned during the War of 1812, subsequently rebuilt, and functioned as a defensive fort and a trading post until 1857.

The name *Chicago* is of Indian derivation and may mean "skunk" or "wild onion." It may also simply refer to the pungent smell of the animal and the plant. The site of Chicago was visited by Jacques Marquette, a Jesuit, and Louis Jolliet, an explorer and cartographer, in 1673. At the time, they noted that there was an Indian village nearby, probably Ottawa. Over a century later, in 1779, Jean Baptiste du Sable, a black man from Sainte Dominique (Haiti/Dominican Republic), started the first permanent settlement. He was a Catholic married to an Indian, and was reputed to be a good husbandman, carpenter, cooper, miller, and probably a distiller.

4. Charles Primeau was a native of St. Louis. He joined the powerful American Fur Company in 1831 as a clerk. He worked for "the Company" at Fort Pierre for fifteen years and was described as "the respected head of an Indian family, a dependable interpreter and an experienced robe and fur trader" (Sunder, p. 92). He was no doubt a friend and longtime associate of Dupuis during their many years at Fort Pierre.

5. In 1846, Primeau, Alexander Harvey, and others formed a partnership known as Harvey, Primeau and Company in opposition to "the Company"

to trade with the Tetons and the Montana Blackfeet. Primeau and Harvey maintained two main posts in "opposition" or competition with Pierre Chouteau's American Fur Company. One post was located near the mouth of the Bad River for the Teton trade, and the other at the mouth of the Marias in Montana for the Blackfeet trade. Primeau and Harvey, later in partnership with a man named Clark, maintained a fur trading operation at the mouth of the Bad River until 1860 when the company folded.

6. Most of the specific biographical information on Fred Dupuis is taken from Calvin Dupree's unpublished manuscript about his great-great-grand-father, Fred Dupuis. A copy of this manuscript was loaned to me by Eugenie Burgee of Dupree, South Dakota, a distant descendant.

7. Sections of the old Dupuis pack trail, incised deeply into the native sod over a century ago, are still visible along state Highway 63 south of the Cheyenne River and along the old Sans Arc road west of Fort Pierre, South Dakota.

8. Calvin Dupree manuscript.

9. *Free Press*, East Pierre, Dakota Territory 5(15) (September 1, 1887).

10. Ibid.

11. Walker D. Wyman, *Nothing but Prairie and Sky*, p. 83.

12. Ibid., p. 156.

13. Walter Knight, who started ranching on the Cheyenne River Reserva-tion about 1917, maintained that Fred Dupuis was referred to as a "black man" (personal conversation with his grandson, Deb Knight, October 2001). A historic portrait of Fred taken late in his life clearly shows features associated with African ancestry. The similarities of Fred's life with those of Jean Baptiste du Sable are remarkable (see note 3). Both men were resource-ful and successful "pioneers" in the true sense of the word. The French were notably different from the English in that they easily intermarried and blended in with the natives, often adopting their ways.

Chapter 14

1. Technically, the elder Riggs was not the first to preach to the western Dakota or Tetons. That honor probably belongs to Father DeSmet, who had come upriver by steamboat in the spring of 1839, preaching from the "white man's Book of Heaven" from the hurricane deck of a steamboat at Fort Pierre to throngs of native onlookers who listened from the shore. It was

later said that some were even baptized in the new faith, but DeSmet tarried only briefly, and his impact must have been negligible.

2. These would have been the Santee or Isanti, a large group of eastern Dakota Indians who occupied most of southern Minnesota and were likely the parent group from which the later Lakota and Nakota Indian Nations split off.

3. According to George Hyde in *Red Cloud's Folk* (p. 13), the term *Saones* is a slur of *Tchanyona* and *Tchankute*, meaning "shooters among the trees," and given to them by their bolder Teton kinsman, who split with them in the Minnesota River valley about 1735, preferring to hunt bison on the open plains as opposed to the tree-sheltered river valley. In 1840 Stephen Riggs was told at Fort Pierre that *Saone* or *Sanyona* was a nickname that the Oglalas and Brûlés applied to five Teton tribes: Mnikojus (Minniconjous), Sans Arc (Itazipcolas), Two Kettles (Oohenumpa), Hunkpapas, and Blackfeet (Sihasapa).

4. Peoria Bottoms was flooded by Lake Oahe in the late 1950s.

5. White men traveling alone or in small groups were attractive targets for Indian marauders, who ambushed small groups of unarmed strangers and outsiders on a regular and frequent basis. That year alone (1872), three men who worked variously at Fort Sully and across the river at the Cheyenne River Agency had been bushwhacked and killed (Riggs, *Sunset to Sunset*, pp. 49–50).

6. Ralph was truly a *kicica*, the Lakota word for companion, partner, and friend, and in his excellent autobiography, *Sunset to Sunset*, Riggs devoted an entire chapter to the many valuable equine *kicicas* he knew and worked with.

7. Although *Oahe* sounds Hawaiian, it means "solid ground or footing" in the Lakota language.

8. *Okikse* in Lakota means "gap" or "opening."

9. The place-name Fox Ridge applied to two different landforms. *Fox Ridge* on the Cheyenne River Sioux Reservation referred to the wide divide that separates the Cheyenne and Moreau River drainages. *Fox Ridge*, as referred to in "Creek of Ghosts" and "the Missouri Plateau," is an eight-mile-long table that begins 19 miles west of Faith and lies south and parallel with U.S. Highway 212.

10. Green Grass, situated near the Moreau River, is where the Sacred Pipe, an old and venerated Northern Teton religious relic, is kept. Hyde noted that "the Saones are reported to have had with them an ancient pipe and some sacred objects which seem to have belonged to the original Teton tribe before it quitted its old home on the upper Mississippi" (*Red Cloud's Folk*, p. 12).

This pipe is still extant and under the care of the "Keeper of the Pipe," who lives on the Cheyenne River Indian Reservation in Green Grass, South Dakota. Green Grass frequently serves as the site for the Cheyenne River Sioux Sundance ceremony.

Chapter 15

1. David A. Dary, *The Buffalo Book*, pp. 66–67.

2. "Flat-iron" refers to the triangular shape on the map of the land area between the Yellowstone and Missouri Rivers from their confluence running west to the Musselshell.

3. The account of this hunt was candidly recalled by Thomas Riggs for his niece, Margaret Kellogg Howard, who probably wrote it down in the early 1930s. This version of the hunt first appeared in *South Dakota Historical Collections*, vol. 29 (1958), as part of a chapter in Riggs's memoir, *Sunset to Sunset: A Lifetime with My Brothers, the Dakotas*. Copyright © 1958, 1997 by the South Dakota State Historical Society. All rights reserved. Reprinted with permission.

Riggs, however, penned an earlier account which appeared in the July 4, 1907, issue of *The Independent*, a newspaper published in New York City. This account was later reprinted as "A Buffalo Hunt" in the *South Dakota Historical Collections*, vol. 5.

What follows is taken verbatim from Riggs's account in *Sunset to Sunset*, while most of the additional notes are from Riggs's earlier newspaper account. Together, the two versions offer a unique, detailed narrative of this fascinating hunt.

4. One mixed-blood came along; he and Riggs were the only two people who spoke English.

5. Riggs's knowledge of Lakota thought and his use of Lakota speech and idiom were so flawless that Indians often remarked, "I heard you talking before I entered the tent and thought you were a Dakota."

6. Although Riggs never mentioned the other English speaker by name, it was likely Clarence Ward.

7. This was recalled by the Lakota as the winter of "the big snow," not only in the Missouri River valley country, but over the entire western buffalo country.

8. He covered a distance of about 60 miles in two days and probably followed Dupuis's well-used pack trail.

9. Big Foot, or *Si Tanka* was a nickname. His proper name was Spotted Elk. Big Foot was chief of a Mnikoju band whose main camp was at the mouth of Deep Creek in northeast Pennington County, South Dakota. He was killed at Wounded Knee in December 1890.

10. The "Moreau people" probably included members of the No Bows, Two Kettles, and Blackfeet bands who lived mainly on the northern and eastern parts of the Cheyenne River Sioux Reservation. The entire hunting party finally gathered near the mouth of Bear Creek on the Moreau River. As the crow flies, the distance from Cherry Creek north across the Fox Ridge to the mouth of Bear Creek is about 45 miles.

11. The Slim Buttes lie near the headwaters of the Grand River (to the north) and the Moreau River (to the south). The actual "buttes" are near Reva Gap, although the entire pine-covered table or ridge that makes up the Slim Buttes runs north and southeast for about 40 miles. The Slim Buttes are located in southeast Harding County, South Dakota.

12. The party consisted of sixty hunters, thirty women, and eleven children. In the newspaper account Riggs noted that "Indians from the Custer battlefield of four years before made up a considerable portion of the hunters."

13. In the news account, Riggs stated that "the Indians organized their 'soldier lodge' where all matters of vital interest were presented and considered. It is by the 'soldier lodge' that runners are sent from time to time to learn and report where game may be found; in the 'soldier lodge' all authority for the hunt rests and by it, the officers of the hunt are commissioned. In this lodge there is much feasting and smoking of the pipe—this or that household being designated as the provider for the next day."

14. In his newspaper account, Riggs detailed the instructions: "It was thought best not to move camp the next day, but to send out scouts in the morning. The two young men selected for this service were to leave camp before daylight and were carefully instructed as to their route. Keeping together, they were to go to certain well-known landmarks; if nothing were seen from there or on the way they were to go to other specified points of outlook, and returning, bring report. These instructions were given by the leading man, he who stood as chief of the council tent; he was assisted by others and all was said in the hearing of those present."

15. Again, Riggs supplies more details for the newspaper account regarding the description of the lodge and what transpired therein. "When Roan Bear and I went in [the soldier lodge] we found Little Bear and one or two

others only. These were seated at the left as we entered. A carefully tended fire in the center made the tent warm and light. By the fire there was a kettle or two of boiled meat and a large iron pail of coffee. Little Bear had his pipe and this he was passing from one to another. As others came in they seated themselves in a circle about the fire. We had but one topic; yesterday a young man had seen what appeared to be the drifted-over trail of a single buffalo, indicated by the broken bits of snow; and today others had seen similar signs and just before we made camp these signs were found plentiful and sure. No shooting had been allowed for two days and even loud talking and the barking of dogs had been repressed. The camp was well in hand and under strict control."

16. Riggs added in his newspaper account that everyone called in a suppressed voice, "They run, they run."

17. Riggs, as a matter of religious conviction, never traveled on Sunday. This is one of the few times he broke with his tradition.

18. In the newspaper account, Riggs noted that "Co-kan-tan-ka expressed my own feelings as he rode up to where we were stopping with a shivery 'I'm cold!' He added after a look to the east: 'We shall all be warm soon and without the sun.'"

19. In his newspaper account Riggs described bison as the meat that has "tang to it."

20. In Riggs's newspaper version he described Sam as an "old buffalo horse of considerable note in those days—and a fast, gamy runner, which I had bought a few years before." Sam, according to Riggs, had earned a wide reputation as both a "buffalo horse" and a "runner" and was "honored and venerated by the Lakota." Riggs noted that "many a time I have seen an Indian go up to Sam, place one hand upon his shoulder, raise the hand to the sky, then place the hand on the ground, a prayer gesture signifying adoration."

21. Riggs noted in his news article that "when this has not been done, horses have been known to get away, and never be recovered."

22. The original plan of attack against the bison, which Riggs described for the newspaper, was a variation of the surround. He noted that "two or three hunters were to keep along the edge of a little plateau beyond which the game were feeding quietly, and by signals, they were to keep the main body posted as it made a detour and followed up a long, crooked depression to get close in before showing themselves."

23. Riggs wrote in his news account: "A good horse, a magazine gun and an open prairie is all that ordinary man needs with buffalo afield. Formerly

a cut-off smooth bore flint-lock was the weapon. The hunter carried his bullets in his mouth and dropping a ball in on the powder, poured by guess from the horn as his horse raced warily along to the right and slightly in the rear of the game. After he rapped the butt sharply on his thigh to settle the charge and prime the piece, he was ready for his shot."

24. Riggs noted in his news account that "these three make the ordinary complement and they are spoken of as 'first', 'second', and 'third' killer, respectively. Should a fourth man render assistance his share is as shall be given by the others. Often disputes occur over who killed the animal and sometimes quarrels and bad blood result, but there is never a question regarding the law of division."

25. Again Riggs wrote in his news account that "when the work of the field is over, the extra horses are packed with the hides and meat and some astonishingly heavy loads are carried, though but little of the bone of the animal is taken, and the hunters make their way back to camp. It is not always that the labor of the day ends as you leave the field."

26. Riggs noted that an accurate translation of his nickname was very difficult. "'Tanka' means large, but 'Co-kan' carries the idea of a central figure of authority ... or power, force or influence, and suggested the terms of Supreme Court, Head Umpire or 'Big Shot.'"

27. Generally speaking, horses have a natural aversion for bison and with good reason. In 1976, while I was working at Blue Mounds State Park in Minnesota, a horse grazing in the same pasture as the bison was gored to death by them. Another horse I tried to ride up to a half dozen young bison bulls on the Terry Bison Ranch in Wyoming snorted and balked at every attempt I made to get him to move closer to the herd.

28. It may have been the BXB ranch or the Crawford road ranch, which was located on the Bismarck to Deadwood trail during the late 1870s and through the 1880s. BXB was the brand owned by the Vermont Cattle Company which, according to Ed Lemmon, ran about 12,000 head of cattle on the Moreau River. The ranch headquarters was located near a ford on the Moreau River north of present-day Maurine, South Dakota. In 1895 the BXB became the Bixby post office. All vestiges of the old BXB and Bixby have since disappeared.

29. In his news account Riggs wrote that "when we started on the hunt in late November, it was expected that we would be gone from three to four weeks and we provisioned accordingly. As we were out twelve weeks our supplies were insufficient. Sugar, coffee and flour hardly lasted the time which we expected they would. Corn was parched and used instead of coffee for a

day or two and that was the last of the corn. Then rosebush tea was made (boiling the buds or the roots and in some cases the wood itself) so long as any sugar was left. I recollect that we had six weeks of straight meat diet with nothing but soup or water to drink. After a while there was no salt. The older Indians cared not for the lack of sugar, coffee and flour but the loss of tobacco caused no end of sorrow. Little Bear cut up his old nicotine-soaked pipe stem, shaved the pieces thin and powdered them in the palm of his hand that he might smoke it in a borrowed pipe. 'I can stand hunger,' he said, 'and thirst, but without tobacco I am dead.' "

30. Riggs noted that the Lakota name for this place was *Okikse*, which means "a gap." It may have been the long, winding, scenic draw South Dakota Highway 63 formerly followed from the south to gain the top of Fox Ridge. As a highway route, it was a dangerous series of ascending, sharp, blind curves and has since been obliterated by a new roadcut.

31. A final historical note of this hunt was the capture of five live bison calves by two of Fred Dupuis's sons. These calves formed the genesis of the Dupuis (Dupris) bison herd, which roamed Fox Ridge for the next two decades. Stamped with Dupuis's famous Circle D brand, the entire herd was later acquired by James "Scotty" Philip of Fort Pierre after old Fred's death in 1898. Under Philip's care the herd grew to 500 animals over the following twenty years. Part of this herd became the genesis of the Custer State Park herd as well as the late Roy Houck's famous Standing Butte Ranch herd.

Houck's bison herd and ranch, located near Mission Ridge, South Dakota, about 35 miles northwest of Fort Pierre, provided the setting and animals for the famous bison-hunting scenes in Kevin Costner's Academy Award–winning film, *Dances with Wolves*.

32. Thomas Lawrence Riggs, *Sunset to Sunset*, p. 156.

Chapter 16

1. Rex Alan Smith, *Moon of Popping Trees*, p. 67.

2. Wovoka said he "turned red with a whiteman's disease" (scarlet fever?), which brought on the trance (Hittman, p. 25). Actually, Wovoka was not the first Indian prophet who received a vision that condemned the white man. In 1805, Tenskwatawa, the "Shawnee prophet" from northern Ohio, received a series of revelations he hoped would revitalize Indian people and culture. In his revelations, whiskey and some aspects of European culture were

banned along with certain traditional dances and medicine bundles. The faithful were also required to refrain from intertribal warfare. Explicit in his teaching was that Americans alone (as opposed to the French and English), among non-Indians, were evil.

3. Effie Florence Putney, *In the South Dakota Country*, p. 159.

4. Rex Alan Smith, p. 68.

5. Putney, p. 160.

6. Rex Alan Smith, p. 68.

7. Riggs, *Sunset to Sunset*, p. 168.

8. Rex Alan Smith, p. 74.

9. Ibid.

10. Beef rations were cut on Pine Ridge from 8,125,000 pounds in 1886 to 4,000,000 pounds in 1889. James Mooney, *The Ghost Dance Religion and the Sioux Outbreak of 1890*, p. 845.

11. Rex Alan Smith, p. 87. Little Wound's vision also echoed the words of Wovoka, who based on his earliest vision predicted that the whites and the Indian unbelievers would be buried under the new order.

12. *South Dakota's Ziebach County*, p. 603.

13. Ibid.

14. In fact, Sitting Bull was shot when he resisted arrest and many of his followers fled to Hump's and Big Foot's band, creating more tension for the Mnikojus.

15. Pass Creek in the badlands was to be the destination for a Ghost Dance gathering so that the military would not interfere with the dancers as they ushered in the new millennium. Sitting Bull was planning to leave for this gathering in the badlands when he was arrested and subsequently killed.

16. *South Dakota Historical Collections*, vol. 2, p. 493.

17. Ibid.

18. Renee Samson Flood, *Lost Bird of Wounded Knee*, p. 28.

19. Ibid., p. 29.

20. *South Dakota Historical Collections*, vol. 2, pp. 494–495.

21. James Mooney, *The Ghost Dance Religion*, p. 869. Mooney wrote that "there can be no question that the pursuit was simply a massacre, where fleeing women, with infants in their arms, were shot down after resistance had ceased and when almost every warrior was stretched dead or dying on the ground."

22. James Mooney, the eminent anthropologist who made a thorough, detailed study of Wovoka, his prophecy, and the events leading up to the

Wounded Knee debacle in *The Ghost Dance Religion*, referred to Kicking Bear as the "chief high priest of the Ghost Dance among the Sioux" (p. 847). Kicking Bird and Short Bull, a Rosebud (Brûlé) Sioux, were the organizers in charge of the Ghost Dance gathering in the badlands. Black Elk, the pre-eminent Oglala medicine man/spiritual leader, was also in attendance.

  23. Putney, p. 164.
  24. Rex Alan Smith, p. 200.

Chapter 17

  1. Bob Lee and Dick Williams, *The Last Grass Frontier*, p. 141.
  2. W. M. Pearce, *The Matador Land and Cattle Company*, p. 96.
  3. Ibid., p. 69.
  4. Lee and Williams, p. 231.
  5. Ike Blasingame, *Dakota Cowboy*, p. 231.
  6. Winter seasons like the one Blasingame described are not just a phenomenon of the past. The last big blizzard season to strike the Cheyenne River Reservation country was in 1996–97. The first blizzard hit with a vengeance on November 11 and was followed by a series of a half dozen blizzards without letup well into January. Sections of U.S. Highway 212 from the Missouri River to Faith were closed a good deal of this time with 12- to 15-foot snowdrifts. The areas worst hit were Timber Lake and Eagle Butte, South Dakota, where schools were closed for weeks at a time and power outages were common. It took large National Guard rotary snowplows to break through the drifts leading into many rural areas. The worst blow to the cattlemen, however, came in early April 1997 when a final spring blizzard killed thousands of already weakened cattle. Wild animals such as pronghorn and deer also suffered severe die-offs that approached 90 percent.

  Old-timers in their eighties who had spent their entire lives in this country remarked to me that this was the worst season of storms they had ever witnessed. It was a terrible winter physically and emotionally for every creature on the plains that had to endure it.

  7. Lee and Williams, p. 231.
  8. Remnants of the old Diamond A shipping corrals at the old Mossman siding still exist and can be seen on the south side of U.S. Highway 212 about 15 miles east of Eagle Butte.

Chapter 18

1. Hamlin Garland, the noted prairie writer, won the Pulitzer Prize for biography in 1921 for his book *A Daughter of the Middle Border*. An eloquent narrative writer and chronicler of the late nineteenth and early twentieth centuries, Garland has regrettably been largely forgotten today.

2. Timber Lake and Area Historical Society Newsletters, printed by *Timber Lake Topic*, 1996 and 1997.

3. The years 1910 and 1911 were the two greatest ones for entering a homestead claim in South Dakota. In 1910, 6,739 entries were recorded on 1,035,512 acres. In 1911, claims peaked at 8,584 entries covering 1,313,234 acres.

4. In regard to the Fox Ridge, the best land *is* on top and *was* nearest the tracks, which have long since been pulled up. Moving north or south off the ridge crest, one leaves the better, sandy soils that had once been the old reef for the heavy, gumbo clays.

5. *The Prairie Yearbook*, Faith High School, South Dakota, 1926.

6. Ibid.

7. The Garlands came from La Crosse, Wisconsin, and homesteaded near Ordway in Brown County, Dakota Territory, in 1881.

8. Garland, *A Son of the Middle Border*.

9. Garland, *Moccasin Ranch*.

10. Josef Kindwall, *A Swedish American Odyssey*. Excerpts taken from the Timber Lake and Area Historical Society Newsletters, printed by *Timber Lake Topic*, 1996 and 1997.

11. Ibid.

12. The term *buzzard*, a common misnomer for this soaring bird, is still in usage in the West. A buzzard is actually an African bird. The correct name for the bird Kindwall was probably watching, the largest of northern plains raptors, is *turkey vulture*.

13. Isabel, like Faith, South Dakota, was named for a daughter of the president of the Milwaukee Road.

14. Kindwall, *A Swedish American Odyssey*.

15. Garland, *Back-Trailers from the Middle Border*.

16. Ibid.

Chapter 19

1. Ash seems to have been an informal friend and confidant of the general. He noted that during the spring of 1874, Custer told him he wanted to take the Seventh Cavalry on a "vacation" field trip, and if he got permission from Washington, he planned "to slip into the Black Hills." Years later, Ash said he believed that Custer never hinted in his request to the government of what he planned to do.

2. The place where Ash first sighted the Black Hills is marked by the Trail Blazers Monument, as per Ash's final wish. It is located about 7 miles east of Mud Butte on Highway 212.

Chapter 20

1. John Bradbury, *Travels in the Interior of North America*, pp. 189–190.
2. Andrew Isenberg, *The Destruction of the Bison*, p. 25.
3. Ibid., p. 26.
4. Francis Haines, *The Buffalo*, p. 204.
5. Tom McHugh, *The Time of the Buffalo*, pp. 292–294.
6. The Big Sheep Mountains are not mountains but a high clay ridge that runs down the center of the flat-iron essentially separating the drainages of the Missouri to the north and the Yellowstone to the south.
7. Harold P. Danz, *Of Bison and Man*, p. 125.
8. Daniel Licht, *Ecology and Economics of the Great Plains*, p. 12. This quote was taken from Licht's book and is from R. L. Barsh's book *The Struggle for the Land: Indigenous Insight and Industrial Empire in the Semi-arid World* (University of Nebraska Press), 1990.
9. The late L. Roy Houck of Fort Pierre, South Dakota, was one of the first of the modern buffalo ranchers. He purchased 400 head of bison from the Custer State Park herd in 1963. His Standing Butte Ranch herd now numbers 3,500. Danz, p. 157.
10. A bison's rumen might also be described as a 45-gallon fermentation tank in which bacteria go to work, breaking down grass into food and energy.
11. Richard Manning, *Grassland*, p. 120.
12. Joseph Epes Brown, *The Sacred Pipe*, p. 70.

Bibliography

Abel, Annie Heloise. 1939. *Tabeau's Narrative of Loisel's Expedition to the Upper Missouri*. Norman: University of Oklahoma Press.

Athearn, Robert G. 1967. *Forts of the Upper Missouri*. Lincoln: University of Nebraska Press.

Bamforth, Douglas. 1988. *Ecology and Human Organization on the Great Plains*. New York: Plenum Press.

Blasingame, Ike. 1958. *Dakota Cowboy: My Life in the Old Days*. Lincoln: University of Nebraska Press.

Blegen, Anne H. 1925. *The Verendrye Explorations*.

Bluemle, John P. 1991. *The Face of North Dakota*. Rev. ed. Bismarck: North Dakota Geological Survey.

Bodmer, Karl. 1984. *Karl Bodmer's America*. Omaha: Joslyn Art Museum.

Boller, Henry A. 1972. *Among the Indians: Four Years on the Upper Missouri, 1858–1862*. Lincoln: University of Nebraska Press.

Bradbury, John. [1819] 1904. *Travels in the Interior of North America in the Years 1809, 1810, 1811*. Edited by Reuben Gold Thwaites. Reprint, 1986, Lincoln: Bison Books.

Brown, Joseph Epes. 1953. *The Sacred Pipe: Black Elk's Account of the Seven Rites of the Oglala Sioux*. Norman: University of Oklahoma Press.

Brown, Lauren. 1979. *Grasses*. New York: Houghton Mifflin.

Burpee, Lawrence J. 1922. *A Chronicle of La Verendrye and His Sons, Pathfinders of the Great Plains*. Toronto: Glasgow, Brook & Company.

Carrels, Peter. 1999. *Uphill Against Water: The Great Dakota Water War*. Lincoln: University of Nebraska Press.

Coues, Elliot, ed. 1893. *History of the Expedition Under the Command of Lewis and Clark*. New York: F. P. Harper.

Crouse, Nellis M. 1956. *La Verendrye: Fur Trader and Explorer*. Port Washington, NY: Kennikat Press.

"Crow Creek Massacre." 1999. *Future of the Plains Environment*. www.usd.edu/anth/crow/ccwarn.

Cy, Martin. 1973. *The Saga of the Buffalo*. New York: Hart Pub. Co.

Danz, Harold P. 1997. *Of Bison and Man*. Niwot, CO: University Press of Colorado.

Dary, David A. 1974. *The Buffalo Book*. New York: Avon Books.

DeMallie, Raymond J., ed. *Handbook of North American Indians. Plains* vol. 13, pts. 1 and 2. Washington, DC: Smithsonian Institute.

DeVoto, Bernard. 1952. *The Course of Empire*. Boston: Houghton Mifflin.

Dorsey, George H. [1905] 1975. *The Cheyenne*. Fairfield, WA: Ye Galleon Press.

Driving Hawk Sneve, Virginia. 1973. *South Dakota Geographic Names*. Sioux Falls, SD: Brevet Press.

Dupree, Calvin. *The First Dupree into South Dakota*. Unpublished manuscript.

Edelson, Zelda, ed. 1993. *The Age of Mammals*. New Haven, CT: Yale University Press.

Faith Country Heritage. 1985. Pierre, SD: The State Publishing Company.

Flood, Renee Sansom. 1995. *Lost Bird of Wounded Knee*. New York: Scribner.

Gard, Wayne. 1959. *The Great Buffalo Hunt*. New York: Alfred A. Knopf.

Garland, Hamlin. 1961. *Dakota Homesteader*. Sioux Falls, SD: O'Connor Commercial Printers.

Geist, Valerius. 1996. *Buffalo Nation: History and Legend of the North American Bison*. Stillwater, MN: Voyageur Press.

Greever, William S. 1963. *Bonanza West: The Story of Western Mining Rushes 1848–1900*. Norman: University of Oklahoma Press.

Gries, John Paul. 1996. *Roadside Geology of South Dakota*. Missoula, MT: Mountain Press.

Grinnell, George Bird. 1915. *The Fighting Cheyennes*. New York: Charles Scribner's Sons.

———. [1928] 1973. *Two Great Scouts: The Experience of Frank J. North and Luther H. North*. Lincoln: Bison Books.

Haines, Francis. 1970. *The Buffalo*. New York: Thomas Y. Crowell Co.

Hall, Bert. 1956. *Roundup Years: Old Muddy to the Black Hills*. Pierre, SD: The Reminder, Inc.

Hamilton, W. H. [1941] 1998. *Dakota: An Autobiography of a Cowman*. Pierre: South Dakota State Historical Society Press.

Hassrick, Royal B. 1977. *The George Catlin Book of American Indians*. New York: Watson-Guptill.

———. 1964. *The Sioux: Life and Customs of a Warrior Society*. Norman: University of Oklahoma Press.

Hittman, Michael. 1997. *Wovoka and the Ghost Dance.* Lincoln: Bison Books.

Hoebel, E. Adamson. 1960. *The Cheyennes: Indians of the Great Plains.* New York: Holt, Rinehart and Winston.

Hoxie, Frederick E. 1979. *Jurisdiction on the Cheyenne River Indian Reservation: An Analysis of the Causes and Consequences of the Act of May 29, 1908.* A report for presentation in *United States v. Glen Dupris,* No. CR 77-30056-01, United States District Court for South Dakota.

Hyde, George E. 1962. *Indians of the Woodlands from Prehistoric Times to 1725.* Norman: University of Oklahoma Press.

———. 1951. *The Pawnee Indians.* Norman: University of Oklahoma Press.

———. 1937. *Red Cloud's Folk: A History of the Ogalala Sioux Indians.* Norman: University of Oklahoma Press.

———. 1961. *Spotted Tail's Folk, A History of the Brule Sioux.* Norman: University of Oklahoma Press.

Isabel Territory. Golden Jubilee, 1960.

Isenberg, Andrew C. 2000. *The Destruction of the Bison: An Environmental History, 1750–1920.* Cambridge, UK: Cambridge University Press.

Jackson, Donald. 1985. *Voyages of the Steamboat Yellowstone.* New York: Ticknor and Fields.

Kavanagh, Martin. 1967. *La Verendrye: His Life and Times.* Brandon, Manitoba: M. Kavanagh.

Kindwall, Josef. *A Swedish American Odyssey.* Excerpts taken from the Timber Lake and Area Historical Society Newsletters, printed by *Timber Lake Topic.* Timber Lake, SD: 1996 and 1997.

King, F. G. 1926. "Early History of Faith." *Yearbook.* Faith High School, Faith, South Dakota.

La Verendrye. [1889] 1925. *Journals of the La Verendrye Trips to the Mandan Villages on the Missouri River in 1738–39 and to the Foothills of the Rocky Mountains in 1742–43.* Translated by Douglas Brymner from a Report on Canadian Archives being an appendix to Report of the Minister of Agriculture, Ottawa, 1889. Reprinted by *The Quarterly of the Oregon Historical Society* 26(2) (June): 47.

Lass, William E. 1977. *Minnesota: A History.* New York: W.W. Norton.

Lawson, Michael Lee. 1975. "Reservoir and Reservation: The Oahe Dam and the Cheyenne River Sioux." *South Dakota Historical Collections* 37 (1974). State Publishing Co.

Lee, Bob, and Williams, Dick. 1964. *Last Grass Frontier: The South Dakota Stock Grower Heritage.* Rapid City, SD: Black Hills Publishers.

Lehmer, Donald J. 1971. *Introduction to Middle Missouri Archaeology.* Washington, DC: National Park Service, GPO.

Lemmon, G. E. 1969. *Boss Cowman: The Recollections of Ed Lemmon, 1857–1946.* Lincoln: University of Nebraska Press.

Levin, Harold L., 1988. *The Earth Through Time.* New York: Holt, Rinehart and Winston.

Licht, Daniel S. 1997. *Ecology and Economics of the Great Plains.* Lincoln: University of Nebraska Press.

Little, Paul. 1983. *River of People: A Multicultural History of the Cheyenne River Reservation Area.* Eagle Butte, SD: Eagle Butte Public School.

Maisey, John G. 1996. *Discovering Fossil Fishes.* New York: Henry Holt.

Manning, Richard. 1995. *Grassland.* New York: Penguin Books USA.

McCracken, Harold. 1959. *George Catlin and the Old Frontier.* New York: Dial Press.

McHugh, Tom. 1972. *The Time of the Buffalo.* Lincoln: University of Nebraska Press.

Mead, James R. 1986. *Hunting and Trading on the Great Plains, 1859–1875.* Edited by Schuyler Jones. Norman: University of Oklahoma Press.

Mooney, James. [1896] 1991. *The Ghost Dance Religion and the Sioux Outbreak of 1890.* Originally published as part 2 of the 14th Annual Report of the Bureau of Ethnology, 1892–1893, by the Government Printing Office, Washington, DC. Lincoln: Bison Books.

O'Harra, Cleophas C. 1920. *The White River Badlands.* Bulletin 13. Rapid City: South Dakota School of Mines.

Parks, Douglas. "Arikara." In *Handbook of North American Indians,* ed. Raymond J. DeMallie. *Plains* vol. 13, pt. 1, p. 366.

Pearce, W. M. 1964. *The Matador Land and Cattle Company.* Norman: University of Oklahoma Press.

Peters, Virginia Bergman. 1995. *Women of the Earth Lodges: Tribal Life on the Plains.* Norman: University of Oklahoma Press.

Putney, Effie Florence. 1922, 1927. *In the South Dakota Country.* Vols. 1, 2. Mitchell, SD: Educator Supply Company.

Raventon, Edward. 1994. *Island in the Plains: A Black Hills Natural History.* Boulder, CO: Johnson Books.

Raymo, Maureen. *Cracking the Ice Age.* NOVA Online, 9-30-97. www.pbs.org.

Riggs, Theodore Foster. 1961. *A Log House Was Home*. New York: Exposition Press.

Riggs, Thomas Lawrence, with Howard, Margaret Kellogg. [1958] 1997. *Sunset to Sunset: A Lifetime with My Brothers, the Dakotas*. Pierre: South Dakota State Historical Society, vols. 5, 29.

Robertson, R. G. 2001. *Rotting Face: Smallpox and the American Indian*. Caldwell, ID: Caxton Press.

Robinson, James M. 1974. *West from Fort Pierre*. Los Angeles: Westernlore Press.

Smith, G. Hubert. 1980. *The Explorations of the La Verendryes in the Northern Plains, 1738–43*. Lincoln: University of Nebraska Press.

Smith, Rex Alan. 1975. *Moon of Popping Trees*. New York: Reader's Digest Press.

Stewart, Alexander M. 1934. *René Menard, 1605–1661*. Rochester, NY: Heindl Print.

South Dakota Historical Collections (and Reports). Vol. 1, 1902; vol. 2, 1903; vol. 7, 1908; vol. 13, 1926; vol. 23, 1947; vol. 24, 1949; vol. 25, 1950. South Dakota State Historical Society. Pierre.

South Dakota's Ziebach County: History of the Prairie. 1982. Pierre, SD: The State Publishing Company.

Sullivan, Noelle, and Nicholas Peterson Vrooman. 1995. *M-e Ecci Aashi Awadi: The Knife River Indian Villages*. Medora, ND: Theodore Roosevelt Natural History Association.

Sully, Langdon. 1974. *No Tears for the General: The Life of Alfred Sully, 1821–1879*. Palo Alto, CA: American West Publishing Co.

Sunder, John E. 1965. *The Fur Trade on the Upper Missouri, 1840–1865*. Norman: University of Oklahoma Press.

Thwaites, Reuben Gold. 1905. *France in America, 1497–1763*. New York: Harper and Brothers.

Timber Lake and Area Historical Society Newsletters, printed by *Timber Lake Topic*. Timber Lake, SD: 1996 and 1997.

Timber Lake Area History. Timber Lake, SD.

Townsend, John K. *Journey Across the Rocky Mountains to the Columbia River*. Philadelphia: Henry Perkins, 1839. *Early Western Travels, 1748–1846*. Vol. 21. "Townsend's Narrative (1833–1834)," edited by Reuben Gold Thwaites. New York: AMS Press, Inc., 1966.

Trimble, Donald E. [1980] 1993. *The Geologic Story of the Great Plains*. Geological Survey Bulletin 1493. Bismarck, ND: Richtman's Printing.

Verendrye Overland Quest of the Pacific. 1926. *The Quarterly of the Oregon Historical Society* 26(2).

Weltfish, Gene. 1965. *The Lost Universe: Pawnee Life and Culture.* Lincoln:
University of Nebraska Press.

Wilson, Edward O. 1992. *The Diversity of Life.* New York: W.W. Norton.

Wyman, Walker D. 1954. *Nothing but Prairie and Sky.* Norman: University of
Oklahoma Press.

Index